Breakfast in Texas

UNIVERSITY OF TEXAS PRESS ⌄ AUSTIN

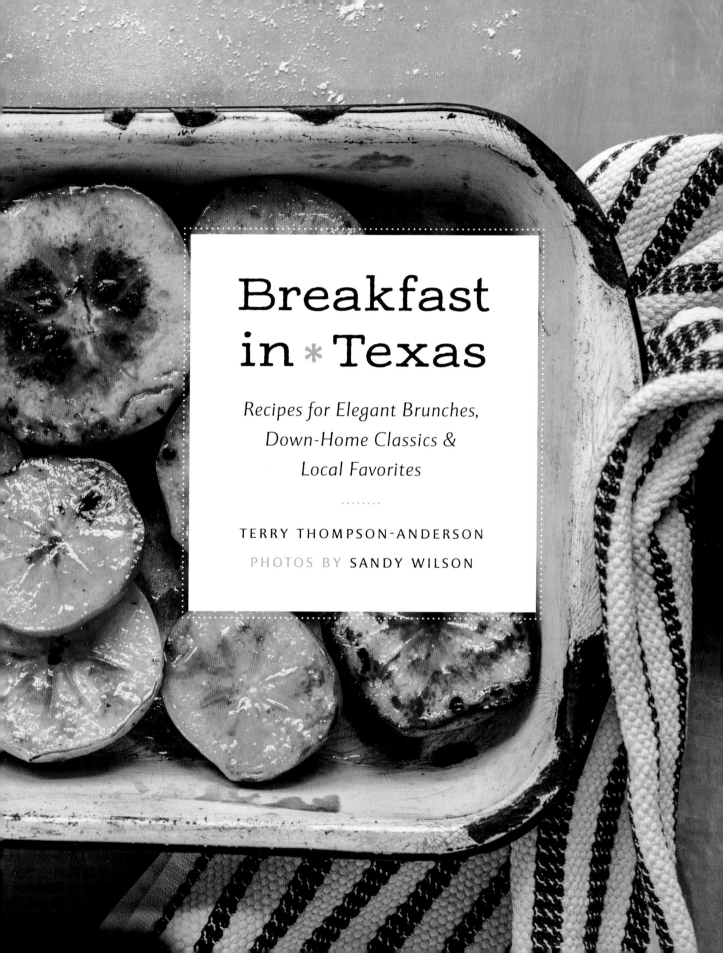

Breakfast in * Texas

*Recipes for Elegant Brunches,
Down-Home Classics &
Local Favorites*

TERRY THOMPSON-ANDERSON

PHOTOS BY SANDY WILSON

Copyright © 2017 by
Terry Thompson-Anderson
and Sandy Wilson

All rights reserved | Printed in China | First edition, 2017

The recipes appearing on pages 46, 144, 166, and 223 originally appeared in
Fonda San Miguel by Tom Gilliland and Miguel Ravago. Copyright © 2005, 2016 by
Cuisines de Mexico, Inc. Used by permission from the University of Texas Press.

Requests for permission to reproduce material
from this work should be sent to:
Permissions
University of Texas Press
P.O. Box 7819
Austin, TX 78713-7819
http://utpress.utexas.edu/index.php/rp-form

The paper used in this book meets the minimum requirements
of ANSI/NISO Z39.48-1992 (R1997) (Permanence of Paper). ∞

Design by Lindsay Starr

LIBRARY OF CONGRESS CATALOGING-IN-PUBLICATION DATA

Names: Thompson-Anderson, Terry, 1946– author.
Wilson, Sandy, 1952– photographer.
Title: Breakfast in Texas : recipes for elegant brunches, down-home classics, and
local favorites / Terry Thompson-Anderson ; photos by Sandy Wilson.
Description: First edition. Austin : University of Texas Press, 2017.
Includes index.
Identifiers: LCCN 2016025871 (print)
ISBN 978-1-4773-1044-1 (cloth : alk. paper)
ISBN 978-1-4773-1267-4 (library e-book)
ISBN 978-1-4773-1268-1 (non-library e-book)
Subjects: LCSH: Breakfasts–Texas. Brunches–Texas. LCGFT: Cookbooks.
Classification: LCC TX733 .T525 2017
DDC 641.5/209764–dc23
LC record available at https://lccn.loc.gov/2016025871

doi:10.7560/310441

CONTENTS

INTRODUCTION

A morning meal, the nutritionists tell us, is essential. It kick-starts our brains so that we can think, function, and work productively until lunchtime. But the morning meal that we know of as breakfast is much more than intellectual stimulation, well-being, or bacon and eggs. The history of breakfast in America parallels the history of the country. The North developed breakfasts featuring sausage and hash brown potatoes, while the South added grits, ham, and its beloved biscuits. The Creole culture of New Orleans introduced the concept of *brunch* to America with grand, leisurely, multi-course meals served later in the morning with exotic cocktails and special coffee concoctions, while westward expansion introduced Mexican and Czech influences and cooking the breakfast meal over open fires in cast-iron cooking vessels.

When settlers from other countries, with varied ethnic and cultural backgrounds, first began to colonize Texas, they found a thriving Mexican culture in place with its tradition of rich, hearty, and spicy morning meals. For example, German immigrants who came to Texas in the mid-1800s brought their skills as sausage makers, and introduced potato pancakes and Apfelpfannkuchen (German puffy pancakes with apples). Czech immigrants introduced their timeless pastries, such as kuchen, kolaches, and klobasnikis (sausage-filled pastries). Today, though the definitive history of brunch in Texas is far from documented, Texas is a melting pot of breakfast styles reflecting the cultural diversity of the state itself.

In our travels researching, photographing, and interviewing people in the Lone Star State, Sandy and I ate a lot of breakfasts, and often shared some heavenly brunches, across the many miles we covered. We were struck with the regional and cultural diversity of the dishes served for the morning meal, both in mom-and-pop diners in the small towns and in luxury hotels and eateries in the big cities. We fell equally in love with the breakfast tacos in San Antonio, the saag paneer omelets in Houston, the pon haus in Austin, the delicious shrimp and grits in the unlikely location of Lubbock, the goat curry in Fort Worth, the caramel-drizzled donuts made from biscuit dough in El Paso, the blintzes in Dallas, and the many unique and innovative versions of eggs Benedict everywhere. We began to realize that breakfast is the all-day meal. And it often substitutes for dinner.

We shared an enthusiasm for trying many of these dishes at home to serve to our families and friends. Then we thought perhaps others, too, might like to make their morning meals more of an "experience" to be shared with the special people in their lives. In writing and providing the photographs for this book, we hope to inspire a breakfast revolution celebrating the many cultures of Texas—a revolution that will bring our readers together as families or groups of friends for a morning meal, or a leisurely Sunday respite before returning to the workplace on Monday. For those times, we've included a selection of tasty libations so that you can start your brunch experience off with a toast to many more shared morning meals.

Along the way, we also noticed that breakfast and brunch are getting a lot of attention these days. And it's certainly not the same old bacon and eggs or bowl of dried cereal swimming in milk and sugar. Savory ingredients like meats (even game meats and fowl), fish and shellfish, and veggies, often topped with rich sauces, are being added to the breakfast table. Even when they're in a hurry, it seems people are wanting a memorable taste sensation in the morning so they can start the day with a satisfied smile—even if it's a mobile handheld breakfast in this day of *mobile everything* lifestyles.

Anthony Bourdain, America's popular chef/food adventurer, is a great fan of the morning meal. We certainly agreed with his sentiments when he said, "What nicer thing can you do for somebody than make them breakfast?"

ENTERTAINING THOUGHTS ON BREAKFAST AND BRUNCH

Make-Ahead Breakfast and Brunch Dishes

There are many recipes within this book that can be made completely ahead, or partially ahead of time and assembled and cooked just before serving. Several of the completely made-ahead dishes can be frozen, making a homemade breakfast, as opposed to one picked up at the Golden Arches on the way to work or to your kids' school, possible for busy parents. This is true of more complex brunches as well: many of the component parts of the dishes can be made ahead of time, making it a breeze to serve a spectacular brunch with little last-minute hassle. For information on those recipes that can be made ahead, or those elements of recipes that can be pre-prepared and assembled just before serving, see the individual recipes throughout the book.

Celebration Brunches

Brunch is one of my favorite ways to celebrate special occasions, holidays, birthdays, and especially Mother's Day and Father's Day. You can pick and choose your brunch spread from the many recipes in this book or try the following suggestions.

NEW YEAR'S BRUNCH

New Year's brunch is one of my all-time favorites, and it always involves oysters, which are at the peak of their season around this time of year.

Well-chilled Shucked Oysters on the Halfshell and Red Cocktail
 Sauce with a Zing (page 217)
Brennan's of Houston's Gumbo Z'Herbes with Cornmeal Drop
 Biscuits (page 218)
South Texas Heritage Pork Menudo (page 130)
Ocean Grille & Beach Bar's Bourbon French Toast (page 93)
Brennan's of Houston's Venison Hash with Fried Eggs (page 163)
Frizzled Sweet Potatoes (page 232)
Fancy Lucky Peas (page 227)
Brennan's of Houston's Bananas Foster (page 220)
Bloody Shiner (page 14) and/or Hot Buttered Rum (page 21)

IT'S FINALLY SPRING BRUNCH

I truly dread cold weather, so winter is not my favorite season. When those first signs of spring show their green little tips, I, too, bloom anew. And I love to herald the arrival of warm with a great brunch of fresh ingredients.

Edible Flower and Herb Frittata with Fried, Stuffed Squash
 Blossoms and Guacamole-Filled Nasturtiums (page 68)
Melon and Berry Compote with Raspberry–Poppy Seed Sauce
 (page 225)
UrbanHerbal's Planet to Plate Cooking School's Brioche Breakfast
 Buns with Scented Geranium Pesto (page 266)
The Driskill Hotel's 1886 Café & Bakery's Orange-Currant Scones
 with Lemon Curd (page 257)
Basil Mojito (page 20) or Chillin' in Galveston Bubbly Punch
 (page 6)

If you'd like to delight the heart of the mother (or mothers) in your life, then prepare a homemade brunch and serve it with all the bells and whistles and pull out the good china and silver. Be willing to bet that the appreciation will reverberate for months.

Helen Corbitt's Cheese Soup with Garlic Croutons, as Adapted
by the Driskill Hotel's 1886 Café & Bakery (page 222)
St. Charles Bay Crab Cakes and Poached Eggs on Fried Green
Tomatoes with Orange-Ginger Hollandaise Sauce (page 194)
Brunch Biscuits with Paula's Texas Lemon Butter (page 252)
Ramos Gin Fizz (page 19)

FATHER'S DAY BRUNCH

It's been my experience that dads are not too impressed by being taken out for brunch on Father's Day. But set him down to a sumptuous, meaty home brunch spread complete with a cocktail or two, and, who knows, you might even see him tackle that "honey-do" list!

Quail in Country Ham on Scrambled Eggs with Peppered Coffee
Gravy (page 148) or Garden Café's Flatiron Steak and Eggs with
Homestead Gristmill Herbed Grits (page 154)
Spicy Candied Bacon (page 116)
Honey-Baked Tomatoes (page 228)
Pecan-Praline Rolls (page 273)
Texas Whiskey Milk Punch (page 7)

BIRTHDAY CELEBRATION BRUNCH

If it were my birthday, I would be so impressed to have someone prepare this brunch for me! It has such an exciting range of flavors. Happy day, indeed.

Brennan's of Houston's Smoked Catfish Mousse (page 177)
Vaudeville's Supper Club Sunday Brunch Crawfish Relleno
(page 185)
MargieBeth's Bake Shop's Apricot-Ginger Scones (page 259)
Bill Varney's Lemon-Rose Martini (page 17)

Slumber parties, or "sleepovers," are a rite of passage for teenaged girls. Although, of course, there's very little actual sleeping done, they are so much fun. As a mom hosting one, you can earn serious brownie points with your daughter if you go out of your way to lay out an impressive spread of goodies for the party crew in the morning.

Breakfast Chalupa Bar (page 213)
Crispy Italian Sausage Scrambled Egg Muffins (page 120)
Mac & Ernie's Roadside Eatery's Lemon and Blueberry Pancakes
    (page 99)
Tucker's Kozy Korner's "Chicken"-Fried Grits (page 237)
Spudnuts (page 281)
La Gloria's Mexican Hot Chocolate (page 25) and/or
    Agua de Horchata (without liqueur) (page 8)

FOURTH OF JULY BRUNCH

The Fourth of July, of course, is one of the most symbolic holidays in America. It's a great mid-summer celebration in which families and friends join together to pay homage to our country. So, what better way to start the day than with a grand brunch to set the stage for the evening's festivities?

Jeff Balfour's Southerleigh Fine Food & Brewery Brunch

Jeff Balfour's Southerleigh Fine Food & Brewery Brunch Cornmeal-
    Crusted Gafftop with Smoked Tomato, Country Ham, Fried Eggs,
    Spring Peas, and Béarnaise Sauce (page 179)
What's a Breakfast Without Good Biscuits? And Perhaps Some
    Sausage Gravy? (biscuits only) (page 250)
Southerleigh Fine Food & Brewery's Peach, Wheat Beer, and
    Sparkling Rosé Cocktail (page 11)

Breakfast in Texas

ONE

Breakfast and Brunch Libations

*

A BOOZY BRUNCH

....

Whence I prepare a weekend brunch for overnight guests or for invited friends, I like to serve some sort of cocktail beverage. This chapter includes a variety of festive drinks that make for great conversation starters. Brunch cocktails also serve as a time buffer, allowing time for the host and/or hostess to put the finishing touches on the brunch dishes while guests sip away. Most of the recipes contain alcohol, with the exception of La Gloria's Mexican Hot Chocolate (see recipe on page 25); the Don Strange Hot White Chocolate, which is delicious, and to which you can add alcohol if desired (see recipe on page 22); and the Agua de Horchata, to which you can also add alcohol (see recipe on page 8). For make-ahead cocktails, try the Chillin' in Galveston Bubbly Punch (see recipe on page 6) or the Texas Whiskey Milk Punch (see recipe on page 7).

My favorites for serving with brunch during the winter are La Gloria's Mexican Hot Chocolate on page 25, the Hot Buttered Rum on page 21, and the Don Strange Hot White Chocolate, either with or without the booze.

For spring and summer, I really love the Basil Mojito on page 20, the always popular Ramos Gin Fizz on page 19, and the Southerleigh Fine Food & Brewery's beer-based cocktails (see the Watermelon–Wheat Beer Cocktail on page 10 and the Peach, Wheat Beer, and Sparkling Rosé Cocktail on page 11). All have fresh, zesty flavors, which blend perfectly with brunches that might begin with cocktails on the patio and continue into the dining room.

For a truly unique brunch cocktail experience, pick up some moon-shine from Texas's legal 'shine producer, Texas Hill Country Distillery in Comfort, Texas, and try the Bloody Shiner or the Watermelon-Mint Shine, both on page 14; the latter is also great for spring and summer, especially when made with Texas-grown Black Diamond watermelons. (Check with your favorite liquor store, as many are now carrying Texas Hill Country Distillery's moonshines.) Mighty tasty and definitely different!

Sparkling wines, rosé (especially sparkling rosé), and crisp, dry white wines are also generally great with brunch.

When you opt to serve alcohol-laced beverages with your brunch, as on any other occasion, serve them judiciously to avoid the possibility that any of your guests will become inebriated and get behind the wheel of a vehicle.

Chillin' in Galveston Bubbly Punch

MAKES 15
8-OUNCE
SERVINGS

One of my favorite summertime outings is to rent a condo on the seawall in Galveston for Girlfriends' Weekend Out. We sunbathe by the pool, shop on the Strand, walk on the beach, or stroll the Pleasure Pier. But mostly we cook, eat, and drink, in addition to solving all of the world's problems and analyzing men. Whatever the agenda, the grand finale is always a decadent brunch on Sunday before we pack up to head back to the real world. Chillin' in Galveston Bubbly Punch is our official Sunday-morning libation. It's said that American Southerners consume more champagne per person than people in any other region in the world—including France, where most of it is produced, and where the process originated. I wonder if that statistic was calculated before, or after, we started the girlfriends' weekends?

Texas is now producing a few really nice sparkling wines. Of course, in Texas they can't legally be called "champagne," but many Texas wineries are producing sparkling wines using the same methods used by the French—with some dandy results.

2 bottles good-quality dry Texas
  sparkling wine, well chilled
1 cup fine cognac, well chilled
1 cup Cointreau, well chilled
½ cup Paula's Texas Orange liqueur,
  well chilled
1 quart club soda
4 medium oranges, cut into
  thin rounds
Ice ring, if using a punch bowl

Combine the sparkling wine, cognac, Cointreau, Paula's Texas Orange liqueur, and club soda in a large punch bowl or one-gallon pitcher. Stir in the orange slices. If using a punch bowl, float the ice ring in the punch. Serve in champagne flutes.

Texas Whiskey Milk Punch

MAKES 12
8-OUNCE
SERVINGS

Texas Whiskey Milk Punch is a time-honored favorite brunch libation. It's such a civilized way to get the conversation going while you put the finishing touches on your brunch. Milk punch is generally made with brandy, but Texans are more generally fond of good whiskey. In recent years, the distilled spirits industry in Texas has virtually exploded since Tito Beveridge, founder of Tito's Vodka in Austin, paved the way by jumping through state and federal government hoops to obtain the first legal license to distill liquor in Texas. In the lineup of Texas-made vodkas, gins, rums, liqueurs, whiskey, and even moonshine, one whiskey stands alone on my list of favorites—Rebecca Creek whiskey, distilled in San Antonio. Its smooth, heady taste is perfect in this rich and delightful punch. Be sure to use nutmeg grated freshly from the pod. Once grated, this wonderful spice has a very short optimal taste shelf life. I never buy grated nutmeg, which I find to have an almost metallic taste. Nutmeg graters are easy to use and inexpensive, so do yourself a favor and grate it fresh each time you use it. The incredible taste will be your reward.

2 cups Rebecca Creek whiskey
1 cup white crème de cacao
1 teaspoon vanilla extract
1⅓ cups Simple Bar Syrup
   (see recipe on page 18)
½ gallon whole milk
1 quart whipping cream
Crushed ice
Freshly grated nutmeg

Combine all ingredients except crushed ice and nutmeg in a large pitcher or punch bowl. Whisk to blend well. Fill serving glasses with crushed ice and fill with punch. Grate a small dusting of nutmeg pod on top of each glass and serve at once.

Agua de Horchata

SERVES 10 TO 12

This tasty and refreshing Mexican drink is generally known simply as horchata, which translates as "rice water." There are many opinions on the making of horchata and its ingredients. Some recipes call for using no water, but only milk; this is how it is made in Oaxaca, according to Miguel Ravago–chef and co-owner of Austin's legendary Fonda San Miguel restaurant, where the drink is served at its Sunday brunch. The beverage has a long history, having migrated to the New World from the Arab region, then by way of Spain to the Yucatan peninsula. Most versions today use either a combination of milk and water or water only. Miguel prefers to use a mixture of milk and water in his preparation, along with cinnamon and vanilla beans.

During the many days I spent researching the various methods of making horchata, my kitchen was a cauldron of assorted concoctions. The recipe that resulted is quite pleasing, and especially refreshing when served over ice. Fonda San Miguel offers the option of adding coffee-based liqueur or dark rum to its horchata. I tried it with several coffee-based liqueurs, as well as with the rum, but preferred the version with Patron XO coffee liqueur.

When preparing horchata, try to get your hands on some Mexican canela cinnamon. Technically known as *ceylon*, or "true" cinnamon, it's more light-natured and delicate than other varieties, with a subtle note of citrus. Note that the making of true horchata is a 2-day process.

2 cups long-grain white rice

3-inch sticks of Mexican canela cinnamon, broken into pieces and toasted in a dry skillet until aromatic

7 cups hot water

¼ cup sugar

½ of a vanilla bean, seeds removed and reserved

2 cups whole milk

Patron XO coffee liqueur (or other coffee-based liqueur) or dark rum, optional

Ground Mexican cinnamon and/or cinnamon sticks for garnishing

Grind the rice in a spice or coffee grinder to a fine powder. This is an important step. Transfer the rice to a large jar and add the cinnamon stick pieces. Pour the hot water over the rice, stirring to blend well. Cover with plastic wrap and set aside at room temperature overnight, or a minimum of 8 hours.

The next day, remove the pieces of cinnamon stick and transfer the rice and water mixture to blender. Blend until the mixture is smooth. Line a wire-mesh strainer set over a bowl with three layers of cheesecloth. Pour the pureed rice mixture through the cheesecloth. Squeeze the cheesecloth to extract all of the liquid. Discard the solids left in the cheesecloth. Stir in the sugar, vanilla bean seeds, and milk until the sugar is dissolved. Refrigerate to chill before serving. Stir well before serving over ice, adding a liqueur if desired. Garnish with a light dusting of ground cinnamon and a cinnamon stick, if desired.

Kir Royale

MAKES 6
COCKTAILS

The Kir cocktail originated in Dijon, France, during World War II, a creation of the Canon Felix Kir, who was both a priest and the mayor of Dijon. The Kir was originally a combination of dry white wine and Crème de Cassis, a deeply colored sweet liqueur made from black currants. At some point, champagne was substituted for the white wine and the cocktail was then called a Kir Royale. It is considered one of the most popular aperitif cocktails, and is perfect for serving to several people at brunch. I remember when I first discovered the Kir Royale, in my early days of discovering the art of drinking in general. I considered myself to be very sophisticated when ordering the cocktail while out for a "drink" with the girlfriends at some of the fine old bars in Houston.

There should be just a touch of the liqueur—just enough to color the champagne and lighten its acidity. The cocktail is served in a champagne flute. When opting for white wine to prepare a Kir, use a bone-dry white wine and serve it in a white wine glass. I have come to really love the Texas Albarino produced by Lost Draw Cellars, and it makes a great Kir. You can also vary the cocktail by using peach, blackberry, or raspberry liqueur in place of the Crème de Cassis.

1 (750-ml) bottle good-quality dry champagne, sparkling wine, or dry white wine, well chilled
3 to 4 teaspoons Crème de Cassis

Place ½ teaspoon of the Crème de Cassis in each of 6 champagne flutes (or white wine glasses if you are using wine). Fill the glass with sparkling wine or white wine and serve at once.

Southerleigh Fine Food & Brewery's Watermelon-Wheat Beer Cocktail

SERVES 4

This cooling and refreshing cocktail is the perfect drink for the torrid summers in Texas. Makes a great brunch cocktail. Southerleigh uses organic watermelons from Martinez Organic Farms in Floresville to make the cocktail.

½ of a smallish (7- to 8-pound) chilled watermelon, rind and seeds removed, roughly chopped
Equal parts of flaky sea salt, such as Maldon, and a good chili powder, tossed to blend well
4 Southerleigh Seawall Belgian Wheat beers, well chilled
Sprig of fresh thyme

Chill four tall highball glasses. Puree the watermelon chunks in a high-speed blender, such as a Vitamix, until smooth. Dip the rims of the glasses in the pureed watermelon just to moisten the edges. Place the sea salt and chili-powder mixture in a shallow bowl. Dip the moistened rims of the glasses into the dry mix to coat well. Pour a portion of the puree into each glass, filling them about ⅓ of the way. Pour in the beer to fill to the top, stirring lightly so that you don't cause the beer to foam, and scatter some of the thyme leaves over the surface. Serve at once.

Southerleigh Fine Food & Brewery's Peach, Wheat Beer, and Sparkling Rosé Cocktail

MAKES 12 TO 14
COCKTAILS

This is another delicious libation created by Chef Jeff Balfour and brewmaster Les Locke at Southerleigh's in the Pearl Brewery complex. It goes down mighty smooth on a hot summer day and makes a terrific pre-brunch cocktail. This is a good place to use up those peaches that are not picture-perfect!

3 medium-sized fresh peaches, peeled, pitted, and roughly chopped
3 cups good-quality vanilla ice cream such as Blue Bell Homemade Vanilla
1 cup Southerleigh Seawall Belgian Wheat beer
½ teaspoon vanilla extract
1 bottle well-chilled Graham Beck sparkling rosé
Fresh raspberries for garnishing

Combine the chopped peaches, ice cream, beer, and vanilla extract in a high-speed blender, such as a Vitamix. Puree until smooth. Transfer to a storage container with a tight-fitting lid and refreeze overnight.

To serve, scoop a portion of the frozen mixture into champagne flutes and fill with the sparkling rosé. Garnish each flute with a fresh raspberry. Serve at once.

TEXAS HILL COUNTRY DISTILLERY— LEGAL MOONSHINE

L et's make it very clear here that this is not your grandpappy's corn squeezins we're talking about. And, by the grace of the Texas Legislature, it's legal, and it's made in Comfort, Texas.

John and Cayce Kovacs never intended to become moonshiners. But one day back in 2012, Cayce visited a friend (who shall remain nameless) in Bandera and was treated to some homemade distillation made from prickly pear cactus! She was so impressed by the smooth taste of the liquor, despite its high level of alcohol, that she urged her husband to consider trying to make some of it.

To learn the process the right way, the couple made a forage into the deep woods of Kentucky, where moonshine still reigns, and sought out the best of the moonshiners to study their operations. Many, of course, would not allow any photos to be taken of them or their equipment. Although these distillers were using corn to make their 'shine, the couple queried them about the possibility of making it with a mash of prickly pear cactus from Texas. After sending samples of the pureed cactus mash they made to several of the distillers, the couple heard back from the distillers—all of whom agreed it was entirely doable. So John and Cayce decided to do it!

In September 2013, Texas state laws changed to allow retail sales of distilled spirits at the location of the distillery, including tastings. The Kovacses named their operation Texas Hill Country Distillers and received their state license in December of the same year. It took another six months to get their federal license, and their label was finally approved in October

2014, allowing them to actually sell their products. John chuckled as he recalled the legal process. "Well, what we wanted to do really didn't fit into any of the government categories, so they didn't know how to classify us. We weren't making vodka, or gin, or whiskey. So we applied to make 'moonshine' and were finally approved. Because we don't have a formulaic process like other distilled spirits makers, we can do pretty much as we wish. Our operation is much closer to those guys in the woods in Kentucky making 'shine than to big distilleries."

Texas Hill Country Distillers make seasonal moonshines. Currently they are producing prickly pear cactus and jalapeño moonshine. And these are 100%-handmade Texas products. The cactus is hand-harvested on Texas ranches, and the jalapeños are grown for John and Cayce by a farmer in Comfort. The prickly pear pads (thorns and all) and the jalapeños (seeds and all) are chopped by hand in the fermentation room at the distillery by two guys in rubber slicker suits who wear very heavy gloves and goggles. Sugar (rather than corn) is used as the "fuel" for the fermentation, along with yeast and a secret ingredient. The water is purified Texas rainwater that comes from a 30,000-gallon rainwater collection system at the Kovacses' home. After the fermentation, which involves a two-week process to produce the alcohol, the mash is strained and distilled only once. The finished product is unfiltered. Big distilleries distill their spirits eight or ten times to remove impurities and bad tastes, but the moonshine tastes great after just one distillation.

The Kovacses purchased the Comfort Cellars Winery property, situated in a charming old home on Comfort's Front Street, and renovated the tasting room. Visitors can taste the straight moonshine, or meander over to the cozy bar and purchase from a selection of mixed drinks made from the moonshine.

These two have become brunch favorites at my house.

Bloody Shiner

The Bloody Mary, generally made using vodka, is certainly the cocktail most often imbibed in the morning. Give your Bloody Marys a true Texas touch by making them with Texas legal moonshine. This is the recipe that's served at the cozy bar at Texas Hill Country Distillers in Comfort, Texas.

MAKES 1 DRINK

4 ounces Zing Zang-brand
    Bloody Mary Mix
1½ ounces Texas Hill Country
    Distillers cactus or jalapeño
    moonshine
Squeeze of fresh lime juice
1 dash Tabasco
Celery stick or pickled jalapeños
    for garnish

Add all ingredients to highball glass filled with ice, and stir to blend and chill. Garnish with a celery stick or a couple of slices of pickled jalapeños.

Watermelon-Mint Shine

I've found this tasty cocktail to be the perfect libation for a spring or summer brunch, especially when served outdoors. The fresh, summer flavors of the lime and watermelon mixed with the tequila nose of the cactus moonshine pair well with just about any brunch or breakfast.

MAKES 1 DRINK

5 fresh mint leaves
1 ounce agave nectar
3 lime wedges
4 large chunks of fresh, ripe
    watermelon
2 ounces Texas Hill Country
    Distillers cactus moonshine
Small watermelon slice and mint
    sprig for garnish

In a cocktail shaker, muddle the mint leaves, agave nectar, lime wedges, and watermelon chunks. Add ice and the cactus moonshine. Shake vigorously to blend the flavors and chill. Strain into a rocks glass filled with ice. Garnish with a small watermelon slice and a mint sprig.

Bill Varney's Lemon-Rose Martini

MAKES 1 DRINK

Bill Varney is one of my best friends. He is a self-taught, very good cook. But his true genius lies in growing and using fresh flowers and herbs. He founded the legendary Fredericksburg Herb Farm in Fredericksburg, Texas, from humble beginnings in a tiny herb shop on Main Street in 1985. The herb farm grew into a Fredericksburg destination. Bill sold the herb farm in 2007 and created a wonderful little herbal haven in Fredericksburg adjacent to the original herb farm property, which he named UrbanHerbal. There's a greenhouse with herbs and other plants for sale, a beautiful grounds with themed raised beds, a boutique shop where he sells handmade herbal products, and the Planet to Plate Cooking School, which he created in 2013. Bill teaches a variety of herb-centric classes in this small intimate classroom setting, and I join him in teaching when time permits. Then–food editor Karen Harem featured the school in a 2013 Sunday issue of the *San Antonio Express-News* Taste section.

Bill is always creating delicious herbal- or flower-oriented things to eat and drink. This luscious martini is a great example. I first tasted it one afternoon when Bill and I were relaxing in one of the inviting outdoor seating spaces on the grounds of UrbanHerbal, surrounded by fresh herbs and flowers. It's a perfect accompaniment to a simple, egg-based brunch dish.

2½ ounces Texas-made vodka
½ ounce Thatcher's Organic Artisan Liqueur
3 drops rose flower water
¼ teaspoon fresh-squeezed lemon juice
1 ounce Rose Simple Syrup (see recipe next page)
1 lemon peel strip (with no white pith)
Pink or red rose petal

Combine all ingredients except lemon strip and rose petal in a cocktail shaker with ice. Shake vigorously until icy cold. Rub the lemon peel around the rim of a martini glass, then twist it over the glass and drop it in. Strain the martini into the glass and serve, garnished with a floating rose petal.

Rose Simple Syrup

MAKES 1½ CUPS

1 cup of extra-fine granulated
   sugar
4 ounces organic red rose petals
1 cup distilled water
Juice of 1 lemon

In a food processor, grind the sugar and the rose petals until the mixture is finely ground with beautiful rose specks. In a small saucepan, bring the water and the rose sugar to a boil and immediately reduce to a simmer. Add the lemon juice and stir until dissolved. Allow to cool. Bottle and store in the refrigerator for up to a month.

Simple Bar Syrup

Simple Bar Syrup will keep indefinitely when placed in a jar with a tight-fitting lid and stored in the refrigerator. It's handy to have on hand to sweeten various drinks as the need arises.

MAKES 1 QUART

2⅓ cups sugar
1⅓ cups water

Combine sugar and water in a heavy-bottomed medium-sized saucepan. Bring to a full boil and simmer for 3 to 4 minutes, or until sugar is completely dissolved. Remove from heat and cool before using.

Ramos Gin Fizz

MAKES 1 DRINK

The frothy smooth and creamy Ramos Gin Fizz cocktail was created in New Orleans in the late 1880s by bartender Henry Ramos. Legend has it that Ramos employed a line of "shaker boys" at his bar. The cocktail was processed and put into a shaker at one end of the line and passed down the line, shaken vigorously by each shaker boy and then poured into the serving glass at the end of the bar. The secret to the texture of a properly executed Ramos Gin Fizz is in the shaking, which must be very vigorous to froth the egg white and cream, giving the drink its silky texture. Because of its delicate citrus notes and creamy texture, it is a grand drink for brunch and it slips on like a fine silk dress. But be forewarned, the drink packs a wallop. Brennan's of Houston, with its New Orleans roots, serves the Ramos Gin Fizz. Its bartender, Ronnie Stidvent, uses London Dry Gin. He says that you should serve the drink "with a wicked glint in your eye." The cocktail, often called the "famous Ramos," is legendary but also has been enjoying a trendy resurgence.

In making Ramos Gin Fizzes at my house, I like to give them a taste of Texas, so I use Waterloo gin, which is produced by the Treaty Oak Distillery in Austin. The name of this gin has nothing to do with Napoleon and his infamous battle; rather, it is named after the city of Austin's original name—Waterloo. The gin has a true taste of Texas *terroir*; even the botanicals used in the distilling process are sourced locally. *Note:* Orange flower water, which comes in a fairly small bottle, can be found at major liquor stores throughout the state.

2 ounces half-and-half
2 ounces Waterloo gin
½ ounce freshly squeezed lemon juice
½ ounce freshly squeezed lime juice
1 large egg white
1 ounce orange flower water
2 to 3 drops pure vanilla extract
Club soda
Orange wheel as garnish

Combine all ingredients except club soda and orange wheel in a cocktail shaker filled with a few ice cubes. Shake it with all you've got until the mixture is very frothy and creamy. Strain into a tall, thin glass filled with ice. Top with club soda and stir vigorously to blend. Garnish with orange wheel and serve at once before the froth dies down.

Basil Mojito

MAKES 1 DRINK

While the exact date and impetus for creating the mojito cocktail are unclear, most food and beverage historians credit its geographic origin to Cuba. The story that seems most logical is that the drink was created by African slaves working in the sugarcane fields in Cuba as a refreshing respite after a day of hot, arduous work. The name *mojito* stems from the African word *mojo*, meaning to "cast a little spell." Imbibing several mojitos will certainly do that! The drink gained international attention when it became a favorite of Ernest Hemingway, who discovered it in a bar in Havana. I first discovered the drink at the lovely poolside bar at the regal Galvez Hotel in Galveston. It became my favorite poolside libation.

Being a fan of experimenting with fresh herbs, I was working in my herb beds on a particularly hot Texas day in the early summer when I picked an armful of fresh basil. I had invited a few friends over for an early patio supper later that day and intended to serve mojitos, my favorite cocktail for chilling out on a hot afternoon. Since I had not picked any mint, I decided to try the mojitos with some of that gorgeous basil I had picked. Wow, were they ever a hit! The rich and bracing flavor of the herb really adds an incredible zing to the drink. I particularly love the clear rum produced by the Treaty Oak Distillery in Austin.

6 to 7 large fresh basil leaves
½ ounce freshly squeezed
   lime juice
¾ ounce Simple Bar Syrup
   (see recipe on page 18)
Ice shards
1½ ounces Treaty Oak Distillery
   rum
Club soda

Muddle the basil leaves, lime juice, and Simple Bar Syrup in a highball glass using a muddler or the back of a large spoon (also called the "nape") to bruise the leaves and release their flavor. Fill the glass with ice shards, and add the rum. Top off the glass with club soda. Stir vigorously to blend well and distribute the flavors. Enjoy!

Hot Buttered Rum

MAKES ABOUT
2½ CUPS OF
BATTER, ENOUGH
FOR 32 DRINKS

Normally we think of brunch or breakfast cocktails as being chilled, but there's nothing better on a blustery winter day than brunch in front of a roaring fire with mugs of Hot Buttered Rum. Throughout the south, it's a Christmas holiday tradition to serve the warming cocktail. It actually predates the American colonies, as it was the drink enjoyed in England where it was made using brandy. The early colonists brought stocks of brandy with them and continued the tradition of the hot drinks. When trade routes to Jamaican ports were established, sailors discovered the heady local rums, which, being easier to obtain, were soon substituted for brandy in the winter cocktail.

During the winter I always have a container of the buttery base for the cocktail in my freezer. I particularly like to make the comforting libation using Pecan Street Rum, produced by the Spirit of Texas Independent Distillery in Pflugerville, Texas. The rum is actually aged in oak with Texas pecans. It has a great nose of butterscotch with a whiff of orange that promises a hint of sweetness on the pecan base.

. . . .

HOT BUTTERED RUM BATTER

½ cup (1 stick) unsalted butter, room temperature
1 pound dark brown sugar
½ teaspoon ground cinnamon
¼ teaspoon freshly ground allspice berries
¼ teaspoon freshly ground whole cloves
1 cup good-quality vanilla ice cream, slightly softened

PER DRINK

2 ounces Pecan Street Rum
1 heaping tablespoon Hot Buttered Rum Batter (see recipe above)
1 cup boiling water
Cinnamon stick as garnish

Prepare the Hot Buttered Rum Batter. In the bowl of a stand mixer, cream the butter and brown sugar at medium speed until light and fluffy, about 5 minutes, stopping to scrape down side of bowl 2 or 3 times. Add the spices and ice cream. Beat just to blend well, about 1 minute. Pack the batter into freezer containers with tight-fitting lids and store in freezer.

To prepare individual drinks, place the rum and 1 tablespoon of the batter in a large mug and add boiling water to cover. Use a small whisk to dissolve the butter. Add cinnamon stick garnish and serve hot.

Don Strange Hot White Chocolate

MAKES 5
8-OUNCE
SERVINGS

Don Strange, a San Antonio native, was a Texas icon who founded, with his parents, one of the largest catering companies in Texas. Don's company catered events from coast to coast and points in between—including Henry Winkler's birthday party at his home in Hollywood for four years in a row, the Congressional Barbecue on the lawn of the White House, and a Texas-style extravaganza at the home of onetime NFL Commissioner Pete Rozelle in New York—in addition to staging various shindigs at remote ranches all over West Texas. He created this great winter beverage for several events that were held during the Christmas holidays in 2009. As the drink is pristinely white, it makes a beautiful presentation when served in white mugs with silver and white holiday decorations. The addition of the optional liqueur is purely my improvisation, but it's quite tasty!

2 cups whole milk
2 cups evaporated milk
½ cup whipping cream
1 cup white chocolate chips
1 teaspoon white vanilla extract
⅛ teaspoon freshly grated nutmeg
⅔ cup peppermint schnapps or Godiva white chocolate liqueur, optional
Sweetened whipped cream, beaten to stiff peaks
5 large mint leaves
5 raspberries

Combine all ingredients except nutmeg and garnishes in a heavy-bottomed 2-quart saucepan over medium-low heat. Cook, stirring often, until all ingredients are blended and chocolate chips are melted. When the mixture is hot, but not boiling, stir in the nutmeg (and the peppermint schnapps or Godiva white chocolate liqueur, if desired), mixing well. Serve hot in mugs, topped with a rosette of the whipped cream. Garnish each mug with a single mint leaf and a raspberry.

Adapted with permission from *Don Strange of Texas: His Life and Recipes,* by Frances Strange and Terry Thompson-Anderson (Shearer Publishing, 2010).

La Gloria's Mexican Hot Chocolate

Perfect for brunch on a chilly winter day, or for serving to the kids. This recipe is the personal hot chocolate recipe of Johnny Hernandez, owner of San Antonio's popular La Gloria restaurants and La Fruiteria.

SERVES 8

48 ounces whole milk
1½ (3-inch-long) Mexican canela cinnamon sticks
2 teaspoons Mexican vanilla
1¼ teaspoons freshly ground allspice berries
1 cup piloncillo
20 whole, skin-on almonds
1 pasilla chile, stem, seeds, and veins removed
1 cup cacao nibs

In a heavy-bottomed 3-quart saucepan, combine all ingredients and bring to a simmer. Remove from stove and set aside to steep for 30 minutes.

Transfer to blender and puree to a smooth consistency. Strain and return to medium heat. Bring to a low simmer and serve hot.

TWO

Crack an Egg

SIMPLE, CLASSIC, AND
FANCY PRESENTATIONS

*

THE
BASICS OF
COOKING
EGGS

R egardless of the method by which you wish to cook eggs, the most important factor in achieving optimum success and flavor is the eggs. Use fresh, cage-free, preferably pastured eggs whenever possible. "Yard eggs," as fresh eggs from free-ranging hens were called when I was a kid, can be found at your local farmer's market, and cage-free, pastured eggs are now appearing in supermarkets, too. I've read a few opinions that say the taste of fresh, pastured eggs is no different than that of caged mass-produced eggs, but my own taste tests prove otherwise. And the peace of mind that comes from knowing where the chickens who laid the eggs I eat are raised, and under what conditions, and what they are fed, is worth the trouble of seeking them out. We all know the adage that we "are what we eat." But it's also true that fresh eggs produce the best shape, which is important if you want your fried eggs to look good on the plate and your poached eggs to have a nice, round look with no flyaway strands of white. Fresh eggs are elongated, with a thick white closely hugging— rather than spreading around—a high-standing yolk.

Regarding the temperature of eggs to be cooked, there are devotees on both sides of the issue. Some say it's best to have eggs at room temperature, while others see no difference. I personally have tried them both ways, and must say that I see no difference.

Using good pans to cook eggs is also essential to success. Thin metal pans tend to overcook eggs and cause sticking. Invest in a couple of good heavy sauté pans—an 8-inch and a 10-inch for the best results. I have become very fond of the ceramic pans for cooking eggs. And you can't beat a well-seasoned cast-iron skillet. I do not recommend cooking eggs in the microwave.

The fat in which you cook eggs is another important component to achieving optimum taste. You can fry an egg in a nonstick pan with no fat and it will slip out of the pan easily, but without fat, it will look like a rubber toy egg and have about the same flavor. Fat—whether butter, lard, bacon drippings, vegetable oil, grapeseed oil, or olive oil—adds moisture and flavor. You don't need much, but don't compromise the flavor of those precious eggs by scrimping on the fat.

– FRYING EGGS –

There are many methods by which you can fry an egg—basted (with hot fat), steam-basted (with water in a covered pan), over easy (lightly cooked on the second side), or over hard (fully cooked on both sides with a set yolk). While eggs are generally fried gently over medium heat, it is often desirable to cook them over high heat, which produces brown, lacy, crisp edges and great flavor.

For 1 to 2 servings of simple fried eggs (over easy or over hard), heat 1 tablespoon fat of your choice, or according to recipe, in an 8- or 10-inch skillet over medium-high heat until just hot enough to sizzle a drop of water. Break and slip 2 eggs into the pan and immediately reduce heat to low. Cook slowly until the whites are completely set and the yolks begin to thicken, but are still quivery. Gently lift the eggs with a spatula and flip upside down into the pan to cook the second side to desired degree of doneness. Invert onto a serving plate yolk sides up.

For sunny-side-up eggs, fry them as above, only cook them on one side only until the whites are set and the yolks are still fairly runny.

For steam-basted eggs, reduce the initial fat to just enough to grease the bottom of the skillet. Heat as for over-easy eggs, then break and slip the eggs into the pan. Immediately reduce heat to low. Cook until the edges begin to turn opaque, about 2 minutes. Add 1 tablespoon water. Cover the pan tightly with a lid to hold in the steam. Cook until the whites are completely set and the yolks begin to thicken, but are not hard.

For fat-basted eggs, increase the cooking fat to 2 tablespoons and cook until the whites are beginning to set and the yolks are still very uncooked. Using a long-handled spoon, spoon the fat from the pan over the surface of the eggs continuously until the whites are completely set and the yolks are covered with a white glaze. Cook to desired degree of doneness.

In his classic work, *Beard on Food*, James Beard wrote: "There are few things as magnificent as scrambled eggs, pure and simple, perfectly cooked and perfectly seasoned."

When scrambling eggs in large batches, you may find that they turn an unattractive greenish shade. This outcome, although harmless, is not altogether desirable! It is simply a chemical reaction—the formation of ferrous sulfide from iron in the yolks and sulfur in the whites. It can occur when eggs are cooked in an iron skillet or when they are cooked at too high a temperature, held too long, or both. Use a nonstick pan to scramble eggs and, when cooking a large batch, add a teaspoon or more of fresh lemon juice when beating the eggs and cook as usual over low heat.

I learned to cook the perfect scrambled egg not in culinary school but from Julia Child—quite simply because I was in the right place at an opportune time. At an early 1980s conference of the newly founded International Association of Cooking Schools (now the International Association of Culinary Professionals, or IACP) held at San Francisco's elegant St. Francis Hotel, the group was quite small and we all fit in one banquet room. It was the era when omelet stations had become *de rigueur* at hotel banquet breakfasts, so at our breakfasts that year there were omelet stations. One morning, Julia entered the room with her husband, Paul, and proceeded to an omelet station where she asked the chef, a jacket-clad young man behind the butane burner, "Might I get just a perfectly scrambled egg instead of an omelet?"

Now, although Julia could have had anything she wished, it was when she asked him "So, young man, do you know how to perfectly scramble an egg?" that he began to stammer, eventually admitting that he probably did not. Julia said she would teach him, and strode behind the table to his station, commandeered his sauté pan, three fresh eggs, and an inordinate amount of butter, then asked for some tepid water and a whisk.

Seizing an opportunity that we'd most likely never have again, several of us fledgling chefs collectively slid into a space close enough to see and hear Julia's mini-seminar. She broke the eggs into a mixing bowl and added some of the water and a little salt—emphasizing that the salt should always be added while whisking the eggs, never after they were cooked! Then, in her vigorous, exaggerated style, she whisked the eggs into a frenzy, with bits of yolk and white flying out of the bowl at every angle. When she was satisfied that the eggs had a full head of froth, she added some of the butter to the nonstick sauté pan, took a look at it as it melted, and added just a bit more. When the buttery foam subsided, she poured in the beaten eggs and began to stir them over medium-low heat.

Patiently she stirred—bending her six-foot-plus frame over the low table and telling the young chef the eggs could not be rushed. As she stirred—making sure that she scraped the sides of the pan with each pass of the spoon, then the center, ever so diligently—the eggs began to coagulate and form little yellow, puffy curds. She stirred for almost 10 minutes, and now admonished all of us to notice how the eggs began to change. Then she announced that they were done. We craned our necks to look at Julia's "perfectly scrambled egg" as she lifted the pan from the burner. They were, in fact, the most beautiful, perfectly scrambled eggs I had ever seen. They had just reached the point of being completely coagulated, but we could see that they were soft, almost cloud-like. I was actually salivating for a bite and I just had to ask her about all that butter, which had disappeared. Being always the teacher, she explained that in the process of the slow cooking, the eggs actually form an emulsion with the butter—as eggs and butter do when you make hollandaise sauce. The butter, in all its delicious golden goodness, was now an integral part of the puff of scrambled eggs that she slid effortlessly onto the plate that Paul held out for her.

I've never forgotten that chance lesson in scrambling eggs, and I've never scrambled one since without thinking of Julia.

Perfectly Scrambled Eggs for Two

4 tablespoons (⅓ stick) unsalted butter
6 eggs, preferably free-range
⅓ cup tepid water
½ teaspoon kosher salt

Melt the butter in a 10-inch nonstick sauté pan over medium heat. Meanwhile, break the eggs into a fairly large mixing bowl and whisk them until the whites and yolks are well blended. Add the water and salt, and whisk them vigorously until frothy.

When the butter foam subsides, pour the eggs into the pan, lower the heat to medium-low, and begin to stir, making sure to stir all parts of the pan to keep the eggs from sticking. Be patient and stir just until the point when the eggs have coagulated and no liquid egg is visible—about 10 minutes. Stir for another few seconds, just to be sure; then slide the eggs onto 2 serving plates and feast, courtesy of Julia Child.

An omelet is a beautiful creation made by simply beating eggs, then cooking them until almost set, then filling them with ingredients as simple as shredded cheese or as complex as combinations of seasoned cooked meats and/or vegetables. Sometimes omelets are topped with additional cheese or simple garnishes, or a sauce or salsa.

A fairly plain cheese-filled omelet can be served for a simple but satisfying breakfast, or omelets can be gussied up as elegant brunch dishes. They also make for fine dinners.

To prepare omelets for two, beat four large eggs with ¼ teaspoon kosher salt, and pinches of freshly grated nutmeg and cayenne pepper, until quite frothy. Melt two tablespoons of unsalted butter each in two 7-inch nonstick skillets over low-medium heat. When the buttery froth subsides, pour half of the beaten eggs into each skillet. Cook until the eggs begin to set, then lift up the edges of the omelet using a flat spatula, letting the uncooked eggs slide underneath. Do this two or three times and gently scrape the spatula under the eggs to keep them from sticking. When the eggs are almost set, place half of desired filling slightly to the right of the center of the omelets. If using cheese, it should be shredded for easy melting. Vegetable and/or meat fillings should be completely cooked and chopped before adding. Flip the left bare half of the omelet over the filling, covering it. Cook to melt cheese and/or heat the other fillings, then slide the omelets onto serving plates and brush a bit of melted butter over them. Top with cheese, sauce, or garnishes as desired and apply your fork to that half-moon of heavenly taste.

– POACHING EGGS –

Sounds like a simple enough task, but there is an art to it. And to be a great brunch cook, you must master the technique of poaching eggs. To give yourself a "leg up" on the process, use the freshest eggs you can find. They will hold their shape better and produce fewer unruly strands of white meandering off from the main body of the egg. You can also add a bit of white vinegar to the poaching water to aid in keeping the whites corralled. But never add salt to the poaching liquid, as it will toughen the eggs.

Fill a heavy, deep-sided 12-inch skillet ⅔ full of water. Add ¼ cup of plain white distilled vinegar. Bring the water to a bare simmer. Break the eggs, one at a time, into a small bowl; then slide them into the barely simmering water. Add up to 6 eggs to the water at a time. Cook the eggs for 3 minutes for a nice, soft yolk, or longer if you wish to set the yolks to a firmer texture.

Remove the eggs from the pan carefully, using a slotted spoon and taking care not to break the yolks. Gently blot off excess water before using the eggs. Let the water return to the gentle simmer before poaching additional eggs.

A restaurant trick that can save time when poaching eggs for a crowd is to poach all of the eggs that you will need, using the method above, but poach them for only 2 minutes. Carefully remove them with a slotted spoon and float them in a large bowl filled with ice water. Set the iced eggs aside, finishing them at the last minute by returning the eggs to the simmering water and poaching for 1 additional minute, or longer, as desired. The eggs can be held for an hour or two in the ice-water bath, as long as you keep replenishing the melting ice. Remove the eggs from the final minute's poaching, blot dry, and use as desired. If you really want your poached eggs to be very uniform in size and shape, cut off any unruly edges using a sharp 3-inch biscuit cutter.

– SHIRRING EGGS –

Shirred eggs are simply eggs that are baked in the oven individually in a flat-bottomed dish. They make an excellent brunch dish because they're so easy to prepare for a lot of people. Traditionally the eggs were cooked in a vessel called a *shirrer*; hence the name of the dish. However, the name applies today regardless of the type of dish in which the eggs are cooked. They are usually baked simply with some butter and maybe a tablespoon or two of heavy cream.

Innovative chefs today, however, have taken great liberties with the cooking of shirred eggs. Often, pre-cooked meats, fish or shellfish, or vegetables are added to the bottom of the dish, with the eggs broken over them, then baked. Alternatively, the eggs are sometimes covered with cheese and/or a sauce.

To prepare shirred eggs, preheat oven to 350 degrees. Grease a 6- to 8-ounce gratin dish with butter, oil, or nonstick cooking spray. Add cream and melted butter to the bottom of the dish and any pre-cooked flavoring ingredients that you like—crumbled bacon, slices of ham or sausage, smoked or baked fish or shellfish, vegetables (such as sautéed mushrooms, asparagus tips, leftover ratatouille)—and shredded cheese. You can also add more complex, cream-based pre-cooked preparations. Break an egg over the top and season with kosher salt and/or freshly ground black pepper.

Place the dishes on a baking sheet and bake in preheated oven for 10 to 12 minutes, or just until the whites are set and the yolk is beginning to thicken. Serve at once.

Huevos con Migas

SERVES 6 TO 8

This dish, whose name translates roughly as "eggs with tortilla strips," is a Tex-Mex classic, and one of my go-to dishes to cook for overnight guests or an early-morning crowd. But when I started investigating the dish, I discovered that its origins actually trace to Spain, where the word *migas* means "crumbs," and that it is a very old traditional Spanish dish. It was created as a way to use stale bread, and was often the mainstay of shepherds who ranged far from home to tend their flocks. They flavored the stale bread with garlic and olive oil or lard and toasted it over their campfires.

The Tex-Mex version of migas is generally considered to have originated in Austin, Texas, as a use for leftover hardened tortillas. (But I must add that there are also some great migas to be found in San Antonio.) There are no specific recipes for making migas. Every Tex-Mex cook has his or her own version, and the ingredients vary. I've adapted the traditional cooking method by baking the dish, rather than scrambling it right before serving. This way, all of the component parts of the dish can be prepared ahead, then assembled and popped into the oven in the morning right before serving. Makes a really good, easy-to-serve breakfast. Serve with Mexican chorizo links or bacon and heated corn or flour tortillas.

Canola oil for pan frying

7 corn tortillas, cut in half, then into ½-inch-wide strips

12 eggs

⅓ cup medium-hot water

2 teaspoons kosher salt

1 teaspoon toasted, then ground cumin

2 large poblano chiles, blistered, peeled, seeded, and cut into 1½-inch dice

1 medium white onion, cut into ¼-inch dice

1 large homegrown tomato, peeled, seeded, and cut into ¼-inch dice

1½ cups (6 ounces) shredded Asadero cheese or Monterey Jack cheese

Your favorite salsa or pico de gallo

Preheat oven to 350 degrees; spray a 9 × 13-inch baking dish with nonstick spray; set aside. Heat the canola oil in a heavy-bottomed 10-inch skillet over medium heat. Fry the tortilla strips until they are light golden brown and crisp, about 3 to 4 minutes. Using a skimmer, remove the tortilla strips and drain them on a paper-towel-covered wire rack set over a baking sheet.

Break the eggs into a large bowl and whisk them with the hot water, salt, and ground cumin until very frothy. Add all remaining ingredients, including the tortilla strips, but not the salsa or pico de gallo. Turn the mixture out into prepared baking dish and bake in preheated oven for about 25 to 30 minutes, or until eggs are set to desired consistency. Stir the eggs every 5 minutes while they're baking. Serve hot, passing the salsa or pico de gallo separately.

Fried Eggs with Sage Brown Butter

SERVES 2

My herb bed sits right outside the side door to my kitchen, so it's easy to step out and pick a few leaves of wonderfully tasty fresh sage to cook up this ridiculously easy dish when I need a breakfast in a hurry. Eggs are such a perfect protein, and it seems that they have now been taken off the list of "do not eat" foods. Add some fresh fruit and/or berries and you've got a great start to your day. When my tomatoes are ripe, I often add a couple of slices of one of those deep red beauties to this plate instead of fruit.

This is a very simple and delicious dish that should be prepared right before serving.

4 tablespoons unsalted butter, divided
8 fresh sage leaves, divided
4 eggs, divided
Kosher salt and freshly ground black pepper
Fruit or sliced tomatoes

You will need two small (7-inch) non-stick skillets (I'm especially fond of the ceramic "green" ones) with lids or something that will suffice as a lid. Melt 2 tablespoons of the butter in each skillet. As soon as it has melted, toss 4 of the sage leaves into each skillet. Cook over medium heat to brown the butter, about 2 minutes. Crack 2 eggs directly into each skillet. Season the eggs with salt and pepper, lower the heat slightly, and cover the pans. Cook for 3 minutes, or until the egg whites are set.

Using a flexible metal or nonstick spatula, scoop the eggs out onto two serving plates. Drizzle that luscious brown butter and sage leaves over the eggs, add fruit or sliced tomatoes, and enjoy.

Arepas with Olive Oil–Fried Eggs and Salsa

SERVES 6

Arepas, simple or complex corn cakes, are a Central and South American (especially Colombian) breakfast tradition that have recently become very trendy in many parts of the United States. The trend has really taken off in Texas with our sizable population of Central and South American residents. There are many variations, but I especially like this version with its great nubby texture and sensational flavor. Arepas are generally fried in olive oil, so what better accompaniment than eggs fried in olive oil? This is a great dish for either breakfast or brunch.

The arepas may be prepared ahead through the stage of frying, then gently reheated in the oven prior to serving. The salsa can also be made ahead of time. Fry the eggs and assemble the plates when ready to serve.

. . . .

SALSA

5 Roma tomatoes, preferably homegrown, cut into small dice
3 serrano chiles, seeds and veins removed, minced
2 tablespoons freshly squeezed lime juice
½ of a smallish red onion, cut into tiny dice
3 tablespoons minced fresh cilantro
Salt to taste

AREPAS

1 cup half-and-half, divided
¾ cup frozen corn kernels, thawed
1 cup canned hominy, well drained
2 tablespoons sugar
1 cup shredded Asadero cheese
1 cup maseca (tamale dough flour)
1 teaspoon kosher salt
All-purpose flour, as needed
Extra-virgin olive oil for frying

OLIVE OIL–FRIED EGGS

Extra-virgin olive oil for frying
12 eggs
Kosher salt and freshly ground black pepper to taste ››

Begin by making the salsa. Combine all ingredients except salt in a medium-sized bowl and stir to blend well. If you are going to use the salsa now, add salt to taste. If you wish to refrigerate it for use later, don't add the salt until ready to serve. (The salt will cause the tomatoes to "weep" and make the salsa watery.)

Prepare the arepas. Combine ½ cup of the half-and-half, corn kernels, hominy, and sugar in work bowl of food processor fitted with steel blade. Process until mostly smooth, leaving a little bit of texture. Turn out into a medium-sized bowl. Stir in the Asadero cheese, maseca, kosher salt, and remaining ½ cup of half-and-half. Stir just to blend well, but don't get heavy-handed, or the arepas will be heavy. If the dough is too sticky to form cakes, add some all-purpose flour, 2 tablespoons at a time, stirring in thoroughly but gently, until the consistency is right. Set the dough aside to rest, covered with a clean towel, for about 20 minutes.

Divide the dough into twelve portions and roll into balls. Cover work surface with a sheet of parchment paper and place the rounds about 3 inches apart on the parchment. Use a large cutting board to cover the dough balls, pressing down on it to form cakes about ½ inch thick.

Heat a thin glaze of olive oil in a heavy-bottomed nonstick skillet. (I've grown fond of ceramic skillets for their great nonstick properties.) When the oil is hot, add some of the arepas, but don't crowd the pan. They should not be touching. Fry them for 2 to 3 minutes, depending on the amount of browning desired, keeping in mind that they should be crispy on the outside. Turn and fry until browned on the other side. Drain on absorbent paper towels placed on a wire rack and repeat with remaining cakes, adding additional olive oil to the pan as needed. Keep warm while frying the eggs.

Wipe out the skillet and heat 3 tablespoons of olive oil. When the oil is screaming hot enough to make a drop of water sizzle, slide in two eggs. Season them at once with salt and freshly ground black pepper. Cook over slightly medium-high heat, spooning some of the oil over the eggs, until the edges of the eggs begin to get bubbly and lacy and golden brown. The yolks should be nice and runny and the bottoms slightly browned. Set aside to keep hot and repeat with the remaining eggs, adding additional olive oil as needed. *Note:* If you can multi-task, you can have two (or more) skillets going at once to cook the eggs quickly.

To serve, place two of the arepas on each plate, slightly overlapping. On the opposite side of the plate, place two of the fried eggs. Spoon a portion of the salsa into the middle of the plate and serve at once.

Aldaco's Breakfast Rellenos

SERVES 6

Blanca Aldaco is a gem among fans of upscale Tex-Mex food in San Antonio. Known for her sassy ponytail and referred to as a "fiesta in heels" for her habit of wearing stylish high-heeled shoes even when working in the kitchen, Blanca was born in Guadalajara, Mexico, long known as a city of distinctive cuisine. Bringing those traditional flavors and techniques with her to San Antonio, she opened the first Aldaco's restaurant in 1989 on San Antonio's Commerce Street, serving what she refers to as "cantina food." But as the spot became a local favorite, it quickly outgrew the original location and Blanca moved to a large location at San Antonio's historic Sunset Station. In 2008 a second location was opened in the Stone Oak area, followed even more recently by a third location near The Dominion. This is one of Blanca's most popular brunch dishes, which she serves at both Saturday and Sunday brunch at her restaurants, and to guests in her own home, where she serves it with Mimosas and Bloody Marys. To lighten the last-minute preparation, you can stuff the chiles and make the crema poblano ahead of time, then bake the chiles and heat the sauce just before serving.

Blanca serves refried beans and chunks of potatoes fried golden brown with the dish– a very attractive presentation. To make this a tasty vegetarian dish, simply omit the ham from the filling.

CHILES

8 medium-sized poblano chiles, blistered, peeled, and deveined, divided

12 ounces shredded Monterey Jack cheese

Scrambled egg filling (see recipe below)

½ cups diced tomatoes, salted

½ cups thinly sliced green onions, including green tops

SCRAMBLED EGG FILLING

12 eggs

1 teaspoon kosher salt

4 tablespoons unsalted butter

6 ounces thinly sliced smoked ham, cut into small dice

2 green onions, chopped, including green tops

2 serrano chiles, stemmed, seeded, and minced

CREMA POBLANO

2 reserved, blistered, and peeled poblano chiles

½ cup whole milk

1 teaspoon kosher salt

2 tablespoons canola oil

½ medium onion, sliced very thin

2 large garlic cloves, minced

1 cup whipping cream

. . . .

Begin by preparing the chiles. Preheat oven to 350 degrees. Spray a baking dish large enough to hold the 6 chiles in a single layer with nonstick spray. Set aside 2 of the chiles for making the crema poblano. When the remaining 6 chiles have cooled after being blistered and peeled, cut a 2-inch slit in each chile, beginning at the very top and continuing lengthwise for 2 inches. Taking care not to tear the chile, carefully remove the seeds and veins. Repeat with all 6 of the chiles and set aside.

Make the scrambled egg filling. Beat the eggs and salt together vigorously until the eggs are frothy. Melt the butter in a nonstick skillet over low-medium heat. When the foam subsides, add the eggs all at once. Begin to stir, keeping the eggs moving until they are starting to take shape. Do not rush them! Stir in the ham, green onions, and serrano chiles while stirring. Continue to cook just until the eggs are barely done. Don't overcook them, as they will be further cooked when the chiles are baked. Set aside.

Make the crema poblano. Roughly chop the 2 reserved poblano chiles and place them in blender jar along with the milk and salt. Puree until very smooth; set aside.

Heat the oil in a medium saucepan over medium-high heat. Add the onion and garlic. Cook just until the onion is wilted and transparent, about 5 minutes. Add the pepper puree and the whipping cream. Simmer, stirring often, just until the mixture is slightly thickened and is very aromatic, 3 to 5 minutes. Remove from heat.

To assemble the dish, carefully open the slits in the chiles and scatter 1 tablespoon of the shredded cheese in the bottom of each. Spoon in about 2 heaping tablespoons of the scrambled egg mixture on top of the cheese, followed by another layer of the remaining cheese—again, about 1 tablespoon per chile. Form the chiles into their original shape and place them in the prepared baking dish, slit sides down. Pour the crema poblano over the chiles and bake in preheated oven until heated through, about 15 minutes.

Using a flat spatula, transfer the chiles to individual serving plates and pour some of the remaining crema poblano in the dish over each serving. Top with a scattering of the diced tomatoes and green onions. Serve at once.

Mama's Breakfast

SERVES 4 TO 6

The Barrios family has long been respected as one of San Antonio's purveyors of great Tex-Mex food. When matriarch and mother of three children Viola Barrios lost her husband and the debts began to mount, she turned to what she knew best—cooking from her heart. After scraping together the sum of $3,000, Barrios converted what had been an old garage used for repairing outboard motors into her restaurant, Los Barrios, opening it in 1979. Although its beginnings were humble, Los Barrios grew to the point where it was named one of the "100 Best New Restaurants in America" by *Esquire* magazine. Viola expanded her operations in 2004 with the opening of La Hacienda, which continued her tradition of offering *casero*-style, or "homemade," Tex-Mex foods. Viola Barrios was the victim of a violent crime that took her life in 2008. Her three surviving children, Diana Barrios Trevino, Louis Barrios, and Teresa Barrios Ogden, continued their mother's dream, opening Viola's Ventanas in 2013. Diana remembers eating this simple breakfast dish often at her mother's table.

Mama's Breakfast is a simple dish to prepare, but you can save a little last-minute time by chopping and preparing the ingredients according to the recipe instructions ahead of time.

¼ cup canola oil, divided
½ onion, chopped
1 serrano chile, seeds and veins removed, minced
4 tomatoes, halved and grated on the large holes of a box grater, and their juice
6 eggs, well beaten
Kosher salt to taste

Heat 2 tablespoons of the oil in a smallish, heavy-bottomed skillet over medium heat. Add the onion and chile and cook until the onion is wilted and translucent, 3 to 4 minutes. Add the tomatoes and simmer for 3 to 5 minutes. If the mixture looks dry, add a little water. Remove from heat and set aside.

Heat the remaining 2 tablespoons of the oil in a medium-sized, heavy-bottomed skillet over medium heat. Add the eggs and scramble for just 2 minutes; they should still be runny. Stir in the tomato mixture and season to taste with salt. Cook until the eggs are cooked through, but not overcooked.

Serve with refried beans, hot fried potatoes, and warm flour tortillas, bolillos (small, elongated hard rolls), or sliced French bread.

Fonda San Miguel's Huevos en Rabo de Mestiza

EGGS POACHED IN
MEXICAN SAUCE

SERVES 6

Austin's much-loved Fonda San Miguel Restaurant, a bastion of true interior Mexican cuisine, was founded by partners Tom Gilliland and Miguel Ravago as the San Angel Inn in Houston in 1972. Miguel's grandmother, Guadalupe Velasquez, born in Sonora, Mexico, came from her home in Phoenix to help set up the kitchen and get things started. San Angel Inn was discovered by Diana Kennedy, a leading authority on Mexican cuisine, and a relationship was formed that continues today, with Ms. Kennedy mentoring the pair. The San Angel Inn was the first restaurant to advertise in a new publication by the name of *Texas Monthly*. By 1975 San Angel Inn had outgrown its fifty seats, and the pair turned their attention to Austin, where they opened the present Fonda San Miguel in the space formerly occupied by a failed Tex-Mex restaurant in November 1975. In October 2015, Tom and Miguel celebrated the fortieth anniversary of Fonda San Miguel.

At a time when Austin was ground zero for lovers of Tex-Mex foods, it was a hard sell for the partners to get Austinites interested in the complex and markedly different dishes of interior Mexico. Tom and Miguel tell about the legions of customers who would come in, peruse the menu, and leave, being completely confused by the menu offerings, asking why there were no "combination plates." Sourcing the unusual ingredients was also problematic. But as adventurous customers—mostly university professors, hip graduate students, and visitors from Mexico, or Austinites who frequently traveled there—began to spread the word, the rest, as is said, "was history," and the restaurant became one of the city's most popular dining destinations.

Fonda San Miguel's Hacienda Sunday Brunch Buffet, which was introduced in 1985, has been consistently rated the best in Austin. Huevos en Rabo de Mestiza, which originated in the Mexican state of San Luis Potosí, is a favorite on the Sunday brunch table. This recipe reflects the way the dish was originally prepared at the restaurant.

This dish can be prepared ahead of time up to the point of poaching the eggs in the tomato sauce. Reheat the sauce and poach the eggs according to the directions on page 32. ››

⅓ cup canola oil

1 medium white onion, sliced

8 poblano chiles, roasted, peeled, seeded, and cut into ¼-inch strips

2 garlic cloves, minced

7 red, ripe tomatoes, roasted, peeled, and chopped

2 cups chicken broth

1 teaspoon sea salt

12 eggs

½ cup crumbled queso fresco

Warm corn or flour tortillas for serving

In a heavy Dutch oven, heat the oil over medium heat and fry the onion slices until wilted and transparent, about 3 to 5 minutes. Add about ⅔ of the chile strips and the garlic and cook an additional 3 minutes. Puree the tomatoes in a high-speed blender and add to the onion and chiles. Cook over medium heat, stirring often, for about 10 minutes. Add broth and sea salt and cook for another 3 minutes. Carefully break the eggs, one at a time, into the hot sauce. Poach uncovered over medium heat for 3 to 5 minutes for soft eggs, or cover the pan and poach 5 to 8 minutes for firmer eggs.

With a slotted spoon, transfer the eggs to individual serving bowls, 2 eggs per bowl. Top each serving with a portion of the reserved chile strips and the sauce. Garnish with a scattering of the queso fresco.

Fried Eggs with Lemon Asparagus and Queso Fresco

SERVES 2

When fresh asparagus begins to appear at the farmer's markets, it's a sure harbinger of spring. I love the crunchy texture of quickly cooked asparagus and its delicate taste. To my way of thinking, that taste is like the very taste of spring peeking out from the soil after the bolder flavors of winter crops have receded. This easy-to-prepare dish makes for a nutritious light breakfast that pops with flavor, and it looks great on the plate!

Any of my recipes in which asparagus appears call for peeling the asparagus. We know that the lower portion of the asparagus stalk is tough and woody, and that it is lopped off and discarded (well, mine goes to the chickens), but even the top portion has a slightly leathery skin. I remember Julia Child admonishing that the stalks must be peeled to remove that layer, and that's always been good enough for me! You'll find that the stalks are tenderer when peeled, and that their color is much more brilliant and striking on the plate. Use a sharp vegetable peeler—I like the ceramic ones—and do just one swipe around the stalk.

Peel and microwave the asparagus ahead of time. The dish is then easy to finish and serve.

---

10 medium-thick asparagus stalks, lower tough portion sliced off and discarded

Kosher salt

4 tablespoons unsalted butter, divided

2 heaping teaspoons grated lemon zest

2 eggs

Additional kosher salt and freshly cracked black pepper

½ cup (2 ounces) crumbled queso fresco cheese

Using a sharp vegetable peeler, peel the bottom half of the asparagus spears. Place them in a single layer in a microwavable baking dish. Scatter a fairly generous amount of the kosher salt over them and add cold water to not quite cover the spears. Microwave on high for 1 minute, then drain and plunge into ice water. When the spears are totally cool to the touch, drain and pat them dry.

Divide the butter among two 7-inch nonstick skillets and melt it over high-medium heat. When the foam subsides, add half of the asparagus spears to each skillet and scatter 1 teaspoon of the lemon zest over each. Cook for 1 minute. Crack one of the eggs directly over the asparagus in each skillet. Cover and cook for 3 minutes, or until the egg whites are set.

Using a flexible metal spatula, slide the asparagus and eggs onto serving plates, taking care not to break the yolks. Drizzle any buttery remains from the skillet over each serving. Then top each with salt, pepper, and half of the crumbled cheese. Serve at once.

Pondicheri Café's Saag Paneer Omelets

SERVES 6 TO 8

Indian cuisine has taken a strong foothold in Houston, due in great part to the efforts of Anita Jaisinghani, who opened Indika in 2001 and Pondicheri Café in 2011. Jaisinghani was born in Gujarat, India; her family's roots are in Sindh, Pakistan. In 1982 she moved to Canada, where she married; eight years later, in 1990, she moved to Houston. Claiming a lifelong passion for food, especially the food of her country, Jaisinghani opened Indika, an upscale restaurant featuring classic Indian cuisine. Believing that food reflects national identity, she felt that Indian cuisine was not represented well in the United States and wanted to open a restaurant that would showcase the foods of her culture while also allowing Americans to discover new foods. Indika has become one of Houston's top dining spots, having survived the vagaries of the Houston economy. But Jaisinghani also longed to offer Indian cuisine that appealed to a broader audience at a modest price. Pondicheri Café introduced Mumbai street food to Houston. Jaisinghani says that "it's the way everyday people eat in India." The café offers food that is easily accessible in a comfortable, modern setting. An especially impressive aspect of the offerings at Pondicheri is that traditional Indian breakfast dishes are served—and they're unlike anything Westerners are used to eating for breakfast. Pondicheri has changed the perception of how people feel about Indian foods. Jaisinghani has shown how it is all about the use of complex blends of spices and the freshest ingredients possible. When she grew up in India, everything was "fresh, local, and organic." She was shocked when she discovered the state of food and eating styles in the United States.

She describes the foods at Pondicheri Café as "nontraditional authentic," including parathas from Punjab, fish curries from Kerala, vindaloos from Goa, and millet rotis from Sindh—foods inspired by the cuisines of different regions of the subcontinent.

Pondicheri Café quickly outgrew its original space with its forty employees. When the space upstairs from the original restaurant became available, Jaisinghani jumped at the opportunity, opening the Bake Lab + Shop, offering traditional Indian pastries, cookies, spices, and condiments. All of the baking for Pondicheri Café is now done in the Bake Lab.

An iconic Indian-restaurant dish, saag paneer is a considered a legendary Punjabi winter preparation. *Paneer* is the only cheese that India can lay any claim to. It is just a simple unripened farmer's cheese, except that it has no rennet, only vinegar. And it has a simple pure milk flavor that blends well with most herbs and spices. The better the quality of the milk, the better the flavor and quality of the paneer. If you can find raw milk, by all means use it to make the paneer. Note that the paneer must be well drained and refrigerated to form a cohesive cheese. ››

2 bunches fresh spinach, stems
  discarded
1 bunch mustard greens, thick
  midribs discarded and leaves
  torn into bite-size pieces
3 serrano chiles
5 tablespoons ghee,* divided, plus
  more for brushing omelets
½ cup caramelized chopped onions

1 tablespoon minced garlic
2 tablespoons pureed fresh ginger
2 tablespoons dried fenugreek
  leaves
2 teaspoons garam masala
¾ cup whipping cream
12 to 16 eggs
Canola oil
Paneer (see recipe below)

½ gallon whole milk
¼ cup white distilled vinegar
1 teaspoon kosher salt
1 teaspoon freshly ground black
  pepper
1 teaspoon cumin seeds, toasted,
  then crushed
2 to 3 tablespoons canola oil for
  oiling baking sheet

* Ghee is essentially clarified butter that is cooked a bit longer until the clarified butter is golden and the milk solids at the bottom are toasted (but not burnt!). It's the butterfat without the lactose and casein, so it's easier to digest.

Another good reason for using ghee is that it has a very high smoke point, so it makes an excellent replacement for oils with low smoke points. Ghee is the traditional fat used in Indian cooking.

To make the ghee, place 1 pound of good-quality unsalted butter in a heavy-bottomed 2-quart saucepan over medium-high heat. Bring the butter to a boil, approximately 2 to 3 minutes. When the butter is boiling, reduce heat to medium. The butter will make a foam on top, which will cook away. Continue to cook until a second foam appears and the butter turns golden, about 7 to 8 minutes. The brown milk solids will settle to the bottom of the pan. Gently pour the mixture through a fine-meshed wire strainer or cheesecloth into a heatproof storage jar. Cover and store at room temperature, using as needed. The mixture will keep for about a month and yields slightly less than 2 cups of ghee.

Begin by making the paneer. In a heavy-bottomed stockpot, bring the milk to a boil over medium heat, stirring frequently. Just when the foam begins to rise, pour in the vinegar and add the salt, pepper, and crushed cumin seeds. Simmer the mixture for 5 to 6 minutes over medium heat. Reduce heat if necessary to maintain a simmer rather than a boil. The milk should form big curds, which should rise to the top, separating from the whey (the clear liquid in which the curds are floating). As soon as the liquid is clear, turn the heat off and let the paneer rest in the liquid for 20 to 30 minutes.

Over the sink, pour as much of the liquid into a cheesecloth-lined colander as you can without disturbing the curds. (A triple layer of Bounty paper towels may be used if you have no cheesecloth.) Using a slotted spoon, gently lift the curds out of the pot and place in the lined colander. Pour the remainder of the liquid over the curds. With the back of the slotted spoon, press the curds lightly to squeeze and discard most of the whey. Fold the cheesecloth over the paneer to cover it completely and let it drain in the sink for 2 hours.

Remove the cheesecloth from the colander with the drained paneer. The paneer should be a round firm wheel. Be careful when lifting—it is still fragile and can crack easily. At this point, you will need to refrigerate the wheel for several days, or up to a week, before proceeding to the next step.

When ready to finish the paneer, preheat the oven to 325 degrees. Oil a baking sheet and gently unwrap the wheel directly onto the baking sheet. Bake for 15 to 20 minutes, or until the paneer top has a nice golden color. Remove and let it cool. Wrap tightly in plastic wrap and store in the refrigerator for up to 2 weeks, or freeze for up to 3 to 4 months.

To prepare the omelets, wash the spinach and mustard greens under cold running water and drain well; set aside. Remove the stem tops of the serrano chiles and slice them into thin rounds crosswise.

In a large, heavy-bottomed stockpot, heat 2 tablespoons of the ghee over medium heat until hot. Add the caramelized onions, garlic, ginger puree, sliced chiles, and dried fenugreek. Sauté for a minute or two.

Add the spinach and mustard greens in batches and cook on high heat until wilted. Stir in the garam masala, turn the heat off, and transfer to a bowl so it does not continue to cook. Let the greens rest for 10 to 15 minutes. Don't discard any of the liquid that the spinach and mustard greens may have rendered. In small batches, puree the greens and their liquid in a blender until smooth, but evenly grainy, adding a portion of the whipping cream to each batch. Stir the batches together in one bowl. At this point, you may

refrigerate or freeze the saag. When ready to cook the omelets, heat the saag and drizzle the remaining ghee over it before using.

To make the omelets, grate the paneer using the medium blade of a box grater; set aside. For each omelet, thoroughly beat two eggs, then add 2 tablespoons of the saag and ½ cup of the grated paneer; beat to blend well. Heat 2 tablespoons of the canola oil in a 10- to 12-inch nonstick omelet pan. Pour in the saag mixture and cook

for a few minutes on medium heat, or until the bottom is firm. Add the desired amount of additional grated paneer to one side of the omelet, then slide a spatula under the omelet and flip the other half over the top. Cover the pan and cook the omelet for another 2 minutes, or until the omelet is set. Transfer to a platter and keep warm in a low oven while preparing the remaining omelets. Brush each omelet liberally with additional ghee and serve hot.

Bacon and Cheese Omelet

SERVES 2

You can dress up this quick and easy omelet for brunch by serving it with a passed basket of tasty biscuits, pastries, or crusty French bread and a few spears of buttered asparagus. Or serve it simply with toast and jam for a nice weekend breakfast for two.

An omelet is a simple but delicious meal. You can prepare the filling ingredients ahead, however, to save a little time before serving. For details on preparing omelets, see the directions on page 32.

OMELETS

4 large eggs
¼ teaspoon kosher salt
Pinch of freshly grated nutmeg
Pinch of cayenne pepper
2 tablespoons unsalted butter
Additional melted butter for glazing the omelets
Minced parsley as garnish

FILLING

10 slices applewood-smoked bacon
3 shallots, minced
⅔ cup (5 ounces) shredded Gruyère cheese

Prepare the filling. Preheat oven to 350 degrees. Place the bacon slices on a foil-lined baking sheet. Bake in preheated oven until crisp and well browned, about 25 minutes. Drain on absorbent paper towels. Transfer bacon drippings to a small skillet. Crumble the bacon slices into small bits and set aside. Heat the bacon drippings in the skillet and sauté the shallots until wilted and transparent, about 5 minutes. Toss with crumbled bacon and reserve.

Combine eggs, salt, nutmeg, and cayenne pepper in a medium-sized bowl and whisk until very frothy. For each omelet, melt 1 tablespoon of the butter in an 8-inch nonstick sauté pan. (I love ceramic pans for making omelets.) Prepare the omelet according to the directions on page 32. When the eggs are set in the pan, spread half of the bacon/shallot mixture across the omelet on the opposite side of the handle. Scatter half of the cheese over the bacon mixture. Tip the pan away from you, slide a spatula under the unfilled half of the omelet, and lift this half to cover the filling. Slide the omelet back to the center of the pan to allow the underside to brown. The side that is now on the bottom will become the top when the omelet is served. Take a serving plate in your left hand and grasp the handle of the omelet pan with your right hand. Tip the plate and pan at 45-degree angles to each other and invert the pan to cover the plate completely. The omelet will slide smoothly onto the plate. Brush the omelets with some of the melted butter and scatter minced parsley over the tops. Serve hot.

Herb and Cheese Omelet Panini

MAKES 2 OMELETS
AND 2 PANINIS

I am a great fan of focaccia bread, and it is so easy to make from scratch. So I try to always have several sandwich-size pieces in my freezer to make paninis (which originated in Italy) or other sandwiches. A panini is a sandwich that is compressed by pressure in a panini grill—or, if you don't have one, after the sandwich is browned, flip it and place an empty cast-iron skillet on top of it, cooking to sear the bottom side. This particular panini is the perfect breakfast-on-the-go hand food. It can be made using store-bought Texas toast, but is so much better on focaccia—even though the most time-consuming component of this dish is making the focaccia. Once you have the bread, however, it can be cut ahead of time and even frozen. Then it's easy to crank out the sandwiches for the whole family to have a "fast-food" breakfast with the peace of mind that comes with knowing what it's made of!

FOCACCIA BREAD

2½ teaspoons instant-rise yeast
½ cup warm water (105 to 115 degrees)
5 cups bread flour
2 teaspoons kosher salt
1½ cups whole milk
4 tablespoons olive oil

Oil a large bowl and set aside. Stir the yeast into the warm water in a Pyrex cup. Set aside to proof, or until it is very bubbly, about 4 to 5 minutes. In work bowl of food processor fitted with steel blade, combine the flour and salt. Pulse on/off 2 to 3 times to blend. Add the proofed yeast, milk, and olive oil. Process to bring the dough together. Stop and check consistency of the dough, adding additional flour or water as needed to form a smooth, nonsticky dough. Process for 20 seconds to knead. Turn dough out onto lightly floured work surface and knead several times by hand until smooth and elastic.

Place the dough in the oiled bowl, turning to coat all surfaces with oil. Cover tightly with plastic wrap and set aside to rise in a warm, draft-free spot, until doubled in bulk, about 45 minutes. Oil a 12 × 16-inch baking sheet with olive oil and line bottom only with parchment paper; oil the parchment and set baking sheet aside.

When the dough has doubled, punch it down and transfer to the prepared baking sheet. Flatten the dough out with your hands, covering the bottom of the sheet completely, all the way into the corners. Cover with plastic wrap and let rise until the dough reaches the top edge of the baking sheet. Preheat oven to 400 degrees.

When dough has risen, use your fingertips to make dimples about 1 inch apart and 1 inch deep all over the dough. Bake on middle rack of preheated oven until golden brown, about 20 minutes. Invert onto wire rack and carefully remove parchment paper. Allow bread to cool completely before slicing. When the bread has cooled, use a serrated bread knife to slice it into twelve 4-inch squares. Slice squares in half horizontally (making two thin slices) for use in making panini sandwiches. If you don't use all of the bread at once, wrap the cut squares singly in plastic wrap and place them in a zip-sealing bag. Freeze for up to a month. Thaw before using. ››

HERB AND CHEESE OMELETS

Focaccia bread
4 eggs
1 teaspoon kosher salt
3 tablespoons tepid water
4 tablespoons unsalted butter,
  divided
4 ounces (1 cup) shredded Asiago
  cheese, divided
1 teaspoon minced fresh rosemary,
  divided
1½ teaspoons minced fresh basil
2 green onions, finely chopped,
  including green tops, divided

Preheat panini grill and slice two of the cut focaccia breads in half lengthwise. Brush one side of each cut half with olive oil; set aside. If using slices of Texas toast, don't cut them in half. Just oil one side of each of 4 slices.

Beat the eggs with the salt and water until frothy. Melt 2 tablespoons of the butter in each of two nonstick, 7-inch sauté pans over low-medium heat. When the foam subsides, pour half of the beaten eggs into each skillet. Cook until the eggs begin to set, then lift up the edges of the omelet, letting the uncooked eggs slide underneath. When the eggs are almost set, place half of the cheese on each one, slightly to the right of the center. Scatter half of the herbs and green onions over the cheese on each omelet, then flip the left-bare half of the omelet over the cheese and herbs. Cook just until the cheese has melted. Remove from heat and set aside.

Place two of the cut focaccia halves in front of you, oiled side down, and slide an omelet onto each, folding the omelet in from both sides to fit the bread. Top with remaining bread halves, oiled side up.

Place the sandwiches in the panini grill and cook until golden brown. Enjoy.

Otto's German Bistro Kaiserschmarrn

SERVES 4 TO 6

When longtime Fredericksburg resident John Washburne opened Otto's German Bistro, the city founded by German immigrants in the mid-1800s was introduced to the cuisine of all the Germanic countries of Northern Europe. With Chef Adam Yoho at the helm in the kitchen, the small eatery quickly became a haven for locals. John and Adam share a mission to source their menu ingredients as locally and seasonally as possible, much like the original German settlers did out of necessity. When the pair added a Sunday brunch in early 2015 featuring classic Germanic fare, local fans and tourists alike were delighted to be able to have an authentic German breakfast in the city of such strong German heritage.

Kaiserschmarrn, a sort of cross between a soufflé and a pancake, is generally regarded as an Austrian dish and is served as both a breakfast and a light dessert. Otto's serves the dish with Weisswurst (see recipe on page 119), Potato Pancakes (see recipe on page 236), and a passed platter of Otto's German Bistro Gravlax with Pickled Red Onions and Horseradish Crème Fraiche (see recipe on page 175). Also pass desired bread or pastries.

8 eggs, separated
2 tablespoons sugar
¾ cup all-purpose flour
½ teaspoon kosher salt
½ cup sour cream
⅓ cup crème fraiche
Additional ½ cup sugar
1 tablespoon melted butter
Homemade preserves or fresh, seasonal fruit and berries

Preheat oven to 450 degrees; place oven rack in middle position. In bowl of stand mixer, combine egg yolks and 2 tablespoons sugar. Beat at medium-high speed until yolks are thickened and pale lemon-yellow in color. Combine flour and kosher salt, tossing with a fork to blend. Whisk together the sour cream and crème fraiche. Add to this mixture the yolks, alternating with the flour mixture, one half at a time, beating just to blend after each addition.

In a clean bowl, whip the egg whites until slightly frothy, then begin adding the ½ cup sugar while beating at medium-high speed. Beat until the whites are stiff, but not overbeaten. Fold the whites gently into the yolk mixture, incorporating evenly, but taking care not to deflate the whites.

Melt the butter in a 10-inch cast-iron skillet over medium heat, swirling the pan to coat bottom and sides. Turn the batter out into the skillet and place on middle rack of preheated oven. Cook for 15 minutes, then reduce heat to 350 degrees and continue to cook for 8 to 10 minutes, or until golden brown and set.

Remove from oven and slice into 4 to 6 wedges. Serve at once, topping each wedge with a dollop of preserves or fresh fruit and berries.

Baked Grits and Eggs with Mushroom Ragout

SERVES 6

My husband Roger's take on breakfast is that it's not really breakfast unless grits are involved. I think this is a pretty common line of thinking in Texas, as grits have been a breakfast staple since the days of the chuckwagons on cattle drives, although we've gussied them up considerably since then. It's perfectly acceptable to use *quick-cooking grits*, but avoid the *instant grits*, please. I love to serve this very flavorful dish for brunch in individual gratin dishes. It's always a big hit. You may use whatever combination of mushrooms you'd like, even only white button mushrooms, but the dish has a greater depth of flavor if you can include a few of the earthy woodland varieties. Be sure to serve some hot rolls or biscuits for sopping up all of the good juices that mingle with the grits in the bottom of the dishes!

The mushroom ragout can be made ahead of time and refrigerated, making the dish very easy to assemble and bake.

Mushroom ragout (see recipe at right)

Grits (see recipe at right)

6 large free-range eggs

1½ cups (6 ounces) shredded Brazos Valley Havarti cheese, or substitute another Havarti cheese

Minced Italian flat-leaf parsley as garnish

MUSHROOM RAGOUT

4 large tomatoes, preferably homegrown, about 2 pounds, peeled

¼ cup extra-virgin olive oil

2 ounces chanterelle mushrooms, stems removed, sliced

2 ounces shitake mushrooms, stems removed, sliced

1 large portabella mushroom, stem removed, chopped

4 ounces white button mushrooms, sliced

4 medium garlic cloves, minced

4 shallots, minced

2 teaspoons minced fresh thyme

½ teaspoon freshly ground black pepper

⅔ cup dry white wine

⅔ cup beef stock, preferably homemade

Kosher salt to taste

4 green onions, sliced thin, including green tops

GRITS

2 cups water

2 cups whipping cream

1 teaspoon kosher salt

1 cup quick-cooking grits (never use instant grits)

2 tablespoons unsalted butter

Begin by making the mushroom ragout. Chop the tomatoes into ½-inch dice, reserving all their juice; set aside. Heat the olive oil in a heavy-bottomed 12-inch skillet over medium-high heat. When the oil is hot, add all the mushrooms, garlic, shallots, thyme, and pepper. Cook, stirring often, until the mushrooms begin to brown, about 10 minutes. Add the wine and cook, stirring to scrape up browned bits from bottom of pan, until wine is reduced to a glaze. Add the tomatoes and their juice and the beef stock. Cook, stirring often, until liquids have reduced and a thick sauce has formed, about 15 minutes. Season to taste with salt. Stir in the green onions. Keep warm, or refrigerate if making ahead.

Cook the grits. Combine the water, cream, and salt in a heavy-bottomed 3-quart saucepan over medium-high heat. Bring to a full boil, then slowly pour in the grits, while whisking. Reduce heat to medium-low and continue to whisk the grits until well blended. Cover the pot and simmer the grits for about 30 minutes, whisking often. If they get too dry, add additional water and cream as needed to keep them good and creamy. They should be about the consistency of cream of wheat. Remove from heat and whisk in the butter, blending well. Preheat oven to 350 degrees.

To assemble and bake the dish, divide the grits among 6 (6-inch) individual gratin dishes set on baking sheets. Top with a portion of the mushroom ragout. Break an egg over each serving, taking care not to break the yolks. Place the baking sheets in preheated oven and bake for 10 to 15 minutes, or just until the whites of the eggs are set. Top each dish with a portion of the shredded cheese and parsley. Return to the oven and bake an additional 10 minutes, or until yolks are set to desired consistency and cheese has melted. Place the gratin dishes on individual plates and serve at once.

A Place in Time's Egg Breakfast Casserole with Fresh Ricotta Cheese

A Place in Time is one of Fredericksburg's loveliest bed-and-breakfast inns. Located in a 1914 Arts and Crafts–style home owned by friends Jon and Mary Kaye Sawyer-Morse, the B&B offers great breakfasts for guests in its cozy communal dining room. This casserole dish is perfect for those times when you need to feed breakfast to a group with a minimum number of dishes, yet want it to be memorable. Just add some fruit and a bread or pastry. The ricotta cheese can be made ahead of time and held in the refrigerator.

SERVES 4 TO 6

MAKES 2 CUPS RICOTTA

10 ounces lean bulk-style pork breakfast sausage
¾ cup sliced white button mushrooms
10 eggs, beaten
½ cup all-purpose flour
¾ teaspoon baking powder
2 cups (8 ounces) shredded Monterey Jack cheese
1½ cups fresh ricotta cheese (see recipe at right)

FRESH RICOTTA CHEESE

1 quart whole milk
2 cups heavy cream
1 teaspoon kosher salt
¼ cup freshly squeezed lemon juice ››

Make the fresh ricotta cheese. Bring the milk, cream, and salt to a boil in a medium-sized saucepan. Remove from heat and add the lemon juice. Stir gently until the mixture begins to curdle. Let stand for 5 minutes.

Pour the curdle mixture into a fine-mesh sieve lined with 2 layers of cheesecloth set over a bowl. Chill until the moisture has drained off and the cheese is a spreadable consistency, at least 1 hour or up to 12 hours. The longer it strains, the thicker the cheese will be. Cover and chill for up to 3 days.

To assemble and bake the casserole, preheat oven to 375 degrees. Spray a 13 × 9 × 2-inch baking dish with nonstick spray; set aside. Cook the sausage until it begins to brown, using the back of a spoon to break up any clumps. When the sausage is beginning to brown and has rendered some fat, add the mushrooms and sauté until the sausage is browned and cooked through and the mushrooms are wilted and browned, about 10 minutes.

Combine the beaten eggs, flour, and baking powder in a medium-sized bowl and whisk to blend well, making sure no lumps of flour remain. Stir in the sausage mixture, the Monterey Jack cheese, and the fresh ricotta cheese. Pour the mixture into prepared baking dish and bake in preheated oven for 30 to 35 minutes, or until set. Slice and serve hot.

The Driskill Hotel's 1886 Café & Bakery's Roasted Farm-Fresh Vegetable Quiche with Tomato Jam

MAKES 1
10-INCH QUICHE

Quiche, often thought of as a "ladies who lunch" dish, has come a long way since its introduction to the American table by the French, who have always considered quiche to be a mainstay dish, especially at brunch. Nowadays it's not at all unusual to see a Texas cowboy in boots and jeans bellied up to a brunch serving of quiche. The Driskill Hotel's brunch quiche is vegetarian, but quite rich and hearty. The tomato jam is a unique accompaniment to the quiche. (And, we discovered, equally delicious on your favorite biscuit!)

The tomato jam can be made up to a week ahead of time and refrigerated. The quiche pastry can be made and fitted into the quiche pan and refrigerated the evening before serving. The quiche custard can be made ahead and held in a covered container in the refrigerator overnight. And the vegetables can be cut and roasted ahead of time. Simply assemble the quiche and bake when you wish to serve it.

Quiche pastry (see recipe below)
2 cups seasonal vegetables, cut into
 ¼-inch pieces and oven roasted
Quiche custard (see recipe below)
Tomato jam (see recipe at right)

QUICHE PASTRY

4¼ ounces (1 cup) all-purpose flour
1 teaspoon kosher salt
3 ounces (6 tablespoons) unsalted
 butter, cut into 1-inch cubes and
 well chilled
1 ounce (2 tablespoons) whipping
 cream, nested over ice to chill

QUICHE CUSTARD

3 eggs
2 egg yolks
1¼ cups whipping cream
1 cup shredded mozzarella
2 teaspoons kosher salt
½ teaspoon freshly ground black
 pepper

TOMATO JAM

2 teaspoons minced garlic
2 teaspoons olive oil
1 pint cherry tomatoes
1⅓ cups turbinado (raw) sugar
⅔ cup red wine vinegar
½ teaspoon kosher salt
½ teaspoon freshly ground black
 pepper ››

Begin by making the tomato jam. In a small nonreactive (stainless steel) saucepan, sauté the garlic in the oil on medium heat until fragrant—about 2 minutes. Add all remaining ingredients and bring to a simmer. Reduce heat to medium-low and gently simmer the mixture for about 30 to 40 minutes, or until the liquid is very syrupy.

Remove from heat and let the jam cool to room temperature. Cover and store in the refrigerator for up to 1 week.

Make the quiche pastry. In stand mixer with paddle blade, combine the flour and salt. Beat at low speed just to blend. Add the butter cubes gradually to the dry ingredients until the dough gets a mealy consistency. Add the cream to the mixture and beat on medium-low speed *just* until combined. It is imperative not to overmix the dough. Turn out onto work surface and gather the dough together. Gently form into a disk and wrap in plastic wrap. Let the dough rest for 1 hour.

Preheat oven to 350 degrees. Roll the dough out on a lightly floured work surface to about ¼ inch thick. Transfer to a 10-inch tart pan with removable bottom. Let the pastry fall into place without stretching it. Pan into bottom and side of pan. Line the pastry with parchment paper and fill with dry beans or rice. Place on baking sheet and bake for about 15 minutes in preheated oven. Remove from oven and cool to room temperature.

Make the quiche custard. Mix the eggs and egg yolks together in a large bowl until well beaten. Add the cream, mozzarella, salt, and pepper; mix gently to evenly distribute the ingredients. Set mixture aside to settle for 15 minutes.

When ready to bake the quiche, preheat oven to 375 degrees; place the parbaked pastry on a baking sheet and dump in the roasted vegetables, spreading them evenly over the bottom of the pastry. Ladle the quiche custard into the pastry. Custard should come three-quarters of the way up the side of the pastry.

Bake the quiche for 30 minutes, or until the center is set. (Lightly jiggle the pan to see if the center shakes.)

Remove from oven and cool to room temperature. Remove from tart pan, cut into wedges, and serve with a dollop of the tomato jam on each slice or pass the jam separately.

Edible Flower and Herb Frittata with Fried, Stuffed Squash Blossoms and Guacamole-Filled Nasturtiums

SERVES 4

This is a great vegetarian breakfast or brunch dish that packs a lot of flavor and satisfies even dedicated meat eaters like my husband. You can use blossoms from any variety of squash for the fried blossoms. I especially like to serve the frittatas baked in individual round or oval gratin dishes. I set them on larger underliner plates, tucking the fried squash blossoms and filled nasturtiums with a slice of grilled rustic bread onto the side. Add a salad and this becomes a very lovely brunch! Frittatas make great dinner dishes also, and are quick and easy to prepare. You can use any combination of ingredients—herbs, cheeses, vegetables, or even meat or fish/shellfish—that you like.

This is a fairly labor-intensive dish, but well worth the effort for its delicious taste and beautiful presentation. The frittata egg mixture can be put together ahead of time, as can the fillings for the squash blossoms and nasturtiums. Be sure to preheat the oil for cooking the squash blossoms. The batter for the squash blossoms should not be made ahead.

....

3 tablespoons extra-virgin olive oil, plus more for drizzling while baking

2 medium-sized leeks, white bottom portion only, cleaned, halved lengthwise, and sliced thin

1 small zucchini, sliced very thin, preferably using a mandolin or Japanese Benriner box (my fave)

2 heaping tablespoons minced fresh basil

½ teaspoon freshly ground black pepper, plus more for garnish

Kosher salt to taste

8 eggs, beaten until frothy

1 heaping tablespoon freshly snipped chives

¼ cup fresh calendula petals, or other edible, seasonal flower

2 tablespoons torn arugula blossoms

Pecorino Romano cheese

FRIED SQUASH BLOSSOMS

Batter

¼ cup rice flour

2 cups all-purpose flour

1 tablespoon baking powder

½ cup cornstarch

1 tablespoon salt

1 teaspoon cayenne pepper

3 cups ice-cold club soda

Seasoned Goat Cheese Filling

1 (8-ounce) log of mild goat cheese (preferably local), softened

5 sprigs fresh thyme, leaves removed and minced

1 large-ish garlic clove, minced

2 tablespoons chopped fresh chives

1 teaspoon minced fresh rosemary leaves

Kosher salt

Freshly ground black pepper

1 to 2 tablespoons extra-virgin olive oil

20 squash blossoms

GUACAMOLE-FILLED NASTURTIUMS

8 perfect nasturtium flowers and leaves

Small batch of your favorite guacamole ››

Note: Use only those edible flowers and herbs that you know come from a source that is organic (preferably), or at least grown without the use of pesticides or chemical fertilizers. As with all produce, wash edible flowers and herbs well before using.

Begin by preparing the frittatas. Preheat oven to 400 degrees. Spray 4 individual round or oval gratin dishes with nonstick cooking spray; set aside. Heat the 3 tablespoons of olive oil in a heavy-bottomed skillet over medium heat. When oil is hot, add the leeks and sauté just until they are wilted and transparent. Add the thin-sliced zucchini, basil, and black pepper, and season to taste with salt. Cook, stirring gently, just until the zucchini is wilted, about 3 minutes. Remove from heat and set aside.

Combine the beaten eggs, chives, calendula petals, and arugula blossoms in a bowl and stir together. Spoon an equal portion of the leeks and zucchini into the bottom of each prepared gratin dish. Pour an equal amount of the egg mixture over the zucchini in each dish and place dishes on a baking sheet. Bake in preheated oven. Bake until the eggs are just beginning to set, about 10 minutes. Scatter about a heaping tablespoon of the Romano cheese over each dish, drizzle with a bit of olive oil, and add a grind of black pepper. Cook an additional 3 to 4 minutes, or until cheese has browned and frittatas are completely set, but not stiff.

To make the guacamole-filled nasturtiums, carefully rinse the nasturtiums and leaves and pat them dry. Hold the nasturtiums by the base and fill with about a heaping teaspoon of the guacamole. Arrange each filled flower on a nasturtium leaf. They can be kept very briefly in the refrigerator.

To assemble and fry the squash blossoms, sift together all of the dry ingredients for the batters. Whisk in the club soda, a little at a time, until the right consistency is achieved. The batter should coat the back of a spoon, but some excess batter should run off the spoon. Allow to rest in the refrigerator at least 1 hour before use.

For the seasoned goat cheese filling, combine all of the ingredients and mix well. Shape the mixture into 1-tablespoon balls. Make sure the squash blossoms are well cleaned. Open the flowers and insert 1 goat cheese ball in each flower. Gently press the filling into the base of the flower. Cover with the petals and pinch the top to seal. Refrigerate for 30 minutes. Preheat a fryer or a deep pot halfway filled with canola oil to 375 degrees.

Hold the squash blossoms by the stem. Dip each into the tempura batter, making sure to coat completely. Let any excess batter drip off. Place the blossom in the oil and fry until golden brown, about 1 to 2 minutes, turning often to brown evenly. Remove to a paper-towel-covered wire rack set over a baking sheet to drain.

Eggs Rockefeller in Portabella Mushrooms with Fried Oysters and Browned Butter Hollandaise

SERVES 4

When I want to prepare a really special brunch for friends or family members, this is one of my go-to dishes. It makes a beautiful presentation, but that's just the initial visual. The textural and flavor combinations of the savory spinach filling, the creamy poached eggs, the blast of smoky bacon, and the crisp, faintly marine nuances of the oysters—all topped off with the lemony, browned butter hollandaise with its nutty attributes—are a truly ethereal treat for your palate. I like to serve the dish along with the tiny Brunch Biscuits with Paula's Texas Lemon Butter (see recipe on page 252). A good Texas Albarino rounds out the feast!

For ease in last-minute preparation of this dish, prepare and stuff the mushrooms ahead of time. The eggs can be poached ahead of time, according to the directions on page 32, and finished just before serving. The batter for the oysters can be made ahead of time, although the oysters themselves should be fried at the last minute. The browned butter hollandaise can be made about 30 minutes ahead of time and held over hot (not simmering) water, covered. Whisk well before serving.

Creamed spinach (see recipe below)
Sautéed portabella mushrooms (see recipe below)
8 poached eggs (see directions on page 32), poached for 2 minutes, then held in an ice-water bath
4 applewood-smoked bacon slices, cooked until crisp and drained
Fried Gulf oysters (see recipe at right)
Browned butter hollandaise (see recipe at right)
Lemon wheels as garnish

CREAMED SPINACH

4 tablespoons unsalted butter
2 pounds fresh spinach leaves, thick stems removed, washed and drained well
6 green onions, sliced thin, including green tops
2 large garlic cloves, minced
1½ teaspoons minced fresh marjoram

½ teaspoon cayenne pepper, or to taste
1 tablespoon Herbsaint, or other anise-based liqueur
1¼ cups whipping cream
Kosher salt and freshly ground black pepper to taste

SAUTÉED PORTABELLA MUSHROOMS

4 tablespoons (½ stick) unsalted butter
4 medium-sized portabella mushrooms (about 4 inches in diameter), stems removed
Kosher salt and freshly ground black pepper to taste

FRIED GULF OYSTERS

8 Gulf oysters, patted dry
1 cup buttermilk, beaten with 2 eggs
1 cup all-purpose flour
1 cup yellow cornmeal
1 tablespoon cornstarch

1 tablespoon toasted, then ground coriander seeds
1 teaspoon toasted, then ground cumin seeds
2 teaspoons kosher salt
2 teaspoons granulated garlic
Canola oil for deep frying, heated to 350 degrees

BROWNED BUTTER HOLLANDAISE

12 tablespoons (1½ stick) unsalted butter
3 egg yolks
1 teaspoon grated lemon zest
1 tablespoon freshly squeezed lemon juice
1 heaping teaspoon whole-grain mustard
Pinch of cayenne pepper, or more if you like a little more spice in your life
½ teaspoon kosher salt ››

Begin by making the creamed spinach. Melt the butter in a heavy-bottomed 12-inch skillet over medium-high heat. When the foam subsides, add the spinach leaves, tossing to coat with the butter. You will most likely need to add the spinach in bunches, cooking it down before adding more. When the spinach has cooked down and the watery liquid has evaporated, stir in the green onions, garlic, marjoram, and cayenne pepper. Cook, stirring often, for 2 to 3 minutes to wilt the onions. Add the Herbsaint and whipping cream, stirring to blend well. Cook until the cream has thickened, about 5 minutes, stirring 2 or 3 times to prevent sticking. Season to taste with salt and pepper.

Prepare the sautéed portabella mushrooms. Melt the butter in a large, heavy-bottomed skillet over medium heat. When the foam subsides, place the mushroom caps, gill sides up, in the pan. Season with kosher salt and pepper. Cook for about 4 minutes, or until the caps are browned on the bottom; then turn and cook the gill sides until browned, about another 4 minutes. Season with salt and pepper. Set aside to keep warm.

Make the browned butter hollandaise. Melt the butter in a heavy-bottomed 2-quart saucepan over medium heat. When the butter has melted, continue to cook it, watching very closely, until it turns light golden brown, about 4 to 5 minutes. (It goes brown to golden brown to black to burned in the blink of an eye.) Remove from heat at once and pour into a Pyrex measuring cup. Be sure to get all of the nutty browned bits on the bottom of the pan. Cover with plastic wrap to keep hot. In work bowl of food processor fitted with steel blade, combine the egg yolks, lemon zest and juice, mustard, cayenne pepper, and salt. Process until the mixture is very smooth and the egg yolks are fluffy and light lemon-yellow in color, about 2 to 3 minutes. With the machine running, add the browned butter in a slow, steady stream through the feed tube until all of it, including the browned nubbins, has been added. Process an additional 20 or 30 seconds to form a strong emulsion. Turn out into a metal bowl and keep warm over hot (not simmering) water. Whisk well when ready to use.

Fry the oysters. Place the buttermilk/egg wash in a small bowl. In a second bowl, combine all remaining ingredients except canola oil. Toss with a fork to blend thoroughly. Be sure the oysters have been patted very dry, then dip them in the buttermilk/egg wash, coating well all over. Next, dredge them, one by one, in the flour mixture, coating well, and shaking off excess breading. Fry the oysters in the preheated oil for about 2 to 3 minutes, or just until they turn golden brown. Do not overcook them. They should have a crisp crust, but still be almost liquid inside. Drain on a wire rack set over a baking sheet.

To assemble the plates, poach the eggs for the final minute in simmering water. Place one of the sautéed portabella mushrooms in the center of each serving plate. Fill each mushroom with a portion of the creamed spinach, allowing some of it to drape over two sides of the mushrooms. Pat the poached eggs dry and nest two of them in the spinach. Lay a strip of the bacon across the eggs, then top each egg with a fried oyster. Drizzle a liberal portion of the browned butter hollandaise over each serving. Garnish with a lemon wheel and serve at once.

THREE

Heavenly, Syrupy Pancakes, French Toast, and Waffles

*

Since my earliest recollections of foods that I loved, pancakes have been at the top of the list—with French toast and waffles right up there also. When we were kids, on busy days our mother would often make one of the three for our dinner and no one ever complained. I still love a pancake dinner now and then.

I also love to try pancakes at different restaurants that serve breakfast when I travel. The variety of tastes and textures I experience is amazing. Sadly, I don't often find a pancake that lives up to my own expectations—that light-as-a-feather, puffy cake that would float off the plate if it weren't weighed down with a couple tablespoons of butter and syrup. And make sure that it's real maple syrup, please—not the sugar-based, artificially flavored and colored glop sold alongside the real thing in supermarkets. Now, I do admit that there is a lot to be said for an occasional pancake, waffle, or French toast doused with cane syrup—Steen's, of course—or blackstrap molasses, which is how my grandfather enjoyed his pancakes.

Pancakes are an ancient food first made when humans ground wheat that could be mixed with bird's eggs and goat's milk, then cooked. Cooked batter cakes spread throughout Europe—from crepes, the classic thin French pancake, to the apple-filled Apfelpfannkuchen in Germany. The first colonists in the New World learned to make a sort of maize griddlecake from the Native Americans. It is reputed that George Washington was an ardent lover of pancakes literally floating in prodigious amounts of syrup.

Waffles, likewise, date to as early as the eleventh century, when they were made from unleavened batter in some sort of heated iron. Their popularity spread throughout Europe and to the west when the Caribbean sugar plantations began to proliferate, bringing down the price of sugar to the point that it could be used in large quantities in the waffle batter. Waffle culture in America began to take hold when Thomas Jefferson brought a waffle iron from France to Monticello in the late 1700s and began making waffles for his guests.

A dish made from bread dipped in milk was recorded in *Apicius*, a collection of Latin recipes from the fourth or fifth century. A similar preparation, with egg added, was known in Medieval Europe by a variety of names. It was often eaten as a soup in Europe. In France, the dish was known as *pain perdu*, or "lost bread," so named because the dish was concocted to make use of leftover, or "lost," bread by softening it in an egg wash and cooking it. Whatever its origins, today in Texas, French toast, as it is commonly known, is a tasty, quick breakfast that can be made for a family or a crowd from "lost" Texas toast.

I think that if there is a secret to making good pancakes and waffles, it's in not overbeating the batter, which would make the final results tough. Also, when cooking the pancakes, use just a glaze of your chosen oil in the skillet. Excess oil will be absorbed by the pancakes, making them soggy and heavy. And it goes without saying that you want to be certain that the pancake is cooked completely through. There's nothing worse than cutting into a pancake and having uncooked batter ooze out onto your plate. When you pour the batter into the hot glaze of oil in the skillet, watch for tiny bubbles to begin to appear around the outside edges of the cake. That means it's time to turn the pancake. It should be nice and golden brown on the first side when you flip it. Cook until it's golden brown on the second side, and you should have a perfectly cooked pancake. When cooking pancakes for a large crowd, set your oven to warm and place each batch in the warm oven before starting another batch. Cold or even lukewarm pancakes, French toast, and waffles are not altogether desirable. The butter must melt on contact! And be sure it's real butter, preferably unsalted, softened at room temperature. Also, when preparing multiple batches of either pancakes or French toast, you will need to wipe out the skillet occasionally to remove any overcooked nubbins of batter, egg wash, or bread crumbs in the pan, and add fresh oil. Be sure to let the oil reheat between batches.

Great French toast begins with great bread. No thin-sliced Wonder Bread will ever make great French toast. Use good rustic bread, or French bread sliced on the bias about ¾ to 1 inch thick, or Texas toast. Be sure that your egg and milk mixture (with whatever secret additives you like) are well beaten and poured into a shallow dish or pie pan. Lay the bread slices in the batter and allow them to become very soggy before lifting them out and lowering them into the hot glaze of oil in the skillet. Cook French toast over medium heat, and don't let it brown too darkly. Like a perfect pancake, French toast should be golden brown on both sides. Remember that you're basically cooking an egg wash and if you get it too brown, the taste will be harsh and unpleasant.

There are limitless possibilities for topping pancakes, French toast, and waffles. Be guided by what you love, remembering that eating these sinfully calorie-laden delights should be a pleasurable thing (even if it's an Elvis waffle topped with peanut butter and sliced bananas).

In this chapter, there's a good selection of flavors and styles. Enjoy—and share!

Dallas's Garden Café's Apple-Raisin Blinis with Mascarpone and Texas Honeybee Guild Honey

SERVES 4

Garden Café owner Mark Wooten has long been a champion of using natural, sustainable, and humanely raised food products, extending even to the honey that he uses at the café.

Blinis (see recipe at right)
Apple-Raisin Filling (see recipe at right)
3 ounces Texas artisan mascarpone cheese, such as Dallas's Mozzarella Company's mascarpone
Texas Honeybee Guild Honey, or other natural local honey
Powdered sugar for garnishing
Fresh sliced seasonal fruit and/or berries

BLINIS

⅛ teaspoon kosher salt
1 tablespoon sugar
¼ teaspoon baking soda
2 cups all-purpose flour
1 tablespoon ground cinnamon
2 large eggs, well beaten
2 cups whole milk
1 tablespoon canola oil
4 tablespoons butter

APPLE-RAISIN FILLING

1 tablespoon butter
1 large apple, peeled, cored, and cut into small dice
1 cup golden raisins, also called *sultanas*
1 tablespoon ground cinnamon

Begin by making the apple-raisin filling. Melt the butter in a heavy-bottomed skillet over medium heat. Add the apple and cook until it begins to brown. Add the raisins and cook, stirring, just to heat through. Stir in the cinnamon and set aside to keep warm.

Make the blinis. In a medium-sized bowl, combine the salt, sugar, baking soda, flour, and cinnamon, tossing to incorporate well; set aside. Combine the beaten eggs, milk, and canola oil in a separate bowl, whisking to blend well. Fold the egg mixture into the flour mixture, blending thoroughly.

Using an 8-inch nonstick skillet, heat ½ teaspoon of the butter and add ¼ cup of the blini batter. Use a high-heat plastic spatula to check the underside of the blini after about 30 seconds. When it starts to brown nicely, flip the blini. Cook for another 30 seconds to brown the other side. Remove from pan. Repeat using the remaining blini batter and another ½ tablespoon of the butter for each blini. Stack and keep warm under a paper towel.

Place the mascarpone cheese in a microwavable bowl and slightly heat the cheese in 10-second bursts. It should be slightly warm to make spreading easier.

To serve, generously spread the mascarpone on one side of each blini. Lightly press a portion of the apple-raisin filling into the mascarpone. Roll the blinis and place two on each small serving plate. Drizzle with some of the honey and sprinkle with powdered sugar. Add fruit and/or berries to the plate and serve.

Cinnamon-Spiced Waffles with Broiled Persimmons and Cajeta

SERVES 4 TO 6

I like to prepare this dish for lazy Sunday brunches in the fall, when persimmons are ripe. There are two types of persimmons grown in Texas—Asian persimmons, which are about the size of an average orange and deep orange in color when ripe, and the native persimmon, which is black and grape-size. For this dish I generally use the Asian variety, as they are easier to source, generally at farmer's markets. However, if you are lucky enough to find some of the native persimmons, which grow wild in many areas of Brazoria County, you can substitute them, allowing about 4 to 5 cups in place of the 4 Asian persimmons. Cajeta is a thickened syrup confection that originated in the Mexican state of Guanajuato. It is generally made of sweetened caramelized milk. The syrup has become so popular with Mexican food aficionados that the Hershey Company created a line of flavored cajeta in 2005 under the name "Cajeta Elegancita."

The component parts of this dish can be made mostly ahead of time. The cajeta syrup can be made several days ahead of time and reheated before using. The persimmons can be pre-cooked and reheated, and the waffle batter can be made up to 1 hour ahead of time.

Baked waffles (see recipe at right)
Broiled Persimmons (see recipe at right)
Cajeta (see recipe at right)
Sweetened whipped cream, optional

BAKED WAFFLES

3 eggs, separated
⅜ teaspoon cream of tartar
1¼ cups whole milk
1¾ cups all-purpose flour, sifted
2 teaspoons baking powder
½ teaspoon salt
½ teaspoon ground cinnamon
¼ teaspoon freshly grated nutmeg
2 tablespoons sugar
½ cup (1 stick) unsalted butter, melted and cooled

BROILED PERSIMMONS

4 ripe persimmons
3 tablespoons agave nectar
3 tablespoons unsalted butter, melted
2 tablespoons freshly squeezed lime juice

CAJETA

½ cup sugar
2 cups sweetened condensed milk
¼ teaspoon cinnamon
¼ cup, plus 3 tablespoons Madeira wine, optional
1 tablespoon vanilla extract
4 tablespoons unsalted butter, cut into ½-inch cubes
⅔ cup whipping cream ››

Begin by making the cajeta. Place the sugar in a 6-quart saucepan over medium-high heat. (The large pan size is necessary to prevent overflow when liquid is added to the hot caramel.) Cook, without stirring, until the sugar has melted and a rich, dark caramel has formed, or until a candy thermometer registers about 320 degrees. In a separate bowl, combine the condensed milk, cinnamon, ¼ cup of the wine, and vanilla; add to the caramel all at once. The mixture will spit, sputter, and bubble furiously, and the caramel will harden. Take care that none of the mixture splashes out on you. Lower heat and stir the mixture until it is smooth and the caramel has melted. Remove from heat and cool to lukewarm. Whisk the butter into the lukewarm sauce until well blended. Rapidly whisk in the whipping cream and the remaining 3 tablespoons of wine. Set aside until ready to use or refrigerate, covered.

Broil the persimmons. Preheat broiler and place oven rack 6 inches below heat source. Using a sharp knife, cut the stem end from each persimmon, then cut a small slice from the bottom end. Slice them in half horizontally.

Place the halves, cut sides down, in a shallow baking dish. Whisk together the agave nectar, melted butter, and lime juice, blending well. Spoon a portion over each persimmon half. Place the dish under the preheated broiler and cook until the persimmons are golden brown and starting to wilt, about 6 minutes. Remove and set aside to keep hot while finishing the waffles.

To make the waffle batter, in a grease-free bowl, beat the egg whites with the cream of tartar until they are firm and fluffy, but not dry; set aside.

In a separate bowl, beat the milk and egg yolks until well blended. Add the remaining ingredients and beat to blend well. Gently, but thoroughly, fold the egg whites into the batter. Bake the waffles according to the directions on your waffle iron.

To serve, top each waffle with the desired amount of persimmon halves and drizzle with a portion of the warmed cajeta. Top with a dollop of sweetened whipped cream for a truly decadent delight.

Crave Kitchen and Bar's Churro Waffle

MAKES 5 WAFFLES

Churros, which originated many years ago in Spain as a sweet treat that shepherds would cook while watching their flocks, are usually fried pastries made from a batter extruded through a pastry bag fitted with a large star tip into various lengths and deep-fried, then rolled in a cinnamon-sugar mixture. They have also been popular in Latin America and Mexico. Chef Rudy Valdes, of El Paso's Crave Kitchen and Bar, created this innovative version of the tasty churros he remembered from his childhood in El Paso, only baked in a waffle iron, then deep-fried and rolled in the cinnamon-sugar mix.

Make the candied walnuts ahead of time and store in a zip-sealing bag. The waffles can be made the day before and deep-fried when you are ready to complete and serve the dish. »

⅔ cup waffle batter (see recipe below)

1 cup sugar

¼ cup ground cinnamon

Canola oil for deep frying, heated to 350 degrees

1 (8-ounce) scoop good-quality vanilla ice cream

¼ cup cajeta*

2 tablespoons chopped candied walnuts (see recipe below)

WAFFLE BATTER

2 cups flour

¼ cup sugar

½ teaspoon kosher salt

4 teaspoons baking powder

¼ tablespoon baking soda

2 eggs, well beaten

1½ cups whole milk

1 teaspoon vanilla

¼ cup melted butter

CANDIED WALNUTS

1 cup sugar

½ cup water

8 ounces whole walnuts

Begin by making the candied walnuts. Preheat oven to 350 degrees. Line a baking sheet with parchment paper; set aside. Combine sugar and water in a heavy-bottomed saucepan. Bring to a full boil without stirring to dissolve sugar. Cook until an amber syrup forms, 338 degrees using a candy thermometer. Remove from heat and stir in the walnuts, making sure all are coated with syrup. Turn the walnuts out onto the prepared baking sheet and spread them out in an even layer. Bake in preheated oven for 8 minutes, or until the walnuts are completely dry. Remove from oven and place on wire rack until completely cool before using.

Make the waffle batter. Sift all dry ingredients into a large bowl. Stir to blend well and set aside. Combine the beaten eggs, milk, and vanilla extract in a second bowl. Beat until well mixed. Slowly add the egg mixture to the dry ingredients, mixing only until all ingredients are incorporated. *Do not overbeat.* Stir in melted butter.

To make and serve the waffles, spray waffle iron with nonstick spray and heat to medium-high. Pour ⅔ cup of the waffle batter onto the hot iron. Cook for about 3 minutes, or until set. Combine the sugar and cinnamon in a baking dish, tossing to blend well.

Remove waffle from iron and deep-fry in preheated oil for 45 seconds per side. Remove from oil and immediately toss the waffle in the cinnamon-sugar mix. Repeat with remaining batter, keeping waffles hot as you cook them.

Place waffles on serving plates and top each with a scoop of ice cream, a drizzle of cajeta, and candied walnuts. Serve at once.

* Cajeta is the Mexican version of what is widely known as *dulce de leche* throughout the Latin culture. Much like its cousin, caramel, this thick sauce is made from milk, baking soda, and a whopping amount of sugar, along with other more subtle flavorings like vanilla or cinnamon. Cajeta can be found in supermarkets that carry Mexican foods. Some brands add sherry or brandy.

WHO TAKES CREDIT FOR CHICKEN AND WAFFLES?

Southerners say it's not a Southern dish, although it is very popular in the South. It would seem logical, since the custom of frying chicken is so linked to Southern cooking, that the dish originated in the Deep South. But there was no mention of such a dish in early Southern cookbooks. The subject is even more confusing when you consider that the dish has had a huge following in Los Angeles since the 1970s. A dish containing waffles and chicken was served in Harlem in the 1930s as a soul food dish, with the waffle topped with fried chicken and the usual condiments of butter and syrup, and is still being served in Pennsylvania, where the waffle is topped with pulled chicken in a creamy sauce. In fact, this version of the dish has been served in Pennsylvania Dutch territory and in the Midwest for centuries.

Fried chicken has been a mainstay of the Southern diet, and it is believed that, in the years of Reconstruction following the Civil War, Southern African Americans migrating to the North carried the tradition of fried chicken with them. Food historians generally agree that the waffle was introduced to America around 1790, when Thomas Jefferson brought a waffle iron from France and waffles became a favorite with the landed gentry of the South. At that time Southern African Americans were more accustomed to pancakes (or biscuits and cornbread) than to waffles, which were considered a delicacy. It was after they migrated to the North that waffles topped with fried chicken became a special-occasion dish for African Americans. Eventually, many of the popular Harlem eateries served the dish. The most popular of these was Well's Supper Club, which became a favorite hangout of Sammy Davis, Jr., and Nat King Cole. So how did the dish get to Los Angeles? In the 1970s a former Harlem resident, Herb Hudson, moved to LA and opened a restaurant that he named Roscoe's House of Chicken and Waffles, which eventually morphed into a small chain. Roscoe's became a favorite with Hollywood celebrities, creating a demand for the dish. Today, Los Angeles restaurants vie for the honor of serving the best chicken and waffles. The popular movie *Pulp Fiction* contains scenes filmed at Holly's, one of these LA shrines of chicken and waffles. The chicken and waffles combo has now returned to the South and is embraced as a breakfast favorite in Texas, too.

24 Diner's Chicken and Waffles

SERVES 6

MAKES 1 CUP
BROWN SUGAR
BUTTER

Austin's much-loved 24 Diner celebrated its seventh anniversary in December 2016. Since its inception in 2009, the focus of the downtown restaurant has been a dedication to serving chef-inspired comfort foods made from ingredients sourced from local farmers, ranchers, and food artisans 24 hours a day. In 2011, *Bon Appétit* magazine placed 24 Diner on its "America's Top 6 Destination Diners" list. The seasonal menu, which was derived by Executive Chef and ELM Restaurant Group Partner Andrew Curren, offers something for everyone. Curren comments: "Serving breakfast is rewarding! We love our regulars that show up every morning at 6 a.m. for a cup of coffee and a bowl of oatmeal, as well as the group of friends and families that join us on the weekend to kick off their day with Bloody Marys, Mimosas, eggs Benedict, and chicken and waffles."

That chicken and waffles dish is one of the diner's most popular menu items. I've often heard praise about the crisp and flavorful crust on the chicken. As you peruse the recipe, you'll see why it's so wonderful. As with the other dishes at the diner, the formula for the chicken evolved from many thoughtful culinary details. The waffles are made from a yeast dough with butter, which gives them a subtle sourdough taste. Allow time for marinating and chilling the chicken and proofing the yeast waffles.

There's no question that this is a complex recipe. However, most of its component parts are made ahead. And if you've ever experienced this sinfully caloric dish at 24 Diner, you'll be delighted to serve it to your guests at home. The chicken is an overnight marinating/battering process, which is begun the day before serving. The yeast dough for the waffles must also have an overnight rest in the refrigerator to develop its wonderful flavor. The 24 Diner's Brown Sugar Butter may be prepared ahead and stored in the refrigerator. Bring to room temperature before serving.

CHICKEN

4 pounds mixed boneless, skinless, all-natural (preferably local) chicken breasts and thighs
Canola oil for deep-frying, heated to 365 degrees
24 Diner's Brown Sugar Butter (see recipe facing page)
Grade A Light Amber Vermont maple syrup
Cholula Hot Sauce, optional

BUTTERMILK MARINADE

1 quart whole buttermilk (not low-fat)
1½ teaspoons freshly ground black pepper
1½ teaspoons kosher salt
1½ teaspoons smoked paprika
⅓ cup Frank's RedHot Sauce

CHICKEN DREDGE #1

4 cups all-purpose flour
1 tablespoon smoked paprika
1 tablespoon kosher salt
6 eggs, whisked until frothy

CHICKEN DREDGE #2

4 cups all-purpose flour
1 pound cornstarch
4 tablespoons kosher salt

YEAST WAFFLES

1 tablespoon active dry yeast
4½ cups warm milk (100 degrees), divided
¾ pound (3 sticks) butter, melted
1½ cups whisked whole eggs
1 cup sugar

½ cup light brown sugar
1 cup turbinado (raw) sugar
1½ teaspoons kosher salt
1½ tablespoons Madagascar vanilla extract
8 cups all-purpose flour

BROWN SUGAR BUTTER

½ pound (2 sticks) butter, softened
⅓ cup light brown sugar
½ teaspoon kosher salt
1 pinch freshly ground black pepper

Begin by preparing the chicken breasts and thighs. Separate the breasts and thighs into two batches, placing them in shallow baking dishes in a single layer. Prepare the buttermilk marinade by whisking all ingredients together to blend well. Pour equal portions of the marinade over the two batches, cover with plastic wrap, and marinate, refrigerated, for 24 hours. Prepare the two dredge mixtures and beat the eggs. Remove chicken pieces from marinade, shaking off excess marinade. Dredge the chicken first in dredge #1, coating well on all sides and shaking off excess. Then dip each piece in the beaten eggs, shaking off excess egg, and finally dredge the pieces in dredge #2, again coating well on all sides and shaking off excess flour. Place the chicken pieces on a parchment-lined baking sheet and refrigerate for about 12 hours, uncovered, to form a skin. Save both the dredges, shaking them through a wire-mesh strainer. Save the egg dredge, straining it and keeping it refrigerated until ready to do the final breading.

While the chicken pieces are chilling, make the 24 Diner's Brown Sugar Butter. Whip the butter in bowl of stand mixer until it is fluffy, about 5 minutes. Scrape down side of bowl and add the dry ingredients. Beat until smooth and well blended. Place in a crock or bowl with tight-fitting lid and store in refrigerator.

Make the waffle batter and proof. To make the waffles, combine the yeast and 1 cup of the warm milk in a 2-cup Pyrex measuring cup, stirring gently to blend. Set aside to proof for 5 to 10 minutes, or until the mixture is bubbly and foaming. In a large bowl, whisk the yeast mixture, the remaining 3½ cups of milk, and the melted butter together until well blended. Then add the eggs and whisk to blend. Using a blender, process the mixture, adding the sugars, salt, and vanilla, just until the batter is homogenous. Pour back into large bowl and add ⅓ of the flour to the bowl at a time, whisking well after each addition to distribute the flour and break up any lumps. (The batter does not need to be perfectly smooth.) Cover and let rise for 1 hour at room temperature, then place in refrigerator for 12 hours to slowly proof. Remove from refrigerator 45 minutes before baking the waffles.

When ready to fry the chicken, preheat the canola oil for deep-frying to 365 degrees. (It's best to use a countertop deep-fryer equipped with a thermostat to maintain an even temperature throughout the frying process.) Repeat the breading process with each piece of chicken. Fry the thighs first in preheated oil for about 9 minutes, or until golden brown and crisp and cooked through. Remove thighs to a wire rack placed over a baking sheet and keep warm in low oven while frying the breasts. Fry the breasts for 7 to 9 minutes.

Bake waffles in buttered, preheated waffle iron according to manufacturer's directions. Keep waffles warm in a low oven until all have been baked.

To serve the dish, place a waffle on each serving plate and slather on a portion of the 24 Diner's Brown Sugar Butter. Drizzle with maple syrup. Place a chicken breast and thigh on each waffle, topping with a shake or two of Cholula Hot Sauce, if desired.

Crispy Challah French Toast

SERVES 6

Kids love this simple French toast, which get its crunch from a favorite breakfast cereal. If you don't have an old-world-style bakery that makes the traditional, braided challah bread, you can, of course, make your own or substitute slices of a good-quality sourdough baguette. This French toast is best served right after cooking so that the slices are at their crunchy best.

Cooking spray or canola oil
5 cups crushed cornflakes
12 1-inch-thick slices challah bread, or substitute 1-inch-thick slices of good-quality sourdough baguette, sliced on the bias
3 eggs, beaten with 4 cups milk
Butter, warm maple syrup, and powdered sugar for serving

Preheat a flat-top grill and spray surface for cooking, or heat a thin glaze of canola on it. Place the crushed cornflakes in a shallow baking dish. Dip the bread slices in the egg mixture, making sure they are well soaked. Let the excess egg wash drip off, then lay the slices in the cornflake crumbs, pressing the slice lightly to be sure the crumbs adhere. Flip and repeat, until all bread slices are breaded.

Fry the bread slices on the prepared grill until evenly browned on both sides, flipping once.

To serve, slice each piece of toast in half diagonally, top with butter and syrup, and scatter powdered sugar over the top. Serve hot.

Driskill Hotel's 1886 Café & Bakery's Bread Pudding French Toast

SERVES 6 TO 8

Austin's Driskill Hotel, built in 1886, is an iconic landmark deeply imbedded in the city's history. Colonel Jesse Lincoln Driskill built the hotel as a cattle baron's showcase at a cost of $400,000.00 (the equivalent of $92 million today). The Driskill has hosted numerous governors' inaugurations, election parties, and celebrities and politicians from around the world. Yet, over the years the hotel underwent financial ups and downs under several owners. In 1969, the hotel closed and it looked as if its fate would be at the hands of the wrecking ball. Concerned citizens, led by the Heritage Society of Austin, intervened to save the hotel, getting the Driskill designated as a National Historic Landmark, preserving it in perpetuity.

Today, the hotel is on solid footing under the guidance of the Hyatt Hotels and Resorts, which undertook a monumental refurbishment of the property to restore it to its original grandeur without altering its traditions.

The hotel has long been a favorite breakfast and lunch spot among both guests and Austinites alike. In 1934, an aspiring Texas politician named Lyndon Baines Johnson met his future wife, Lady Bird, at the Driskill for their first date—a sumptuous breakfast. The 1886 "Lunchroom" opened in 1973, operated by the Austin Historical Society, featuring a selection of recipes from the hotel's past as well as personal family recipes. The wait staff were outfitted in period costumes. The current 1886 Café & Bakery opened in 2002. In 2014, following a summer-long update, the Driskill reopened the café for daily breakfast, lunch, and dinner as well as brunch on weekends.

When asked how he felt about being tapped as the Driskill's executive chef, Troy Knapp replied that it was clearly an obligation that was different from any other position he had ever held. "Like a curator of a museum I knew my role would be to ensure that the culinary team embodied the spirit of the ones who preceded us. It would be our responsibility to ensure we looked after it to the best of our ability. All ideas, such as menu items, recipes, tableware, you name it—all needed a reason for existence in order to align with the legacy and tradition already set forth at the Driskill. Sort of like going back in time and understanding how it all connects with the present. Challenging, yet worth it. Every day I am reminded about special experiences that are shared and how the Driskill is cherished by so many."

Certainly no one will dispute that bread pudding is, hands down, a much-loved dessert. But the creative chef's team at the Driskill Hotel's 1886 Café & Bakery, under the tutelage of Knapp, turns it into a splendid French toast for breakfast or brunch. It's a favorite on the brunch menu at the café. First bite, and you'll understand why!

The bread pudding mixture can be made ahead and packed into a loaf pan according to recipe directions. Allow 1½ hours for baking, plus about 30 minutes for cooling before serving. ››

4½ cups whole milk
Pinch of salt
5 tablespoons butter, melted
⅔ cup sugar, divided
½ teaspoon ground cinnamon
½ teaspoon freshly grated nutmeg
½ cup raisins
½ cup dark rum
5 eggs
1 loaf Texas toast, cubed
1 teaspoon vanilla extract
1 pint fresh, seasonal berries
½ cup pecan pieces
1 banana, sliced
Powdered sugar for dusting
Warm maple syrup

Preheat oven to 350 degrees. Prepare a bread loaf pan by spraying with non-stick pan spray. Line pan with parchment paper, then spray the parchment paper with the pan spray and dust with all-purpose flour. Shake out excess flour. Set pan aside.

In a small saucepan, combine the milk, salt, butter, half of the sugar, and spices. Cook over medium heat until sugar is fully dissolved and mixture is well incorporated.

While waiting for the sugar to dissolve, soak the raisins in the rum for 10 minutes.

In a separate bowl, combine the eggs and the other half of the sugar, whisking until fully incorporated and fluffy. Slowly add the milk mixture into the egg mixture while whisking constantly. Drain the raisins, discarding the rum. Add them to a large bowl with the egg/milk mixture, cubed Texas toast, and vanilla. Mix lightly until mixture is fully incorporated.

Turn the pudding mixture out into the prepared loaf pan and pack tightly. Cover with foil and place the pan in a large baking dish. Put the pan on oven rack in preheated oven and fill the bottom dish with hot water to come halfway up the sides of the bread pan. Bake for 1½ hours. To test, remove the foil and poke the middle of the loaf with a toothpick. It should come out clean.

Remove from oven, uncover, and let cool to room temperature. Remove the bread pudding loaf from the pan to a cutting board, discarding parchment paper. Slice the loaf into ¾-inch-thick slices. Finish each serving with a portion of the berries, pecan pieces, and sliced bananas. Dust each serving with desired amount of powdered sugar. Serve with the warm maple syrup.

Ocean Grille & Beach Bar's Bourbon French Toast

The Ocean Grille & Beach Bar opened on Galveston's popular Seawall Boulevard in 2015. Randy Evans, former executive chef of Brennan's of Houston and owner of the late, great Haven Restaurant in Houston, developed the original menu for the laid-back restaurant where you can enjoy a great meal and watch the surf roll in from the Gulf of Mexico across the sand, along with Managing Partner Bryan Davis and Chef Brian Peper. It has quickly become a popular dining spot, with its Sunday brunch an island favorite.

SERVES 4

FRENCH TOAST BATTER

8 cups whole milk
2 cups whipping cream
2 cups light brown sugar
2 cups Texas bourbon, such as Rebecca Creek
1 tablespoon ground cinnamon
1 tablespoon, plus 1 teaspoon vanilla extract
12 eggs
½ teaspoon kosher salt

FRENCH TOAST

1 French baguette, cut on a long bias into slices about 2 inches thick
French toast batter (see recipe at left)
8 ounces clarified butter
8 ounces grade-A maple syrup
2 tablespoons powdered sugar
Fresh seasonal berries or melon ››

Begin by making the French toast batter. Combine all ingredients in a large mixing bowl and mix well, making sure the eggs are well beaten.

Place three pieces of the sliced baguette into the batter at a time, saturating well. In a heavy-bottomed 12-inch sauté pan over medium heat, heat 2 ounces of the clarified butter and sear off the baguette, turning once, until well browned on both sides and cooked through. Keep warm while battering and cooking remaining baguette slices.

To serve, place 3 slices of the French toast on each serving plate, shingling them in a crisscross fashion. Drizzle with a portion of the syrup, sprinkle with powdered sugar, and garnish with fresh berries.

Simple But Delicious Texas Toast French Toast

SERVES 4 TO 6

Often the simplest of meal options turn out to be just what the moment needs for flavor gratification. I adore French toast. It's one of my all-time favorite comfort foods, just as it was my daughter Cory's when she was growing up. Today, I will often reward myself, especially if I've had a less-than-stellar day, with a grand feast of a couple of slices of French toast dripping with butter and maple syrup and a couple of slices of good, crisp bacon alongside. Simple. Satisfying. And as often as not, I make this little feast for my dinner!

8 slices Texas toast, 1 inch thick
4 eggs, beaten until frothy
1 cup whipping cream
½ cup whole milk
2 teaspoons grated lemon zest
½ teaspoon salt
2 tablespoons light brown sugar

2 tablespoons melted unsalted butter
8 tablespoons (1 stick) additional unsalted butter, plus more for slathering on top
Warm real maple syrup

Preheat oven to 300 degrees and place a wire rack over a baking sheet. Lay the Texas toast slices on the rack and place the baking sheet in the oven. Toast the bread for 5 minutes, then turn and toast another 5 minutes. Remove from oven and cool the toast on the rack for 5 minutes.

Combine the eggs, whipping cream, milk, lemon zest, salt, brown sugar, and melted butter in a medium-sized bowl and whisk until well beaten. In a non-stick 12-inch skillet over medium heat, melt 2 tablespoons of the butter. Dip 2 slices of the Texas toast in the egg

mixture, allowing about 15 seconds for the egg wash to soak in. Flip and dip the other sides. As each slice is dipped, add to the melted butter in the skillet. Cook for about 3 minutes, or until the toast is browned and crisp on the bottom, then flip and cook until browned and crisp on the other side for another 3 minutes. Keep warm in a low oven. Do not be tempted to smash the toast with a spatula as it cooks! I never have understood that. One of the secrets to great French toast is to keep it puffy and light-textured—which it won't be if you smash it flat!

Melt another 2 tablespoons of the butter in the skillet, and repeat until all toast slices are done. Re-whisk the egg dip before cooking each batch.

To serve, stack the desired number of slices on each serving plate, adding butter between each slice and some on the uppermost slice. Pour maple syrup on top, and dig in!

Otto's German Bistro Banana-Stuffed Brioche French Toast

SERVES 4

MAKES 1
BRIOCHE LOAF

Adam Yoho, chef at Fredericksburg's Otto's German Bistro, is one of the most innovative and creative chefs I know. Each time I visit the restaurant I am once again delighted by a new slant or unique flavor he has added to a traditional recipe. This rich French toast, created from house-made brioche, is balanced by slathering the toast with tart goat cheese—an amazing flavor combination with the bananas. Chef Adam sources his goat cheese from Honey Doe Goat Farm in Madisonville, Texas. Honey Doe produces stellar, all-natural artisan goat cheeses from its own herd of over one hundred goats. Use a good-quality local Texas goat cheese for the very best taste in this dish.

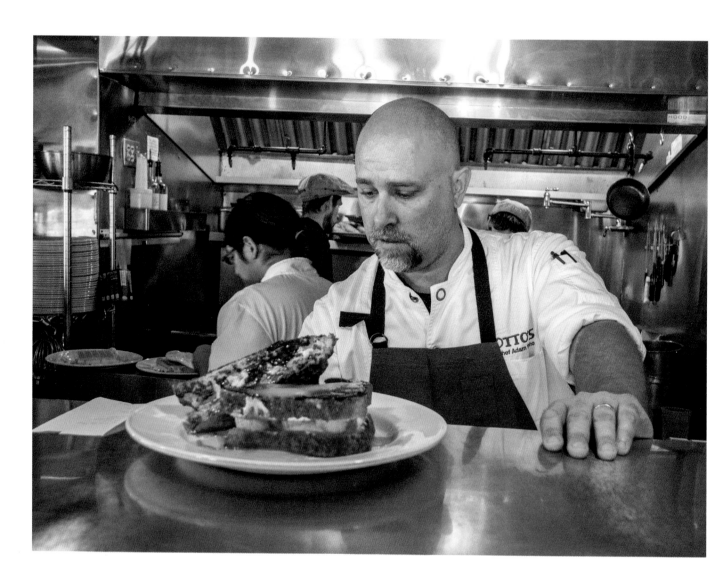

Brioche dough (see recipe below)

French toast batter (see recipe below)

1 cup soft artisan goat cheese

3 to 4 bananas, depending on size

Butter for cooking the toast

Warm maple syrup

Fresh seasonal berries of your choice

Powdered sugar, if desired

BRIOCHE DOUGH

1 tablespoon active dry yeast

1 cup warm water (105 to 115 degrees)

2 tablespoons whole milk

3½ cups all-purpose flour

¾ teaspoon salt

4 eggs

FRENCH TOAST BATTER

4 eggs

1½ cups whipping cream

⅔ cup sugar

1 vanilla bean, slit down the middle to expose the seeds

Begin by making the brioche dough. Combine the yeast, water, and milk in a 2-cup Pyrex measuring cup. Stir gently to activate the yeast. Set aside until the mixture is foamy and all yeast granules on the bottom of the cup have dissolved.

In a stand mixer bowl, combine the flour and salt, beating just to blend. Add the yeast mixture and beat to blend well. Add the eggs and beat with the dough hook to blend. Knead for 5 minutes, using the dough hook until the dough is well blended and just slightly sticky. Turn the dough out into a lightly oiled large bowl, cover the top with plastic wrap, and set aside in a draft-free spot until the dough has doubled in bulk, about 1 hour.

Preheat oven to 375 degrees. Lightly grease a bread loaf pan; set aside. Remove the dough from the bowl and punch down until flat. Form the dough into a loaf and fit into the prepared loaf pan. Cover loosely with plastic wrap and set aside until doubled in bulk, about 30 minutes. Bake in preheated oven for 30 minutes, or until the bread is golden brown and the loaf pan sounds hollow when tapped on the bottom. Turn out onto a wire rack and allow to cool before slicing.

To prepare the French toast batter, begin by combining all ingredients in a shallow bowl and whisking to blend well. Use a sharp paring knife to scrape the beans from the vanilla pod into the batter.

Preheat oven to 375 degrees. When the bread has cooled, slice into 8 (½-inch-thick) slices using a serrated bread knife. Lay 4 slices of the bread on work surface and spread each with 4 tablespoons of the goat cheese. Slice the bananas lengthwise into thin slices to fit on the bread over the goat cheese. Place the remaining 4 slices of bread on top of the bananas and soak the toast in the prepared batter, turning once, for 5 minutes on each side. Heat a glaze of butter on a flat griddle or in 2 large skillets. When the butter is sizzling, add the stuffed bread slices and cook until golden brown and cooked through on the bottom. Flip the toasts and cook until golden brown. Transfer the toasts to preheated oven and bake for 5 minutes. Turn out onto individual serving plates and top with warm maple syrup and berries of your choice. Scatter powdered sugar over the top, if desired.

Mac & Ernie's Roadside Eatery's Lemon and Blueberry Pancakes

MAKES 10 TO 12
PANCAKES,
DEPENDING
ON SIZE

You'd be hard-pressed to find a more perfect embodiment of a Texas diner than Mac & Ernie's Roadside Eatery. Located twelve miles west of Bandera, in Tarpley, Texas, one of those "blink and you miss it" towns that dot the Texas back roads, Mac & Ernie's was founded in 1999 by Naylene Dillingham. At the time, the diner was actually a portable building/taco stand kind of place, where Naylene cooked out back under a tin roof. There were a few picnic tables scattered around in front for seating. The menu started out with cabrito tacos (Naylene raised and butchered the goats), fajitas, sausage wraps, and great beans. But the difference between Mac & Ernie's and an ordinary diner was that Naylene cooked gourmet fare from scratch. The place was an instant hit. Soon she bought a fryer and added catfish to the menu. Later came grilled quail, lamb chops, and salmon. As soon as she could afford steak knives, Naylene added steaks. The reputation of Mac & Ernie's grew, and soon people would be lined up waiting for the place to open on Friday and Saturday for lunch and dinner. They came from everywhere to Tarpley, Texas! The press discovered Mac & Ernie's with features appearing in *Southern Living* and *Texas Monthly* magazines. Then Guy Fieri came to Tarpley and Naylene found herself on the Food Network's *Diners, Dives, and Drive-ins.*

Today Mac & Ernie's is across the road from the original location in a much more permanent structure, complete with an inside kitchen and a real dining room, although the original portable building remains at the core of the new place. When Naylene added Sunday brunch, it was immediately embraced by Mac and Ernie's legions of fans, and diners often wait for tables. You still get your meal on a disposable plate with plastic utensils (except for those steak knives), but now you can enjoy a bottle of champagne with your brunch. Naylene's Lemon and Blueberry Pancakes at Mac & Ernie's are legendary. In Naylene's own words: "These are not wimpy pancakes." ››

4½ cups all-purpose flour
3 tablespoons sugar
3 tablespoons baking powder
3 teaspoons kosher salt
Zest of 4 lemons, or substitute
    orange, grapefruit, or lime juice
    as desired
3¾ cups whole milk
3 eggs, beaten
9 tablespoons butter, melted and
    cooled slightly
1 cup fresh blueberries, or more
    to taste
Butter and real maple syrup

Stir together the flour, sugar, baking powder, and salt in a large bowl. Toss in the citrus zest, blending well. Whisk in the milk with the eggs and butter to incorporate. Pour the wet mixture into the dry mixture, then stir until well mixed. Cover and refrigerate overnight before using. The pancakes will be much fluffier.

Heat a flat griddle to 350 degrees. Spray with nonstick spray. Ladle about ½ to ¾ cup of batter onto griddle for each pancake. Then add blueberries to each. Naylene uses at least 8 per pancake.

Cook until bubbles form around the edges of the pancakes, then flip and cook about another 3 minutes. Each pancake takes approximately 7 minutes from start of cooking to finish. Keep pancakes warm in low oven until all are cooked.

Serve hot, slathered with butter and maple syrup.

Apfelpfannkuchen

GERMAN PUFFY
PANCAKES WITH
APPLES

These puffy and delicious pancakes have long been a winter favorite in German households. They're also sometimes called "Dutch babies." There used to be a couple of German restaurants in Fredericksburg that served hearty breakfast dishes, including Apfelpfannkuchen, but this grand treat, sadly, has since disappeared from menus throughout Texas. Do try them in your kitchen where I'm sure they'll become a favorite weekend breakfast dish. Serve with German-style pan or link sausage.

SERVES 4 TO 6

PANCAKE

6 eggs, room temperature
1 cup whole milk
1 teaspoon vanilla extract
1 teaspoon grated lemon zest
½ teaspoon kosher salt
1 cup sifted all-purpose flour
4 tablespoons unsalted butter
Powdered sugar

APPLE FILLING

½ stick (4 tablespoons) unsalted
  butter
5 Granny Smith apples, peeled,
  cored, and sliced into thin wedges
½ teaspoon ground cinnamon
¼ cup Texas honey

Preheat oven to 450 degrees and place oven rack in middle position. Make the apple filling. Melt butter in a heavy-bottomed 12-inch skillet over medium-high heat. When the buttery foam subsides, add the apples and cinnamon. Cook, stirring, until the apples are quite tender—about 15 minutes. Stir in the honey to blend, and cook an additional 5 minutes; set aside to keep warm while preparing the pancake.

Place a 10- to 12-inch cast-iron skillet on oven rack. In bowl of stand mixer, combine eggs, milk, vanilla extract, lemon zest, and salt. Beat for 5 minutes, or until the mixture is light

lemon-yellow, thickened, and very smooth. Add the flour in thirds, stopping to scrape down side of bowl after each addition; beat for additional 5 minutes. Carefully remove the hot skillet from the oven and add the 4 tablespoons of butter. Return pan to oven.

When the butter has melted and is sizzling, pour the prepared batter into the pan all at once. Quickly return pan to oven and bake for 15 minutes. Reduce heat to 350 degrees and bake an additional 8 to 10 minutes, or until the pancake is puffed and golden brown.

Remove from oven and pour the apple filling over the pancake. Dust with powdered sugar and cut into wedges. Serve at once.

Ginger Pancakes with Lemon Sauce

SERVES 6

MAKES 12
PANCAKES

Ginger pancakes are a Hill Country favorite. One of my favorite 24-hour eateries is the Kerbey Lane Café in Austin, which now boasts seven locations in and around the city. They serve a mean ginger pancake; however, this is not their recipe. Most folks who like ginger pancakes are particular about their toppings. Some like maple syrup, others like molasses or cane syrup, and then there are those of us who like a nice lemony sauce on top. This recipe has the added kick of flavor and a hint of crunch from little nubbins of candied crystallized ginger. If you don't have any on hand, or can't find it, you can omit it without totally ruining the pancakes—but it's worth searching for, as it really adds the icing on the (pan)cake! If you have access to a Penzey's Spice store, they carry it.

Most pancake recipes are a last-minute process, but you could make the lemon sauce ahead of time and very gently reheat it when ready to serve. Just don't let it boil, or it will curdle.

. . . .

Ginger pancakes (see recipe at right)
Butter
Lemon sauce (see recipe below)
Powdered sugar for dusting
Fresh blackberries or blueberries

LEMON SAUCE

1 egg
1 cup sugar
½ cup (1 stick) unsalted butter
¼ cup water
1 tablespoon grated lemon zest
 (about 3 medium lemons)
3 tablespoons freshly squeezed
 lemon juice

GINGER PANCAKES

2 cups all-purpose flour
1½ teaspoons ground ginger
1 teaspoon ground cinnamon
¼ teaspoon ground cloves
2 teaspoons freshly grated nutmeg
 (not pre-ground)
3 eggs
¼ cup brown sugar
1½ cups whole buttermilk
 (not low-fat)
¼ cup strong black coffee
¼ cup molasses
4 tablespoons (½ stick) melted
 unsalted butter
1 tablespoon very finely minced
 candied crystallized ginger

Begin by making the lemon sauce. In a medium-sized bowl, whisk the egg until frothy; set aside. In a heavy-bottomed, 2-quart saucepan over medium heat, combine the remaining sauce ingredients and bring to a boil, stirring constantly. Pour ½ cup of the mixture into the beaten egg, while whisking the egg vigorously. Now pour the tempered egg into the sauce, while whisking the sauce vigorously. Stir for 1 minute, or until thickened enough to coat the back of a metal spoon loosely; remove from heat. Cover and set aside to keep warm while making the pancakes.

To make the pancakes, sift together all dry ingredients, blending well. In bowl of stand mixer, cream the eggs and brown sugar together, beginning on low speed and increasing to medium-high after ingredients are blended. Beat until eggs are thickened and mixture is smooth. Add the buttermilk, coffee, and molasses; beat to incorporate thoroughly. Remove bowl from mixer and whisk in the dry ingredients by hand, just to blend. Don't overbeat the batter, or the pancakes will be heavy. Gently whisk in the melted butter and candied crystallized ginger.

Heat a nonstick skillet and pour slightly less than ¼ cup batter for each pancake. Cook until edges are dry and bubbly. Turn and cook until golden brown on the other side. Serve desired number of pancakes per plate. Top with butter and spoon on a portion of the lemon sauce. Dust with powdered sugar and scatter on some fresh berries. Serve at once.

Light and Fluffy Maple Buttermilk Pancakes with Blackberry Jam

If you're a pancake lover (and who isn't?), then these great little flapjacks will really kick-start your morning. They are wonderful when topped with the easy homemade jam, but if you wish you can simply slather on the butter and more maple syrup.

Make the blackberry jam ahead of time. Reheat the portion you will use to top the pancakes. Prepare the pancake batter and cook the pancakes just before serving.

MAKES 15
3-INCH PANCAKES

MAKES 4 HALF-PINT
JARS OF BLACKBERRY
JAM

2 eggs, beaten until frothy
¼ cup canola oil
⅓ cup real maple syrup
1½ cups whole buttermilk
(not low-fat)
2 cups all-purpose flour
1 teaspoon baking powder
¼ teaspoon kosher salt
Unsalted butter for frying
Powdered sugar
Blackberry jam (see recipe at right)
Butter
Warm maple syrup, if desired

BLACKBERRY JAM

3 cups sugar, divided
2 16-ounce packages of frozen
blackberries
Zest and juice of 1 lemon
1 teaspoon vanilla bean paste
3-inch piece of stick cinnamon
10 fresh sage leaves

Make the blackberry jam first. Place 2 cups of the sugar in a heavy-bottomed 3-quart saucepan. Cook over medium heat, without stirring, until the sugar caramelizes to a rich amber color. Take care not to cook it too long. It should be medium golden colored. Add the frozen berries and stir them quickly into the caramel to coat well. Add the lemon zest and juice. Add the vanilla bean paste to the jam, placing the cinnamon stick and sage leaves on the top. Using a potato masher, mash the berries until they begin to fall apart. Stir to blend well. Add the additional cup of sugar and cook over medium heat, stirring often, until the berries have broken down to a pulpy mass

and the sugar is dissolved, about 45 minutes. Remove the sage leaves and cinnamon stick. Pack the jam into canning jars and seal. Refrigerate after cooling.

To make the pancakes, into the beaten eggs whisk the canola oil, maple syrup, and buttermilk. In a separate bowl, toss together the flour, baking powder, and salt. Gently whisk the dry mixture into the egg mixture just until it's smooth. Set aside for 15 minutes.

Melt 2 tablespoons of unsalted butter in a heavy-bottomed, preferably nonstick skillet over medium heat. When the froth has subsided, pour in

¼ cup of the batter for each pancake. Don't crowd the pan. The pancakes should not touch. Cook for about 2 minutes, or until the cakes are lightly browned around the edges and have big bubbles in the middle. Using a metal spatula, flip the pancakes and cook an additional 2 minutes, or until browned, on the other side. Repeat, using all of the batter and melting additional butter as needed.

To serve, place desired number of pancakes on each serving plate and dust with powdered sugar. Top with a dollop of the jam, or butter them, and drizzle with maple syrup if desired.

FOUR

*Meat Lover's
Breakfast and Brunch
Dishes*

*

My country-born and -bred Texan husband Roger has two caveats regarding breakfast or brunch. It must include grits, and there must be meat on the plate. I've found that most other Texans share his thoughts regarding the first meal of the day.

Southern breakfasts or brunches throughout the nation's history have been heavy on meat. The grand brunches prepared in Southern plantation kitchens consisted of course after course of game meats and fresh fish and shellfish. Most food historians agree that brunch in America originated in New Orleans—and it was there, in 1863, that Madame Begue, at her legendary namesake restaurant, served a mid-morning meal to the butchers from the French Market across the street, after they closed their stalls for the day, that lasted for hours and consisted of several meat dishes and prodigious amounts of wine and brandy.

In Texas, the morning meal, at whatever time it was served, evolved along the lines of the rich ethnic heritage of the state, but almost always contained meat. The Mexican population enjoyed chorizo, a richly seasoned fresh pork sausage. The Germans, many of whom were butchers, who settled in Central Texas, introduced hearty smoked sausages and cured bacon. When the great ranches and cattle drives originated in the western region of the state, the bunkhouse kitchens and chuckwagons served hearty, meat-laden breakfasts to the cowboys who worked the range and tended the herds on the long drives to northern markets. Often offal meats were used in chuckwagon cooking as the cook didn't want to waste any part of a head of beef. One such dish was known as "son-of-a-gun" stew.

When Sandy and I first began researching the subject of breakfast and brunch in Texas and talking with chefs and owners at fine dining restaurants as well as diners that serve breakfast or brunch, we found that the overwhelming majority of their menus featured dishes containing meat. And it wasn't just bacon and sausage, but a wide variety of red meat, including beef, lamb, pork, and even goat, in addition to poultry and game birds. We also discovered that many chefs are curing and smoking their own bacon from pork bellies from free-ranging hogs sourced locally, and in many different styles. They're making great sausages, both smoked and fresh, to include in their breakfast and brunch offerings. And they're curing hams, which are smoked over Texas's abundant pecan wood coals.

This chapter will serve as a go-to resource for Texas meat lovers in search of a carnivore's first meal of the day.

Dai Due
Pon Haus

MAKES 8
SERVINGS

For eight years Dai Due owner Jesse Griffiths operated from a farmer's market pop-up stand in Austin's Republic Square. Over the years the demand for his breakfast dishes, handmade condiments, fresh lard, game sausages, and many, many cuts of meat seasoned and ready for roasting or grilling, plus much more, became too great to handle from the market. In August 2014, Dai Due opened its brick-and-mortar restaurant on Austin's Manor Road to standing-room-only crowds. The shop/restaurant still sells Jesse's great condiments and that wonderful lard, but now they have a butcher counter from which you can purchase meats such as venison, wild boar, antelope, brined chickens, various sausages—all sourced from local producers and suppliers or made in-house.

Dai Due serves one of Austin's most interesting breakfast menus—right through lunch. One of the most popular items is Jesse's Pon Haus. When German settlers arrived on the Texas Gulf Coast to begin their journey to Central Texas, where many had invested in land syndicates, they brought with them the traditional German dishes. Pon Haus is one of those dishes that evolved using the cornmeal that the German housewives found available in Central Texas. The tasty dish has been kept alive in many Texas German families. It is often compared to Pennsylvania Dutch *scrapple*, but German Texans will argue that it is not the same. Jesse's menu changes weekly but Pon Haus is often found among his offerings, served with a perfectly fried egg and cane syrup to drizzle on top.

Pon Haus, by its nature, is made and baked ahead of time. Slice and fry when ready to serve.

MEAT MIX

2 pounds pork butt or shoulder
1 pork kidney, cut into small dice
1¼ cups fine cornmeal
Kosher salt and freshly ground black
   pepper
¼ cup Steen's cane syrup, plus more
   for serving
2 teaspoons chopped fresh sage
1 teaspoon minced garlic
Salt and pepper

SPICE MIX

2 teaspoons freshly ground black
   pepper
1 teaspoon crushed red pepper
¼ teaspoon freshly grated nutmeg
¼ teaspoon dried thyme
¼ teaspoon dried marjoram
1 clove
1 bay leaf ››

Line an 8½ × 4-inch loaf pan with plastic wrap, allowing enough to overhang at the edges. Begin by making the spice mix. Grind all ingredients in a spice mill or clean coffee grinder until finely ground; set aside. Place the pork in a large pot and cover with cold water. Bring to a simmer and cook, uncovered, until very tender, about 3 hours. (Add additional water as needed to keep the meat covered.) Remove meat from the stock and set aside to cool. Reserve the cooking stock. Pick all of the meat from the butt or shoulder and set aside.

In a heavy-bottomed stock pot, heat 1 quart of the cooking stock at a gentle simmer. Whisk in the cornmeal, then add the picked meat, the diced kidney, the cane syrup, the sage, and the garlic. Season with salt and pepper, then add the ground spice mix. Cook at a very gentle simmer until the cornmeal is thickened and begins to come away from the sides of the pan, stirring often to prevent scorching, about 1½ hours. Once the mixture is very thick, pour the Pon Haus into the prepared loaf pan, smoothing it into the corners of the pan. Bang the pan on the counter top a few times to remove any air pockets. Allow the Pon Haus to cool to room temperature on a wire rack, then wrap tightly and refrigerate overnight. Remove the Pon Haus from the loaf pan and slice into 1-inch slices. Heat a little fresh lard in a cast-iron skillet over high heat and sear the Pon Haus on both sides, turning once, until deeply browned and crispy. Serve with a fried egg and more cane syrup drizzled over the top.

Heritage Pork Breakfast Pan Sausage in Caul Fat

MAKES ABOUT 20
3-OUNCE PATTIES

It gives me great pleasure to make my own sausage patties, especially when I know that the ground pork that I buy from South Texas Heritage Pork Farm is meat that came from pastured, well-cared-for animals that haven't been raised with the aid of pharmaceuticals. I add zesty fresh herbs from my garden and a little hit of chiles to make some really flavorful sausages. I finish the sausage patties using an ingredient I learned about many years ago from Cajun French butchers—caul fat, which adds a separate and delicious dimension of both flavor and texture to the patties. I was delighted to discover that many of our Texas charcuterie producers have also discovered the joys of using caul fat and save it when they process their animals. Caul fat is a unique type of pork fat that binds the intestines of the animal together. The French refer to it as *crepine*, and the sausages that they wrap it in are called *crepinettes*. It's a clear membranous fat with lacy fingers of waxy fat spread throughout. The sausage patties are wrapped in sheets of the fat; as they cook, the clear membrane is cooked away, leaving only the lacy fingers, which form a crisp network encasing the patties. In Texas, a good description of the sausages would be to say they're sausage patties wrapped in cracklins.

The sausage patties can be made ahead, wrapped in the caul fat, and refrigerated until ready to cook and serve. They may also be frozen for up to a month. Thaw before cooking.

2 pounds medium-lean South Texas Heritage Pork ground pork
12 ounces smoked bacon, rough chopped, then pulsed in food processor until finely chopped
4 large shallots, finely chopped
3 large garlic cloves, minced
3 large jalapeños, blistered, peeled, seeded, and minced
1 tablespoon crushed red pepper flakes
⅓ cup firmly packed light brown sugar
2 teaspoons smoked sea salt

2 teaspoons freshly ground black pepper
3 fresh bay leaves, minced
1 tablespoon minced fresh thyme
3 tablespoons minced fresh sage
2 tablespoons minced fresh marjoram
1 tablespoon minced Italian flat-leaf parsley
¾ teaspoon freshly ground allspice berries
3 tablespoons Texas ruby port wine
20 (6-inch) squares of pork caul fat
Canola oil

Combine all ingredients, except the caul fat, in a large bowl and mix well, making sure that the ingredients are thoroughly incorporated. I find that using your hands, the original chef's tools, works best for blending ground meat preparations. Using a portion scale, divide the mixture into 20 3-ounce balls. Flatten each ball into a 3-inch round patty. Wrap each patty in a square of the caul fat, tucking the ends under and overlapping them to seal the sausage patty in the fat.

The sausage patties, or a portion of them, can be frozen at this point for future use, when wrapped in individual pieces of plastic wrap and stored in zip-sealing bags. To cook the sausage patties, heat a light glaze of canola oil in a heavy-bottomed 12-inch skillet over medium heat. Add the desired number of sausage patties and cook until the meat is cooked through and the lacy fingers of the caul fat are crisp and golden brown, about 12 minutes, turning once. Drain on absorbent paper towels and serve hot.

Spicy Candied Bacon

A few years ago, "candied" bacon became a big hit with breakfast lovers, and it remains a tasty side dish for a sit-down breakfast or brunch. It's an often-requested dish at events catered by Don Strange of Texas Catering. This version adds an extra dimension of flavor with a spicy seasoned flour dredge, and it forms a crispy slice of bacon.

**MAKES 1 POUND
ABOUT 14 SLICES**

2 cups all-purpose flour
1 tablespoon freshly ground
    black pepper
2 teaspoons cayenne pepper
1 pound thick-sliced applewood-
    smoked bacon
1½ cups firmly packed light
    brown sugar, or more as
    needed

Preheat oven to 350 degrees. Line a large rimmed baking sheet with foil and place a wire cooling rack set over the baking sheet; set aside.

Combine the flour, black pepper, and cayenne pepper in a shallow baking pan; toss to blend well. Dredge the bacon slices, one at a time, in the seasoned flour, coating both sides well and shaking off excess. Arrange the slices on the wire rack on the prepared baking sheet in a single layer so they don't overlap. Using your fingers, pat about 1½ tablespoons of the brown sugar on each bacon slice, covering the entire slice and firming it down with your fingers.

Bake in preheated oven until the bacon is good and crisp and the brown sugar has caramelized, about 40 to 45 minutes. Remove from oven and cool slightly before serving.

OTTO'S GERMAN BISTRO SUNDAY BRUNCH— FREDERICKSBURG- STYLE

O tto's German Bistro opened in Fredericksburg in July 2013, introducing farm-to-table German cuisine to the Texas Hill Country. Tourists come to Fredericksburg expecting to find authentic German food representing all of the German cultures, and Otto's has filled that gap. Owner John Washburne and Chef Adam Yoho collaborated to create an environment that feels like it's always been there. Chef Yoho crafts a seasonally focused menu that not only highlights dishes you can find in Germany and Austria but also explores the Germanic cuisine of Alsace, Bavaria, Northern Italy, and even Texas. When they began serving Sunday brunch in early 2015, offering traditional brunch dishes from various Germanic regions, it was an instant hit. Serve this delightfully delicious brunch with your favorite breads and pastries.

Otto's German Bistro Kaiserschmarrn (see recipe on page 59)
Weisswurst (see recipe on page 119)
Potato Pancakes (see recipe on page 236)

Weisswurst

Weisswurst is a sausage generally prepared in Bavaria and is considered to be separate from the cultural areas of Southern Germany. It can be made ahead of time and refrigerated before cooking.

1 pound veal
12 ounces pork fat
1 tablespoon kosher salt
1 teaspoon ground white pepper
1 teaspoon Colman's dry mustard
  powder
¼ teaspoon ground mace

½ teaspoon grated lemon zest
½ tablespoon minced Italian flat-leaf
  parsley
1 ounce dried whole-milk powder
5 feet pork casings
Canola oil

Combine all ingredients in a large mixing bowl. Using your hands (the original chef's tools!), mix all ingredients together, blending well. Grind the mixture through the small die of a meat grinder twice to ensure a very smooth grind. Stuff into pork casings, making 6 links. Refrigerate until ready to cook.

To cook, heat a glaze of canola oil in a heavy-bottomed 12-inch skillet over medium heat. Cook the sausage links, turning several times, until well browned and cooked through, about 10 to 12 minutes. Drain on paper towels and keep warm in a low oven until ready to serve.

To serve the brunch, place a wedge of the Kaiserschmarrn on each serving plate. Add a link of the cooked Weisswurst and a potato pancake. The Weisswurst is also delicious served simply with fried eggs and potatoes, as shown.

Crispy Italian Sausage Scrambled Egg Muffins

MAKES 15 TO 16
MUFFINS

For the family facing busy, hectic mornings, these scrumptious and filling "muffins" are the answer to providing a hot meal in the form of a hand food that can be enjoyed on the go. You can substitute breakfast sausage for the Italian sausage, or even substitute chopped cooked bacon, and you can vary the type of cheese, too. Try Monterey Jack, Pepper Jack, or Cheddar to change the flavor completely.

The muffins can be assembled and baked ahead of time, then frozen. You may want to make several flavors at one time for future use. To heat, place the desired number of frozen muffins on a microwave-safe plate and cover with a paper towel. Microwave on high for 1 minute.

½ cup melted butter
⅔ cup panko bread crumbs
½ pound bulk-style Italian sausage, hot or mild, your choice
12 eggs
½ cup finely chopped onion

2 large garlic cloves, finely minced
1 small green bell pepper, cut into tiny dice
½ teaspoon kosher salt
½ cup (2 ounces) shredded Asiago or Italian Fontina cheese

Preheat oven to 350 degrees. Brush 16 nonstick muffin-tin cups liberally with the melted butter, using a pastry brush. Dump 1 heaping tablespoon of the panko bread crumbs into each tin. Shake and tilt the muffin tin, coating the bottom and sides of each cup. Tap out excess crumbs. Set aside.

Brown the sausage in a heavy-bottomed skillet, mashing with the back of a spoon to break up any large lumps. The sausage should be in loose crumbles. Drain well and set aside.

Whisk the eggs until frothy and well blended, then add onion, garlic, bell pepper, and salt. Whisk in the cheese, then the sausage, incorporating well. Spoon an equal amount of the mixture into each prepared muffin-tin cup, filling each about ⅔ full. Bake in preheated oven for 25 to 30 minutes, or until a thin knife inserted in the center comes out clean and the eggs feel set to the touch. Run a thin metal spatula around the edges of the cups to remove the "muffins." Enjoy at once, or let them cool, wrap individually in plastic wrap, and freeze for future use.

THE TACO

··

Τ he taco is the Mexican embodiment of "soul food." It is part of the cultural heritage for Mexicans, who hold fond memories of the tacos of their childhoods. In the United States, tacos were first mentioned on a Texas banquet menu as early as 1910; but it is generally agreed that the concept of a "taco-style" concoction probably dates to Mesoamerica, although the word *taco* didn't exist at the time. The breakfast taco, a soft flour or corn tortilla stuffed with fillings made from whatever is available and generally containing scrambled eggs, is the most sought-out of all types of tacos.

After living away from Texas for a number of years, I was amazed to see that the taco had risen from a unique dish that I had often enjoyed in the homes of Mexican friends, and in neighborhood cafés frequented by Mexican-Americans around Houston, to being embraced to cult status by Anglos. Today there are literally hundreds of taco stands, taco trucks, and Mexican restaurants that serve breakfast tacos all over Texas. Food cultures pass from generation to generation, and the Mexican taco continues to evolve. There is no such thing as an *authentic* breakfast taco—all are unique, and every Tex-Mex cook has his or her particular way of making them from various ingredients and with or without sauces. The breakfast taco is normally served with spicy red or green salsa, usually handmade on the premises. I have many memories of early-morning breakfast tacos, but the ones that bring a smile to my face involve fishing. My husband and I are both avid anglers. Nothing beats heading out just at sunrise on a secluded bay to catch a mixed bag of fish that will become dinners for the weekend. In years past, we would hitch up our boat and head out on Friday afternoons from our home in West Columbia—destination Rockport. Driving south on Highway 35, we would anticipate the list of tacos we would order when we got to a taco stand in Old Ocean, at the gates of the Conoco-Phillips Refinery. The place had been there for years, catering to the around-the-clock working shifts at the refinery. It wasn't a place you'd normally go to, unless you knew of its reputation or were intrigued by the crowds always packed around the windows. The folks there had every kind of taco imaginable, or they would make one to your specifications if they had the ingredients you wanted. We would stake a place in line and order a bagful, which we'd store in the refrigerator of our RV when we got to Rockport. Early the next morning, while Roger loaded our gear into the boat, I would heat up a stack of those tacos in the oven and put them in a small cooler to keep them warm. When we arrived at our favorite fishing hole, we'd reach in the cooler and pick out a favorite. They were always marked by initials on the foil as to the fillings—"BBE" for my personal favorite, bean, bacon, and egg. Peeling back that foil, dumping in a hefty dose of hot sauce from the little plastic container, and taking that first bite made the world a better place. The water, with its faintly marine smell; the quiet; and the splendor of the rising sun all came together in that delicious bite of a special part of Texas at its best.

I think it's a safe bet to say that tacos will continue to evolve—plain or fancy, traditional or fusion, high-end or as low-end as that little place in Old Ocean. The breakfast taco is a readily available, and usually delicious, hand food with a good dose of morning protein that feeds thousands of Texans every day. And it's likely here to stay.

Bean, Bacon, and Egg Breakfast Tacos with Red Salsa or Roasted Jalapeño Salsa Verde

MAKES 6
8-INCH TACOS

MAKES ABOUT
2 CUPS RED SALSA

MAKES ABOUT 1¼
CUPS ROASTED
JALAPEÑO SALSA
VERDE

Sounds like a simple breakfast taco—and it is, essentially. But there's a secret to making an outstanding bean, bacon, and egg taco. Each component in the taco is important, beginning with a really good, thin flour tortilla, perfectly scrambled eggs, and good-quality bacon cooked to delicious crispness. But it's even more about the beans. Most devotees of this classic breakfast taco, like me, prefer refried beans, the best of which are prepared using bacon drippings. I learned the true art of making refried beans from a longtime kitchen staff member when I was the chef for a large international corporation in charge of its executive retreats. Her name was Rosa Ramirez, and she was a tiny dynamo from Guanajuato, Mexico, who could do anything in the kitchen, and twice as fast as anyone else, without speaking a word of English. Rosa insisted that all bacon drippings be saved. There was always a large round steam table insert of bacon drippings near her stove. She would use those drippings in a variety of Mexican dishes that she would make when we were lucky enough to have her prepare staff lunch. It was pure magic to watch her cook those smashed beans down in the hot drippings to become a creamy work of art, and heavenly anticipation to smell the aroma of the process. Rosa liked to leave a bit of nubby texture to the beans when she mashed them, and I agree that the resulting *refritos* are preferable to the pureed smooth, limpid version. The beans can be prepared ahead of time, making the tacos a quick and easy breakfast treat. A good salsa is almost a requisite ingredient for breakfast tacos. There are fans of both red salsa (made using tomatoes) and green salsa (made with green chiles and no tomatoes), and I usually serve them both.

As noted, the refried beans can be made ahead of time; just reheat them in the microwave before assembling the tacos. You can also make the two salsas ahead of time and keep them refrigerated until ready to use. Assemble all ingredients, prepped as per the recipe, before you begin assembling the tacos. ››

Red salsa (see recipe at right)

Roasted jalapeno salsa verde (see recipe at right)

3 cups refried beans (see recipe at right)

6 slices thick-cut applewood-smoked bacon, cooked until crisp and drained on absorbent paper towels

6 eggs, scrambled (see directions on page 30)

6 (8-inch) thin flour tortillas

About 1¾ cups shredded Cheddar cheese

REFRIED BEANS

2 cans (15-ounce) pinto beans, not drained

1 white onion, finely chopped

3 tablespoons bacon drippings

Kosher salt to taste

RED SALSA

2 large garlic cloves, peeled and trimmed

1 can (15-ounce) plum tomatoes, and their liquid

2 tablespoons chopped canned chipotle chiles in adobo sauce

¼ cup roughly chopped cilantro leaves and tender top stems

ROASTED JALAPEÑO SALSA VERDE

4 garlic cloves, peeled and trimmed

6 jalapeños, stems removed, blistered, peeled, and roughly chopped

5 tablespoons fresh lime juice

1 teaspoon kosher salt

½ cup canola oil

1 cup firmly packed cilantro leaves and tender top stems

Make the red salsa. With machine running, drop the garlic cloves down the feed tube of food processor fitted with steel blade to puree. Stop and scrape down side of bowl. Add remaining ingredients and process until you have a smooth puree. Refrigerate until ready to use.

Make the roasted jalapeño salsa verde. With machine running, drop the garlic cloves through the feed tube of food processor fitted with steel blade to mince. Stop machine and scrape down side of bowl. Add the blistered jalapeños, lime juice, and salt. Process until well pureed. Again, with machine running, add the canola oil in a slow, steady stream through the feed tube until all has been added. The mixture should be fairly thick and emulsified. Add the cilantro and process until

well blended. Taste and adjust salt, if needed. Refrigerate, covered, until ready to serve.

Next make the refried beans. Combine the beans and their "gravy" with the onion in a heavy-bottomed 3-quart saucepan over low-medium heat. Cook, stirring occasionally to prevent sticking, until the gravy has thickened and the onion is very pulpy, about 45 minutes. Remove from heat. Using a potato masher, or a flat-ended wooden "beetle," mash the beans to desired consistency. I like to leave a texture to them.

Heat the bacon drippings in a cast-iron skillet over medium heat. When the fat is almost smoking, scrape in the beans and stir to blend them into the fat. Cook over medium heat, stirring

often, until the beans have completely absorbed the drippings and are a spreadable consistency, about 15 minutes. Season to taste with kosher salt.

To assemble the tacos, briefly heat the tortillas on a hot comal flat grill or in a dry cast-iron skillet until hot and pliable, about 30 seconds per side. Place the tortillas on a work surface and spread a portion of the beans over each one, leaving about a 1½-inch border at the sides. Divide the scrambled eggs among the tortillas. Scatter a portion of the shredded cheese on the eggs and top each with a strip of the bacon. Fold the tortillas into a half moon, then fold the open side slightly back over the taco. Place on a platter, open sides down, and serve hot. Pass the salsas separately.

Diana Barrios Trevino's Frijoles con Chorizo Tacos

MAKES 8 TACOS

Diana Barrios Trevino is the daughter of legendary San Antonio restaurateur Viola Barrios, who founded Los Barrios in 1979, going on to open La Hacienda in 2004. Her three children carried on her legacy with the opening of Viola's Ventana in 2013 after her death. She was a single mother who raised her family while juggling a busy career (often as a hands-on cook) in the restaurant business. But Diana remembers that there was always a family breakfast on the table, and that they were always delicious. This simple dish was one of her childhood favorites.

Bacon drippings
½ cup chopped onion
½ cup chopped tomato
1 or 2 serrano chiles, seeds and
   veins removed, minced
½ cup bulk-style Mexican chorizo,
   cooked and well drained
2 cups hot refried beans
8 flour or corn tortillas, warmed
8 eggs, softly scrambled
Table salsa, if desired

Heat a thin layer of bacon drippings in a heavy-bottomed 12-inch skillet over medium-high heat. Add onion, tomato, and serrano chiles; cook for 4 to 5 minutes, or until onion is wilted and translucent. Add the cooked and drained chorizo and stir to blend well. Cook for 2 more minutes. Spoon out any excess fat that may have accumulated. Stir in the refried beans and cook to heat through for 2 or 3 minutes, stirring.

Spoon about ⅓ cup of the bean and chorizo mixture down the center of each tortilla. Top each with a portion of the scrambled eggs, fold over, and enjoy. Pass a bowl of table salsa if desired, for an added bonus of heat.

Crave Kitchen and Bar's Eggs Blackstone with Chipotle Hollandaise Sauce

SERVES 4

Crave Kitchen and Bar has become one of El Paso's hottest dining spots in the time since its first location with twenty-eight seats opened in 2008. What began as a small-concept restaurant started by three longtime friends from El Paso with varied backgrounds has now grown to four locations. Octavio Gomez had been in the bar nightlife business, Nick Salgado was the marketing genius, and Chef Rodolfo (Rudy) Valdes had just moved back to his hometown after years of working as a chef in Scottsdale. The group has remained loyal to their original concept of creating a casual, fine-dining restaurant offering a modern American menu with a definitive El Paso twist. Breakfast and brunch at the Crave locations are considered the best in town by locals and visitors alike.

8 eggs
4 English muffins, halved
Softened butter for buttering the muffins
3 additional tablespoons unsalted butter
8 tomato slices, preferably homegrown, salted and peppered on both sides
8 thin slices of Black Forest ham
Chipotle hollandaise sauce (see recipe at right)
Salt and freshly ground black pepper to taste
Minced cilantro as garnish

CHIPOTLE HOLLANDAISE SAUCE

2 egg yolks
2 teaspoons red wine vinegar
1 chipotle chile in adobo sauce, roughly chopped
1½ teaspoons tomato paste
8 ounces hot melted unsalted butter
Salt to taste

Begin by making the chipotle hollandaise sauce. Combine the egg yolks, vinegar, chipotle chile, and tomato paste in work bowl of food processor fitted with steel blade. Process until the yolks are thickened and fluffy, about 2 minutes. Add the hot melted butter in a slow, steady stream through the feed tube until all has been added. Add salt to taste and process another 20 seconds to form a strong emulsion. Turn out into a metal bowl and keep warm over hot (not simmering) water while preparing the eggs.

Poach the eggs according to the directions on page 32, cooking them for 3 to 7 minutes, depending on how you wish to cook the yolks. Drain and set aside to keep warm.

Butter English muffin halves and toast in a heavy-bottomed skillet until light golden brown; set aside to keep warm. Melt the 3 tablespoons butter in the skillet and quickly sear the tomato and ham slices.

To serve, place two English muffin halves on each plate, cut sides up. Top each half with a ham slice and then a tomato slice. Carefully place a drained egg on top of each serving and drizzle with a portion of the chipotle hollandaise sauce. Season with salt and pepper, garnish with a scattering of minced cilantro, and serve at once.

South Texas Heritage Pork Menudo

MAKES ABOUT
1¾ GALLONS

Menudo is a traditional Mexican soup with a variety of preparation methods in different regions of Mexico as well as in the United States, where it has become a popular dish. The dish is very labor-intensive and takes hours to make. It is usually prepared by the entire family to be served in the morning after all-night parties involving alcohol, as it is generally believed to be a cure for hangovers! Menudo is usually served with corn or flour tortillas, or with bolillos, small, oval-shaped hard rolls.

Mark and Kelly Escobedo founded the South Texas Heritage Pork Ranch in Floresville in 2007 and began raising heritage English Large Black hogs and Tamworth hogs, producing quality pork and bacon that they offer at San Antonio's Pearl Brewery Farmer's Market on Saturdays and Sundays. Their excellent products are sought after by many regional chefs. South Texas Heritage Pork Ranch is the only pork producer in the state of Texas to be Animal Welfare Approved. The Escobedos made a huge cauldron of this heady menudo for one of the breakfasts at the 2015 Foodways Texas Symposium in San Antonio, following a Tex-Mex dinner prepared by six legendary Mexican restaurants during which the margaritas and mescal tastings flowed. It was an incredible treat.

The making of proper menudo is a time-consuming process, so it's best done a couple days ahead of time. Reheat when ready to serve.

RED CHILE SAUCE

4 dried ancho chiles
4 dried guajillo chiles
Chicken or pork stock as needed
1 white onion, peeled, trimmed, and roughly chopped
3 garlic cloves, peeled and trimmed

MENUDO

4 pounds honeycomb tripe, rinsed well and cut into 1-inch dice
2½ pounds beef tripe, rinsed well and fat trimmed
¼ cup white distilled vinegar
1 pound pig's feet
1 pound pork shoulder, cut into 1-inch dice
2 large yellow onions, diced
1½ heads garlic, unpeeled
1 tablespoon freshly cracked black pepper
1 teaspoon kosher salt
2½ tablespoons dried Mexican oregano
1½ tablespoons ground cumin

1½ tablespoons Fiesta-brand Menudo Spice Seasoning
1 bay leaf
7 quarts water
2 (15-ounce) cans hominy, drained, then soaked in water for 8 hours, and drained again
1 cup chicken or pork stock

GARNISHES FOR SERVING

Dried Mexican oregano
Lime wedges
Diced onion
Chopped serrano chiles
Chopped cilantro ››

Begin by making the red chile sauce. Remove the stems from the chiles. Toast them in a hot dry skillet for about 30 seconds, turning once, or just until fragrant. Do not overcook the chiles, or the entire pot of menudo will have a bitter, burned flavor! Add enough chicken or pork stock to cover the chiles. Add the onion and garlic cloves. Simmer for 1 hour, or until all ingredients are very soft. Add addi-tional stock if the sauce becomes too dry. Transfer mixture to a high-speed blender and puree. Strain through a fine wire strainer into a bowl, stirring the solids with the back of a spoon to extract all possible liquid. Scrape off any sauce clinging to the bottom of the strainer with a rubber spatula. Discard solids and reserve sauce until ready to use.

Place the diced tripe (both honey-comb and beef) in a large bowl and add cold water to cover. Stir in vinegar and soak, refrigerated, overnight. Drain and rinse the tripe, then blanch in boil-ing water for 10 minutes. Drain and rinse again. This step will eradicate the strong odor that many find very off-putting in making menudo.

Place the tripe, pig's feet, pork shoul-der, onion, garlic, pepper, salt, oregano, cumin, Menudo Spice Seasoning, bay leaf, and water in a large stock or soup pot. Bring to a boil, then reduce heat to a simmer. Simmer the menudo, uncovered, for about 2 hours, or until the tripe and pig's feet are tender. As the menudo simmers, skim fat from the surface and discard.

Add the drained hominy, the reserved red chile sauce, and 1 cup of chicken or pork stock to the simmering menudo and stir to blend well. Cook on low-medium heat for another 3 hours, continuing to skim any fat from the surface.

Serve the menudo in large bowls. Put the garnishes in additional bowls and place them on the table. Serve with warm flour and/or corn tortillas and butter.

Shirred Eggs on Spanish Chorizo and Tomato Stew

SERVES 8

This tasty dish borrows its flavor components from Spain. It is ideal to prepare for overnight or early-morning guests. *Shirred*, or baked, eggs are very simple to make. Just bake them until the whites are firm and the yolks are still nice and runny. Be sure to use Manchego cheese and authentic Spanish, dry-cured chorizo. Texas has its own great brand, Aurelia's Spanish Chorizo, which is produced in Austin and available through HEB Grocery and Central Market stores throughout the state (and Mexico).

The "stew," which is the most labor-intensive aspect of the recipe, can be made ahead of time and rewarmed before assembling the dish. All that's left to do is spoon the stew into gratin dishes, top with an egg, and bake.

---

1 large russet potato, about 8 to 9 ounces, peeled and cut into ½-inch dice

12 ounces Spanish (dry-cured) chorizo, roughly chopped

¼ cup extra-virgin olive oil

3 jalapeños, seeds and veins removed, minced

1 medium yellow onion, cut into small dice

4 ounces white button mushrooms, sliced fairly thin

4 large garlic cloves, minced

1 teaspoon toasted, then ground coriander seeds

2 heaping teaspoons minced fresh thyme

¼ teaspoon pimento de la vera (smoked paprika)

3 large homegrown or heirloom tomatoes, peeled and chopped, with their juice

⅛ teaspoon saffron stirred into 1 cup hot chicken stock

Kosher salt and freshly ground black pepper to taste

1 cup whipping cream

8 eggs

8 ounces shredded Manchego cheese

5 green onions, sliced, thin, including green tops

Place the diced potatoes in a heavy-bottomed 2-quart saucepan and add cold water to cover. Bring to a boil and cook for about 12 minutes, or until barely tender. Drain and set aside.

Place the chopped chorizo in work bowl of food processor fitted with steel blade and process until the sausage is reduced to crumbles; set aside.

Heat the olive oil in a heavy-bottomed 12-inch, deep-sided skillet over medium-high heat. Add the jalapeños, onion, mushrooms, and garlic. Cook, stirring occasionally, until the onions are wilted and transparent and the mushrooms have started to brown, about 7 minutes. Add the crumbled chorizo and potatoes; stir to blend. Cook, stirring often, until the chorizo is very fragrant, about 5 minutes. Add the ground coriander, thyme, pimento de la vera, tomatoes with their juice, and saffron-infused chicken stock, stirring to blend well. Reduce heat to medium and simmer, stirring often, until the stew is reduced and thickened, about 25 minutes. As the stew reduces, skim off any grease that rises to the surface. The mixture should have very little liquid left. Season to taste with salt and pepper. Stir in the whipping cream and cook to reduce slightly and thicken to a medium sauce consistency, about 7 to 10 minutes. Preheat oven to 375 degrees.

Divide the Spanish chorizo and tomato stew evenly among individual gratin dishes. Crack an egg over each dish, taking care not to break the yolks. Place the dishes on baking sheets and bake in preheated oven for about 12 to 13 minutes, alternating the trays halfway through cooking. Scatter a portion of the shredded Manchego cheese over the tops. Return to oven and bake just until the whites are set, leaving the yolks still runny, about an additional 10 minutes. Remove from oven and top each serving with some of the sliced green onions. Place on underliner plates and serve at once.

Brisket, Bacon, and Egg Breakfast Quesadillas

SERVES 8

A quesadilla is a perfect solution when you need a filling breakfast—even for a crowd—in a hurry. In a quesadilla, you have a complete meal sealed together in a tortilla with cheese incorporating whatever is available, and it's a hand food that can be eaten on the go. I always make this particular quesadilla when I have leftover barbecued brisket. I love the flavor of the smoky, bark-crusted slices of beef with the scrambled eggs. Throw in some bacon and good cheese, and you've got a very flavorful start for your day! On those occasions when I anticipate having overnight guests, I've been known to buy brisket from Cranky Frank's in Fredericksburg (some of the best barbecue in the State of Texas) to make these for breakfast!

Slice leftover brisket ahead of time, or purchase sliced brisket if you wish. Assemble all ingredients, prepped as per recipe instructions, before assembling and cooking the quesadillas.

¼ pound (1 stick) unsalted butter

1 large jalapeño, stems, seeds, and veins removed, minced

8 eggs, preferably free-range (also known as "yard eggs"), whisked with ⅓ cup medium-hot water and 1 teaspoon kosher salt until quite frothy

6 applewood-smoked bacon slices, cooked until crisp, then drained well and crumbled

8 (8-inch) flour tortillas

2 cups (8 ounces) shredded Eagle Mountain Granbury Gold Gouda cheese

1 pound barbecued beef brisket, sliced thin and heated

4 ripe homegrown tomatoes, cut into small dice

5 green onions, thinly sliced, including green tops

2 cups salsa of your choice

In a 12-inch nonstick skillet, melt the butter over medium-high heat. Add the minced jalapeño and sauté for a minute or so. Turn the heat down to low-medium and add the beaten eggs, stirring rapidly. Cook, stirring constantly, until the eggs are almost set, then stir in the crumbled bacon. Continue to cook, stirring, until the eggs are softly scrambled, but done; leave no runny, uncooked egg, but don't cook them until they are stiff! Set aside to keep warm.

Place the tortillas on work surface and scatter some of the cheese over each one, covering the entire tortilla. Divide the brisket between the tortillas, allowing about 2 ounces per tortilla. Lay the sliced brisket on one side of the tortillas. Scatter some of the diced tomatoes, green onions, and salsa over the meat, then top each with a portion of the scrambled eggs. Fold the top half of the tortillas down over the fillings to make half-moon shapes. Heat a large dry skillet or comal flat grill over medium-high heat. Cook each tortilla until the cheese is melted and heated through, sticking the quesadilla together, about 2 to 3 minutes per side, turning once.

To serve, cut each quesadilla in half and serve, passing additional salsa if desired.

Chef Johnny Hernandez's Chilaquiles Verdes with Pollo Escabeche

SERVES 6 TO 8

Chef Johnny Hernandez, who learned his passion for food at his father's side in the family restaurant on the west side of San Antonio, is a driving force in the culinary industry in San Antonio. He was encouraged by his dad to become a chef and attended the Culinary Institute of America in New York. As a young chef, Hernandez worked in some of the top resorts in America, including the Mirage Hotel and Casino in Las Vegas and the Four Seasons Biltmore in Santa Barbara, California. But his love of Mexican culture and his keen entrepreneurial spirit brought him back to San Antonio, where he began to establish a restaurant empire. His restaurants today include La Gloria, which has two locations in San Antonio and one in Las Vegas; The Fruteria-Botanero; El Machito; Casa Hernan (his home and the site of pop-up dinners, brunches, and private events); and his catering company, True Flavors Catering.

Chef Hernandez has shared his recipe for this classic Mexican breakfast dish. Chilaquiles are sometimes confused with migas, as both use tortilla strips or chips and both are served for breakfast or brunch. The word *chilaquiles* comes from the native Mexican Nahuatl word *quilaquilitl*. Often, as in Chef Johnny's version of this dish, pulled chicken is added to the *totopos*, or tortilla triangles, after they are softened in green or red salsa or mole. Serve the dish with refried beans, eggs, and guacamole as a side dish.

Both the pollo escabeche and the salsa verde can be made ahead of time. Simply assemble the ingredients in a baking dish per the recipe directions and bake.

. . . .

10 ounces thick-variety fried corn tortilla chips
Salsa verde (see recipe at right)
Pollo escabeche (see recipe below)
½ cup Mexican crema
4 ounces queso fresco, crumbled

POLLO ESCABECHE

¼ cup corn oil
1 ounce julienned onion
1 whole chicken, cooked, skinned, deboned, and shredded
1 Anaheim chile, roasted, peeled, and sliced
¾ cup chicken stock
1 tablespoon each: kosher salt and freshly ground black pepper

SALSA VERDE

3 pounds tomatillos, washed (after paper-like husks are removed)
1 onion, peeled and quartered
6 garlic cloves, peeled and trimmed
2 serrano chiles, stems and seeds removed
¾ cup water
4 ounces crushed ice
1 bunch cilantro, washed
Juice of 1 lime
1 tablespoon kosher salt ››

Begin by making the salsa verde. Combine the tomatillos, onion, garlic cloves, and serrano chiles in just enough water to cover. Boil until the vegetables are tender. Drain and puree the vegetables until smooth. Blend the ¾ cup of water and ice together and add the cilantro; blend until pureed. Mix with the tomatillo mixture and stir in lime juice and salt. Adjust seasoning if needed. Cool and store in refrigerator until ready to use.

Make the pollo escabeche. Heat the corn oil in a medium-sized sauce pan over medium heat. Sweat the onions lightly in the pan. Do not allow them to brown. Add remaining ingredients and simmer gently for about 20 minutes. Adjust seasoning as needed. Cool and reserve.

Preheat oven to 350 degrees. To assemble and serve the dish, place the tortilla chips in a large casserole. Cover with the chicken, followed by the salsa. Bake in preheated oven for 15 minutes. Remove from oven and garnish with the Mexican crema and crumbled queso fresco. Serve hot.

Fonda San Miguel's Grilled Lamb Loin Chops and Quail with Chipotle Rub and a Side of Chipotle Sauce

SERVES 6

MAKES 4 TO 5 CUPS
CHIPOTLE SAUCE

Fonda San Miguel Restaurant in Austin is a local icon serving interior Mexican food. Over forty years ago, when the restaurant first opened, many Austinites were not familiar with the complex dishes of interior Mexican cuisine. In the beginning, the owners, in their quest for authenticity, did not serve the basket of tortilla chips with salsa that is traditional at Mexican restaurants. However, after watching scores of diners leave, they acquiesced on this point, but remained steadfast on the rest of the menu.

Owners Tom Gilliland and Miguel Ravago have always been adamant about serving locally sourced ingredients wherever possible, and certainly about using all-natural, grass-fed meats that have not been exposed to the use of hormones, pesticides, or antibiotics. There is a large herb and vegetable garden on the restaurant grounds that provides the kitchen not only with many herbs unique to interior Mexican cuisine but also with unique vegetables.

Note: Any unused chipotle rub can be stored at room temperature in a sealed container. Regrind before using again. It's also great on corn on the cob!

QUAIL

12 semi-boneless whole quail
Olive oil for glazing
Chipotle rub (see recipe below)
Chipotle sauce (see recipe at right)

LAMB LOIN CHOPS

24 2½-ounce loin lamb chops
Olive oil for glazing
Chipotle rub (see recipe below)
Chipotle sauce (see recipe at right)

CHIPOTLE RUB

¼ cup corn oil
7 dried chipotle chiles, stems, seeds,
   and veins removed
2 ancho chiles, stems, seeds, and
   veins removed
12 garlic cloves peeled
¼ cup coarse sea salt
¼ cup dried Mexican oregano,
   toasted

CHIPOTLE SAUCE

10 to 12 Roma tomatoes, about
   2 pounds
4 chipotle chiles in adobo sauce
4 tablespoons vegetable oil
1 cup beef stock
1 teaspoon sea salt ››

Prepare the chipotle rub. Heat the corn oil in a heavy-bottomed, 10-inch skillet over medium-high heat until hot but not smoking. Fry the chiles, 1 or 2 at a time, turning once, until they puff up and brown, about 10 to 15 seconds each. Do not allow them to burn, or the rub will be bitter. Remove with a slotted spoon and drain on paper towels set on a wire rack. Set aside until chiles are cool and crisp. Once the chiles are cooled, grind them in batches in a spice grinder until they are a fine powder. Combine the ground chiles, garlic, salt, and toasted oregano in a food processor and process until the mixture is coarse and salt-like. If the rub seems overly wet, spread it in an even layer on a baking sheet and allow it to dry in a cool (150-degree) oven until it is no longer moist, about 1 hour. Break up any lumps with your fingers.

Make the chipotle sauce. Put the tomatoes in a large bowl and cover with boiling water. Let stand about 20 seconds, or until skin begins to crack, then drain. Carefully peel the tomatoes. Combine the tomatoes and the chipotles in adobo sauce in blender and puree. Heat the vegetable oil in a nonreactive skillet or Dutch oven over medium heat, and add the tomato puree. Cook, stirring often, for about 5 minutes. Add the beef stock and sea salt and cook to heat through. Keep the sauce warm over low heat.

To grill the quail, preheat a gas grill to medium-low flame, about 300 degrees. Rub the birds with olive oil and a generous portion of the chipotle rub. Place the quail on the grill and cook for 20 to 22 minutes, turning frequently, until the birds are grilled on all sides and the flesh is nicely browned. Serve two per person with a bowl of the chipotle sauce on the side.

To grill the lamb chops, increase the heat of the gas grill to 350 degrees. Rub the chops all over with olive oil and a generous portion of the chipotle rub. Place the chops on the grill and cook for 2 to 3 minutes, or until grill-marked and browned on one side. Turn and cook an additional 2 to 3 minutes on the other side. Serve four chops per person with a bowl of the chipotle sauce on the side.

Garden Café's Mushroom Duxelles and Duck Confit Tart with Poached Eggs and Hollandaise

SERVES 4

Tucked away in the Junius Heights neighborhood in old East Dallas, the Garden Café is a unique restaurant that championed the "farm-to-table" concept long before it had gained much traction in North Texas. Founded in 2002 by Dallas attorney Dale Wooten, the diner opened with a half-acre garden of herbs and vegetables from which it sourced fresh produce for use in the kitchen. Wooten was quoted on the opening of the café: "For someone who's coming here for the first time, I think they'll be a little surprised with what they find. You see this 1920s-era strip mall surrounded by houses, and it feels like another place and time. Then you walk back and see this huge garden back there. It really adds to this feeling of 'where am I?' It doesn't feel like anything else in Dallas."

The garden has since spread to the parking lot, where diners will find cornstalks and asparagus! Dale's son, Mark Wooten, took over the daily operation of the café in 2010 with a continuing commitment to sustainable, ethical food preperation and gardening. He continues to focus on the garden, while also searching for the best local purveyors of meat, eggs, and even honey and maple syrup. Open for breakfast and lunch, the little café is a popular hangout for locals, and it hosts community-centered events as well as poetry readings and small concerts.

All of the component parts of this spectacular recipe can be made ahead of time (and the duck confit must be). Assemble and complete the recipe beginning with the last paragraph of directions when ready to serve.

. . . .

8 poached eggs (see directions on page 32)
Your favorite hollandaise sauce
Minced fresh chives and paprika

DUCK CONFIT

2 duck breasts, skinned and boned
1 tablespoon kosher salt
1 teaspoon minced fresh Mexican oregano, divided
2 teaspoons minced fresh thyme, divided
2 teaspoons minced Italian flat-leaf parsley, divided
2 teaspoons freshly ground black pepper
Duck fat to cover the breasts

PHYLLO TARTS

5 sheets phyllo dough
½ cup melted butter

DUXELLES

2 pounds mixed wild mushrooms of your choice
¼ cup olive oil
2 large shallots, peeled and roughly chopped
3 tablespoons butter
2 tablespoons duck fat
1 teaspoon each: kosher salt and freshly ground black pepper

Begin by making the duck confit. Combine all of the seasonings, blending well. Divide the mixture in half, setting one half aside for use later. Rub the duck breasts well with the remaining herb mixture. Place the breasts squeezed together in a small pan. Cover with plastic wrap and refrigerate to cure for 36 hours. When the duck is cured, rub off all spices and submerge the breasts in the duck fat in a small, heavy-bottomed saucepan over medium-low heat. Simmer for 1½ to 2 hours.

While the breasts are simmering, make the phyllo tarts. Preheat oven to 350 degrees. Spray a medium-sized muffin pan with nonstick spray; set aside. Carefully lay out one sheet of phyllo dough on work surface. Using a pastry brush, brush a generous portion of the melted butter on the sheet. Place another sheet on top and repeat the buttering. Repeat with remaining phyllo sheets. Cut the pastry into roughly 2 × 2-inch squares. Press each dough square into the tins of the prepared muffin pan. Parbake the pastries in preheated oven for 2 minutes. Remove from oven and set aside. You will need 8 perfect tart pastries.

To prepare the duxelles, toss the mushrooms, stems and all, with the olive oil. Spread them out on a large baking sheet, and place in oven set at 175 to 200 degrees. Leave them to bake for 30 to 45 minutes, or until fairly dried. Set aside.

Remove the duck breasts from the duck fat. Sear them on both sides in a very hot cast-iron skillet. Cook for about 2 minutes per side. Remove from pan and set aside to rest on a plate.

Process the shallots in work bowl of food processor fitted with steel blade until minced, but not pureed. Transfer to a mixing bowl. Repeat with the mushrooms, processing them until finely minced, but not to a paste. Combine the mushrooms in bowl with the shallots. Next, cut the duck breasts into roughly 1-inch-sized pieces and process to mince. Place in a separate bowl and set aside. Preheat oven to 350 degrees. Line a baking sheet with parchment paper; set aside.

Heat the 3 tablespoons of butter in a 4-quart, heavy-bottomed saucepan over medium-high heat. When the butter stops bubbling (as most of the water content is cooked off), stir in the shallot/mushroom mixture. Cook, stirring constantly, for about 3 minutes, then lower the heat to medium-low and add the 2 tablespoons of duck fat along with the salt and pepper. Cook another 3 minutes, stirring constantly. Add the minced duck and the reserved herb/spice rub for the duck breasts. Cook just to heat through. Turn off heat. Fill the 8 parbaked tart pastries with the duxelles/duck mixture and place on the prepared baking sheet. Bake in preheated oven for about 3 minutes, or until the pastry is golden brown and crisp. Place two of the hot pastries on each serving plate and top each with a poached egg. Drizzle a portion of the hollandaise sauce over each tart. Garnish with a scattering of paprika and a few of the minced chives. Serve at once.

Fonda San Miguel's Pollo en Mole Poblano

SERVES 6 TO 8

MAKES 9 CUPS
MOLE POBLANO

Chef Miguel Ravago often includes this classic interior Mexican dish, considered by many to be Mexican *haute cuisine*, among the restaurant's Hacienda Sunday Brunch Buffet offerings. Legend has it that the rich sauce composed of chiles, spices, and chocolate was created by the Catholic nuns of Puebla in honor of a visiting bishop. Miguel developed his version of the dish from one that he learned from Diana Kennedy.

Parboil the chicken ahead of time, drain, and reserve the cooking broth. Refrigerate the chicken until ready to finish and serve the dish. Because there are no shortcuts to making a true mole poblano, which takes time and patience, I highly recommend that you make the sauce ahead of time. Reheat the mole poblano and finish cooking the parboiled chicken until cooked through.

4 pounds chicken pieces, skin on
Sea salt and ground black pepper
  to taste
2 tablespoons sesame seeds,
  toasted, for garnish
Cooked white rice

MOLE POBLANO

9 mulato chiles
7 pasilla chiles
6 ancho chiles
1 cup, plus 9 tablespoons vegetable
  oil or lard, plus additional as
  needed
4 or 5 tomatillos, husked and
  cooked until soft
5 whole cloves
20 whole black peppercorns
1-inch piece of a Mexican cinnamon
  stick

1 tablespoon mixed seeds from the
  mulato, pasilla, and ancho chiles,
  toasted
½ teaspoon anise seeds, toasted
¼ teaspoon coriander seeds, toasted
8 tablespoons sesame seeds,
  toasted
4 garlic cloves, roasted
3 tablespoons raisins
20 whole almonds, blanched
¼ cup pumpkin seeds
2 corn tortillas, torn into pieces
3 stale French rolls, cut into 1-inch
  slices
6 to 7 cups reserved chicken broth
  as needed
1½ ounces Mexican chocolate,
  chopped

In a large stock pot, parboil the chicken in water seasoned with salt and pepper to taste. Drain, reserving cooking broth, and refrigerate until ready to assemble the dish.

Prepare the mole poblano. Clean the chiles by removing the stems, veins, and seeds; reserve 1 tablespoon of the mixed seeds. Heat ½ cup of the oil or lard in a heavy-bottomed skillet until it shimmers. Fry the chiles until crisp, about 10 to 15 seconds, turning once; make sure they don't burn. Drain on paper towels. Put the chiles in a nonreactive bowl, cover with hot water, and set aside for 30 minutes. Drain the chiles, reserving the soaking water. Puree the chiles in a high-speed blender with enough of the soaking water to make a smooth paste. It may be necessary to scrape down the side and blend several times to obtain a smooth paste. In a heavy-bottomed Dutch oven, heat an additional ½ cup of oil or lard over medium heat and add the chile puree. Be careful; it will splatter. Cook for about 15 minutes, stirring often. Remove from heat and set aside.

Puree the tomatillos in a high-speed blender. In a coffee or spice grinder, grind the cloves, peppercorns, cinnamon, and toasted seeds. Add the seed mixture and the garlic to the pureed tomatillos and blend until smooth. Set aside.

Heat 6 tablespoons of oil or lard in a heavy-bottomed frying pan. Fry each of the following ingredients and then remove with a slotted spoon: the raisins until they puff up, the almonds to a golden brown, the pumpkin seeds until they pop. If necessary, add enough oil to make 4 tablespoons and fry the tortilla pieces and bread slices until golden brown, about 15 seconds per side; remove from the skillet with a slotted spoon. Add the raisins, almonds, pumpkin seeds, tortillas, and bread to the tomatillo puree and blend, using 1 to 2 cups of the reserved chicken broth, as needed, to make a smooth paste. This may be done in batches. In a heavy-bottomed Dutch oven, heat 3 tablespoons of the oil or lard over medium heat. Add the chile puree, the tomatillos puree, and the Mexican chocolate. Be careful; this will splatter, too. Cook over medium heat for about 15 minutes, stirring often. Add the remaining 5 cups of reserved chicken broth. Cook over low heat for an additional 45 minutes, stirring often enough to prevent the mixture from scorching on the bottom. During the last 15 minutes of cooking time, add the parboiled chicken and heat through.

Garnish with toasted sesame seeds and serve with cooked white rice.

Bird Café's Country Breakfast with Peameal Bacon and Bacon Redeye Gravy

SERVES 6

When I discovered that Chef David McMillan at Fort Worth's Bird Café cured his own peameal bacon in-house, I was very interested in finding out his procedure for this breakfast meat, which is similar to what is generally known as "Canadian" bacon but much tastier. I first learned about "peameal" bacon from a sous chef I once worked with who was from Toronto, Canada. I fell in love with it, as did my guests, so it was interesting to see it served in Fort Worth. Peameal bacon did in fact originate in Canada, where it was first created from boneless, trimmed pork loin that was cured in a wet brine, then rolled in dried, ground yellow peas to extend its shelf life. Today, the method is the same, only the cured loin is rolled in cornmeal.

This is a really scrumptious and hearty dish, and the bacon redeye gravy takes it way over the top in flavor.

Cure the peameal bacon 7 days before you wish to serve it. It can also be frozen after curing and coating in the cornmeal. The bacon redeye gravy can be made ahead of time and reheated before serving. Cook the grits just prior to serving.

12 (3-ounce) slices peameal bacon
   (see recipe at right)
2 to 3 tablespoons canola oil
12 eggs, fried as desired
4 cups cooked grits
Bacon redeye gravy (see recipe at
   right)
12 thin slices Brazos Valley Cheese
   Horseradish and Pecan Cheddar
   cheese
Minced Italian flat-leaf parsley as
   garnish

PEAMEAL BACON

5 pounds trimmed pork loin
3 quarts cold water
1 cup real maple syrup
⅔ cup salt
2 tablespoons curing salt, such as
   Morton's "Tender Quick"
10 whole peppercorns
1 tablespoon mustard seed
1 bay leaf
2 cups yellow cornmeal

BACON REDEYE GRAVY

¾ pound bacon, cut into 1-inch
   pieces
1 onion, roughly chopped
8 garlic cloves, peeled and trimmed
¾ to 1 cup all-purpose flour
4 cups brewed coffee
1 tablespoon cracked black pepper
½ teaspoon kosher salt
½ cup chicken stock, if needed
1 tablespoon apple cider vinegar

Begin by curing the peameal bacon. Cut the pork loin in half and stab with a wooden skewer every inch or so. Combine the water, maple syrup, salt, curing salt, and spices in a deep, non-reactive baking pan. Sink the meat into the brine; rest dinner plates on top to keep the meat submerged. Refrigerate for 5 days.

Remove the meat from the brine and pat dry with a clean cloth towel. Spread the cornmeal on a shallow-rimmed baking sheet and roll the pieces of loin in it. Leave the meat in the cornmeal and refrigerate overnight. The next morning, turn the meat over in the cornmeal and refrigerate for another night. Remove from cornmeal, discarding remaining cornmeal. Place the meat on a wire rack set over a baking sheet and refrigerate overnight.

At this point you can slice off the amount you wish to use. You can pre-slice the remaining meat and freeze in zip-sealing bags for easy use in the future. Refrigerates well for up to 4 days.

Make the bacon redeye gravy. Combine the bacon, onion, and garlic in food processor fitted with steel blade and puree coarsely, stopping to scrape down side of bowl once or twice. Scrape the bacon mixture into a heavy-bottomed saucepan over medium heat and cook, stirring often, until it is well browned and the fat has been rendered. Take care not to burn the mixture.

Add the flour all at once and stir to blend it thoroughly into the fat. Cook to make a medium-dark roux, stirring constantly. Add the coffee and stir to blend. Be sure that no lumps of flour remain. Bring to a boil to thicken. Add

the seasonings, and adjust the texture of the gravy with chicken stock as needed. It should be a thin gravy. Add the vinegar a little bit at a time. You want to taste a very little hint of tartness on the back of the palate—not an outright sour taste, just a bright one. Keep warm on low heat.

When ready to serve the country breakfast, heat the canola oil in a heavy-bottomed 12-inch skillet and sauté the slices of peameal bacon until lightly browned. Set aside to keep warm. Fry the eggs as desired. Place a portion of the hot grits in the center of each serving plate. Place a slice of peameal bacon on each end of the grits, and ladle a portion of the bacon redeye gravy around the outside of the grits and peameal bacon. Place two hot fried eggs on the grits and top with two thin slices of the cheese. Garnish with minced parsley and serve at once.

Quail in Country Ham on Scrambled Eggs with Peppered Coffee Gravy

SERVES 6

Quail is a favorite game bird in Texas. We are also blessed in the fact that even if you're not a hunter, you can still enjoy quail in our state. Bandera Quail in, where else, Bandera, Texas, raises a Texas-cross quail called a *coturnix* quail that has light meat and grows into a plump and tasty bird. Bandera Quail's products are used by chefs all over the country, and they can be ordered online. For ease in cooking and eating, the birds are partially deboned, with the backbone and breastbone removed. During my tenure as executive chef for the Halliburton Corporation at its executive lodges, this was one of the company's most popular brunch dishes. Encourage your guests to eat the tiny leg and wing bones with their fingers. What tasty little morsels they are—and finger licking is certainly permitted. Serve with your favorite biscuits or bread.

This dish is best suited for a late Saturday or Sunday brunch. Be sure to prepare all of the components right before serving, including roasting the quail.

12 roast quail (see recipe at right)

12 eggs, scrambled (see directions on page 30)

Peppered coffee gravy (see recipe at right)

3 green onions, green portion only, sliced thin on the bias

ROAST QUAIL

12 semi-boneless quail (backbone and breastbone removed)

Melted unsalted butter

Kosher salt and freshly ground black pepper

12 thinly cut cured country ham slices

PEPPERED COFFEE GRAVY

½ cup bacon drippings

2 (¼-inch) thick cured country ham slices

1½ teaspoons freshly ground black pepper

4 tablespoons all-purpose flour

1 cup strong black coffee

1½ cups rich beef stock

- -

Begin by roasting the quail. Preheat oven to 350 degrees. Brush each quail liberally with some of the melted butter. Season all over with salt and freshly ground black pepper. Wrap each quail in a slice of the country ham, leaving the wings exposed on top of the ham slice. Overlap the ends of the ham slice on the back side of the quail and secure with a tooth-pick. Place the quail in a single layer in a heavy baking pan, toothpick side down. Roast in preheated oven for 45 minutes, or until quail are just cooked through and juices run clear when pricked with a knife. Remove from oven and set aside to keep warm while making the gravy and scrambling the eggs.

To make the peppered coffee gravy, heat the bacon drippings in a heavy, preferably cast-iron 10-inch skillet over medium heat. Add the ham slices and cook until they are crisp, taking care not to burn them. Remove and set aside, reserving the drippings in the skillet. Add the pepper and flour to the reserved drippings and stir to blend well so that no unblended traces of flour remain. Cook, stirring constantly for about 4 to 5 minutes, until the flour is golden brown to give the gravy a greater depth of flavor. Add the coffee and stir rapidly to blend well. Bring to a boil and cook for 3 to 4 minutes. Stir in the beef stock. Chop the reserved ham slices in crumb-sized bits and add to the gravy. Cook, stir-ring, until thickened.

To serve, spoon a bed of scrambled eggs onto the center of each serving plate. Remove the toothpicks from the quail, and place two quail on the scrambled eggs on each plate. Drizzle a portion of the peppered coffee gravy over the quail and eggs. Garnish with a scattering of the sliced green onions. Serve hot.

Flat Creek Estates Winery Bistro's Wood-Fired Eggs with Scratch-Made Sausage, Herb Butter, and Roasted Tomatoes

SERVES 4

There has been a trend developing at many wineries along the various wine trails in Texas that is not only long past due but a great addition to wine education and appreciation in the state—namely, the fact that wineries are making the investment of adding restaurant operations to their wineries. Wine, as most people know, is intended to be enjoyed with food. However, making the right pairings of food and wine is a confusing matter for many who entertain in their homes. By serving good food at a winery, the owner, winemaker, and chef can work together to spotlight various styles of wine on their lists in pairings with certain foods. This, in turn, makes it easy for consumers to select wines that pair well with the foods they enjoy. Flat Creek Estates was one of the first wineries in Texas to add a full restaurant kitchen to its operation. Today, The Bistro Restaurant at Flat Creek, under the direction of Chef Sean Fulford since 2009, serves sumptuous dinners and regal brunches on Saturday and Sunday. The dishes are made from scratch in The Bistro's kitchen, and much of the produce is grown on the property. The Bistro was named one of the eight best winery restaurants in America by *Vinepair* in June 2015.

This impressive dish is easy to prepare. All of the components can be made ahead. The scratch-made sausage can be prepared, wrapped, and refrigerated up to 3 days ahead. Add the eggs just before serving and cook in your prepared hardwood charcoal grill (hardwood charcoal and no squirt-on fire starter, please) or, if you have the luxury of owning one, your wood-fired oven. The dish can also be prepared in a conventional oven with a good broiler. Be sure that the 6-inch cast-iron skillets are heated until very hot ahead of time. ››

Sean Fulford's Buttermilk Drop
Biscuits (see recipe on page 263)
Pinch of fines herbes (see recipe at
right)
Herb butter (see recipe at right)
Herb-roasted red potatoes (see
recipe below)
Scratch-made sausage (see recipe
at right)
Roasted cherry tomatoes (see
recipe at right)
2 tablespoon extra-virgin olive oil
Pinch of salt and pepper mix (10
parts kosher salt to 1 part ground
white pepper)
4 eggs

HERB-ROASTED RED POTATOES

½ pound small red new potatoes
(about 1½ inches in diameter)
2 tablespoons extra-virgin olive oil
1 tablespoon herb butter (see
recipe at right)
1½ teaspoons fines herbes (see
recipe at right)
Pinch of salt and pepper mix (10
parts kosher salt to 1 part ground
white pepper)

SCRATCH-MADE SAUSAGE

2 pounds pork loin, cut into small
chunks (you can substitute ground
venison, duck, wild boar, or
chicken)
½ pound bacon, cut into small
chunks
2 tablespoons roughly chopped
garlic
¼ cup minced Italian flat-leaf parsley
1½ teaspoons oregano
1 tablespoon fennel seed, toasted,
then ground
1 teaspoon cumin seed, toasted,
then ground
1 tablespoon cracked black pepper,
medium grind
½ to 1 tablespoon salt and pepper
mix (10 parts kosher salt to 1 part
ground white pepper)

HERB BUTTER

1 tablespoon extra-virgin olive oil
2 tablespoons minced garlic
2 tablespoons minced shallot
2 tablespoons minced Italian flat-
leaf parsley
2 tablespoons minced basil
1½ teaspoons minced tarragon or
Mexican mint marigold leaves
¼ teaspoon freshly grated nutmeg
¼ teaspoon crushed red pepper
flakes
½ cup dry white wine
1½ pounds softened unsalted butter
1 teaspoon salt and pepper mix (10
parts kosher salt to 1 part ground
white pepper)

FINES HERBES

¼ cup Italian flat-leaf parsley leaves
1 tablespoon fresh tarragon or
Mexican mint marigold leaves
1 tablespoon fresh chives, roughly
chopped
1 tablespoon fresh chervil leaves

ROASTED CHERRY TOMATOES

1 pound cherry or grape tomatoes
2 tablespoons fresh rosemary leaves
2 tablespoons extra-virgin olive oil
½ teaspoon freshly ground black
pepper
Pinch of salt and pepper mix (10
parts kosher salt to 1 part ground
white pepper)

Begin by preparing the buttermilk biscuits and keep them warm. Make the fines herbes: remove the stems from all of the herbs and finely mince. Set aside.

Make the herb butter by combining all ingredients in work bowl of food processor fitted with steel blade. Process until smooth and well blended. Turn out into a small bowl and set aside.

Next, preheat two 6-inch cast-iron skillets until very hot, or to 500 degrees, in a conventional oven. Make the herb-roasted red potatoes, which can also be prepared in a wood oven. Place 1½ quarts cold water in a large saucepan; quarter the potatoes and add to the water. Bring to a full boil over medium-high heat. Reduce to a simmer and cook for about 20 minutes, or until the potatoes are soft when pierced. Remove from heat and drain. Heat the olive oil in a heavy-bottomed 12-inch skillet over medium-high heat. Sauté the potatoes until golden brown and crispy. Just before serving, toss the potatoes with some of the herb butter, fines herbes, and salt and pepper mix. Serve hot.

Prepare the scratch-made sausage. Grind the pork, bacon, garlic, parsley, and oregano together. (If you don't have a meat grinder, you can use the pulse feature on a food processor to chop the meats to a sausage-like texture, but don't over-process.) Transfer to a mixing bowl and add the ground fennel and cumin seeds, black pepper, and salt and pepper mix. Using your hands, mix together well.

Prepare the roasted cherry tomatoes. Preheat oven to 375 degrees. Place all ingredients in a shallow open roasting pan. Mix well to coat the tomatoes. Roast in preheated oven for 20 minutes, or until softened.

Place 1 tablespoon of the olive oil in each of the two very hot 6-inch skillets. Scatter some of the raw sausage and roasted tomatoes in the skillet and roast in wood oven, in barbecue grill, or under 500-degree broiler for 3 to 4 minutes, or until sausage is cooked. Scrape sausage and tomatoes to the center of the skillets and top with a dollop of the herb butter and a pinch of the salt and pepper mix. Crack an egg on each side of the sausage/tomatoes. Place back in wood oven, in grill, or under broiler and roast the eggs to desired level of doneness. Remove from oven and place the skillet on an underliner plate topped with a paper napkin to keep the hot skillet in place. Top eggs with a scattering of fines herbes. Serve immediately with the herb-roasted red potatoes and hot buttermilk biscuits.

Garden Café's Flatiron Steak and Eggs with Homestead Gristmill Herbed Grits

In my estimation, no book about breakfast and brunch in Texas would be complete without a recipe for the quintessentially Texas "steak and eggs." The dish conjures up images of well-to-do ranchers with Stetsons and custom-made boots, or Texas-made oil barons—both icons of our Texan culture. I have fond memories of laid-back Saturday breakfasts at Austin's former Night Hawk Steak House on Guadalupe, where the steak and eggs plates emerged continuously from the kitchen to the tables of hungry steak lovers. I was delighted when I discovered that the Garden Café in Dallas offers a steak and eggs platter on their brunch menu. It's a true Texas, two-fisted dish made with the wonderful stone-ground grits from the Homestead Gristmill near Waco, Texas. The Garden Café's version features two fried eggs and flatiron steaks that are pan-seared and finished in the oven.

SERVES 4

Pan-seared flatiron steaks (see recipe at right)
Homestead Gristmill herbed grits (see recipe below)
4 eggs, fried your favorite way
Fresh seasonal fruit and/or berries

HOMESTEAD GRISTMILL HERBED GRITS

8 cups chicken stock, preferably homemade
1 cup Homestead Gristmill grits, or substitute another brand of stone-ground grits (not instant)

½ cup whipping cream
2 tablespoons unsalted butter
2 teaspoons kosher salt
2 teaspoons freshly ground black pepper
1 teaspoon cayenne pepper, or to taste
2 tablespoons minced fresh thyme
1 tablespoon minced fresh rosemary

PAN-SEARED FLATIRON STEAKS

4 (6- to 8-ounce) flatiron steaks
Kosher salt and freshly ground black pepper
Olive oil

Begin by making the grits. Bring the chicken stock to a boil in a 4-quart, heavy-bottomed saucepan over medium-high heat. Add the grits and whisk vigorously to blend. Turn heat to medium and cook for about 40 minutes, whisking often, until thickened and tender. Whisk in the remaining ingredients. Cook just to melt the butter and incorporate flavors. Set aside to keep warm while cooking the steaks.

Pat the steaks very dry using absorbent paper towels. Season on both sides with kosher salt and a liberal dusting of freshly ground black pepper. Set aside at room temperature for 15 minutes.

Preheat oven to 350 degrees. Heat a glaze of olive oil in a heavy-bottomed, preferably cast-iron skillet over medium-high heat. When the pan is very hot, sear the steak for 2 minutes on each side, turning once. Remove skillet from stovetop and place in preheated oven for 3 to 5 minutes, depending on how well you like your steaks.

To serve, place a portion of the grits slightly off-center on each serving plate. Place a steak on each plate, slightly overlapping the grits. Place a fried egg on top of the steaks and add sliced fruit and/or berries. Or serve the steak and grits with sautéed spinach and sliced tomatoes as shown.

Bird Café's Duck Egg with Curried Goat and Jasmine Rice Grits

SERVES 6 TO 8

Bird Café, located in Fort Worth's historic Sundance Square Plaza, is a gem of a restaurant. And it serves an amazing Sunday brunch from a menu packed with innovative and adventurous dishes and beverages. The café, which opened in 2013, is located in the original Land Title Block building, which was established in 1889; it is one of the most important and best-surviving Victorian commercial buildings in Downtown Fort Worth. The restoration of the space was done with utmost regard for period authenticity. The structure, now surrounded by buildings that tower over it, has seen many tenants since it first housed the Land Mortgage Bank, the Chamberlain Investment Company (developers of the Arlington Heights subdivision in Fort Worth), and the law firm of Ross, Herd, & Ross. At one point in time, its tenant was a house of ill repute. The café derives its name from the sandstone carvings on the east façade of the building, which feature an owl, a tree, and a mockingbird. The owners carried through on the bird theme inside the restaurant as well. The walls are adorned with an impressive collection of the Texas bird prints of Stuart and Scott Gentling, brother Texas artists who lived in Fort Worth and were greatly influenced by the work of John James Audubon. Their work over their lifetimes greatly influenced the arts in Fort Worth. The café collection also includes prints by the master himself.

Restaurateurs Shannon Wynne and Keith Schlabs, who also own the Dallas gastropub Meddlesome Moth, joined with Chef David McMillan to create Bird Café as a chef-driven concept known for delicious, delectable small plates. The menu focuses on David's innovative take on breakfast and brunch dishes with real Texas-style flavors.

This delicious recipe pulls out all the stops to create an incredibly amazing, complex-flavored dish. But don't be intimidated by the many steps and ingredients. You can prepare all of the component parts of this dish ahead of time, hold them in the refrigerator, and then reheat and assemble them just before serving. After sautéing the pulled goat meat with the peppers, add the duck eggs and scramble just before serving. ››

Goat curry (see recipe below)

6 to 8 duck eggs

Jasmine rice grits (see recipe below)

6 to 8 ounces crumbled Cotija cheese and chopped cilantro as garnish

2 quarts water

¼ cup yellow curry powder (Bird Café uses Madras Hot Curry)

¼ cup Thai fish sauce

2½ tablespoons apple cider vinegar

2 tablespoons soy sauce

2 tablespoons light brown sugar

1 teaspoon cayenne pepper

½ teaspoon chopped garlic

4 kaffir lime leaves, crushed

1 stick lemongrass, crushed

4 pounds goat meat (Bird Café uses leg meat)

Canola oil

¼ cup white wine

12 dried cherries

3 tablespoons unsalted butter

1 red bell pepper, roasted, peeled, and cut into ¼-inch-wide strips

1 poblano chile, roasted, peeled, and cut into ¼-inch-wide strips

1 large shallot, minced

2 tablespoons minced Italian flat-leaf parsley

1 cup jasmine rice

2 cups water

Milk or more water as needed to reach desired consistency

Kosher salt and black pepper to taste

Make the goat curry. Combine the water, curry powder, fish sauce, vinegar, soy sauce, brown sugar, and cayenne in a large nonreactive container. Whisk until smooth. Add the garlic, kaffir lime leaves, and lemongrass. Add the goat meat to the container so that it's fully submerged in the marinade. Use a plate if needed to weigh the meat down so that it stays covered. Refrigerate overnight.

Preheat oven to 325 degrees. Remove the goat meat from the marinade; reserve the marinade. Add a glaze of canola oil to a braising pan and sear all sides of the goat meat until well browned. Add the reserved marinade and cover the pot. Cook for about 3 hours, or until the meat is fork tender. Remove from heat and let the meat cool, covered, at room temperature.

Strain the liquid from the meat into a clean saucepan and add the white wine and dried cherries. Set meat aside. Reduce the marinade/cooking liquid until it is a thin sauce. Taste for seasoning and adjust as desired. Pull the goat meat into bite-sized shreds.

Heat the butter in a large sauté pan over medium heat. Sauté the pulled goat meat, red bell pepper, poblano chile, and shallot. Beat the eggs until well-blended and add to the pan. Cook, stirring often, until the eggs are scrambled. Add the parsley and a little of the reduced goat cooking liquid to the mixture. Or you may fry the eggs by desired method just before plating and serving the dish. (See section on frying eggs, page 29.)

To cook the jasmine rice grits, grind the rice in batches in a spice grinder until the rice is slightly larger than regular corn grits. Using a wire strainer, sift out the fine powdered rice to prevent the grits from becoming pasty. Bring the water to a boil in a large saucepan. Pour in the ground rice and reduce heat to low. Simmer until almost tender, stirring often, about 15 minutes. Continue to cook for 5 to 6 minutes, adding milk or water to keep smooth, or until the ground rice is creamy–like grits. Season to taste with salt and pepper. Set aside to keep warm.

To plate the dish, place a portion of the jasmine rice grits in the center of individual rimmed soup plates. Spoon a portion of the curried goat mixture over the grits, letting it run off the edges of the grits. If you have opted to fry the eggs, place one over the grits in each serving. Ladle a portion of the reduced goat cooking liquid over each serving and garnish with some of the crumbled Cotija cheese and a scattering of the chopped cilantro.

Bird Café's Carne Asada Waffle with Warm Brie and Coffee-Maple Syrup

SERVES 6

Meat-topped waffles have become a popular breakfast and brunch dish. Chef David McMillan created a decidedly different version by topping the waffles with a hearty carne asada and a drizzle of coffee-infused maple syrup. Very tasty, and visually appealing.

Carne asada (see recipe below)
6 freshly cooked waffles, separated into four pieces
6 large cilantro sprigs
5 ounces crumbled Cotija cheese
8 ounces brie cheese at room temperature, cut into 6 wedges
Coffee-maple syrup (see recipe at right)

CARNE ASADA

2 tablespoons canola oil
8 garlic cloves, peeled and trimmed
1 jalapeño
4 tablespoons ancho chile powder, preferably, or substitute regular chili powder
2 tablespoon fresh lime juice

1 tablespoon dried Mexican oregano
2 teaspoons kosher salt
½ cup water
2 pounds beef skirt steak
2 tablespoons canola oil
2 green bell peppers, seeds and veins removed, cut into thin slices lengthwise
1 white onion, sliced about ¼ inch thick

COFFEE-MAPLE SYRUP

2 cups real maple syrup
¼ cup dark coffee grounds, or substitute 1½ teaspoons dark instant-espresso granules
¼ cup water
½ teaspoon kosher salt

Begin by making the carne asada. Heat the canola oil in a heavy-bottomed saucepan over medium heat. When oil is hot, add the garlic cloves and the whole jalapeño. Roast, turning often, until the garlic is lightly browned and the jalapeño is charred. Add the chili powder, lime juice, oregano, salt, and water. Cook on low heat, stirring often for about 5 minutes, or until garlic and jalapeño are softened. Transfer to a blender and puree. Set aside to cool to room temperature.

Place the skirt steak in a nonreactive, deep-sided baking pan. Pour the cooled marinade over the meat and refrigerate overnight. Remove the meat from the marinade and grill/sear in a hot skillet. Cook to desired doneness, then let the meat rest for 5 minutes. While the meat is resting, heat the additional canola oil in a heavy-bottomed 12-inch skillet over medium-high heat. Add the bell pepper and onion slices. Cook, stirring or tossing often, until the vegetables are softened and tender. Slice the skirt steak across the grain to ¼-inch thickness and toss with the sautéed vegetables.

Make the coffee-maple syrup by combining all ingredients in a small saucepan over medium-high heat. Bring to a boil, then lower heat and simmer for about 5 minutes until espresso granules have dissolved and mixture is slightly thickened.

To serve the dish, overlap four waffle wedges down the center of each serving plate. Spoon a portion of the carne asada over the waffles. Lay a cilantro sprig on top of the carne asada on each plate and scatter some of the crumbled Cotija cheese over the plate. Lay a wedge of the brie cheese at the bottom of each plate and drizzle a portion of the coffee-maple syrup around the plate and over the waffles. Serve immediately.

BRENNAN'S OF HOUSTON'S SUNDAY CREOLE JAZZ BRUNCH

Brennan's of Houston, a sister restaurant to New Orleans's famous Commander's Palace, opened in 1967 in its Midtown Houston location, adding an upscale Creole vibe to the Houston dining scene. Like its sister, Brennan's of Houston serves an elegant Creole Jazz Brunch on Sunday. And like many Brennan's of Houston chefs before him, Chef Danny Trace joined the Brennan's of Houston staff as executive chef in 2009, after stints at many of the Brennan family's umbrella of restaurants. Ella Brennan, the matriarch of the Brennan family, always thought that working at the "mother ship" would help the chefs develop a good *la bouche Creole*, or "Creole mouth." Danny grew up just outside of New Orleans, enjoying a childhood spent hunting, fishing, crabbing, and crawfishing. The thrill of the catch and turning it into a fresh, savory meal spawned a passion for cooking that led him to pursue a culinary education at Johnson & Wales University. Under Danny's tutelage, the brunch menu at Brennan's of Houston remains Creole-rooted, though it changes seasonally and has some Texanized touches like the rich venison hash topped with fried eggs and the Creole mustard cream sauce. I asked Chef Trace to put together dishes that he thought would make a perfect brunch for a winter Sunday.

Brennan's of Houston's Gumbo Z'Herbes with Cornmeal
Drop Biscuits (see recipe on page 218)
Brennan's of Houston's Smoked Catfish Mousse
(see recipe on page 177)
Brennan's of Houston's Venison Hash with Fried Eggs
(see recipe facing page)
Brennan's of Houston's Bananas Foster
(see recipe on page 220)

Many of this brunch's parts can be prepared ahead of time, making it easy
to serve the "whole enchilada." One good example of a dish with make-
ahead possibilities is the Texas venison hash, including the Creole mustard cream sauce. To serve, proceed with the preparation beginning with
the next-to-last paragraph. Heat the Creole mustard cream sauce gently
before serving.

Brennan's of Houston's Venison Hash with Fried Eggs

SERVES 4

2 cups finely cubed potatoes
4 tablespoons canola oil, divided
1 cup (¼-inch half-moon-sliced) venison link sausage
½ cup finely chopped yellow onion
¼ cup finely chopped red bell pepper
¼ cup finely chopped green bell pepper
2 tablespoons Louisiana Hot Pepper Sauce
2 tablespoons Worcestershire sauce
Creole seasoning to taste

Water as needed
4 eggs
2 tablespoons thinly sliced green onions
Nonstick spray or unsalted butter as needed.

CREOLE MUSTARD CREAM SAUCE

¾ cup whipping cream
¼ cup Creole mustard
Salt and freshly ground black pepper to taste

Place the potatoes in a heavy-bottomed medium-sized saucepan and add cold water to cover. Bring to a boil and simmer until potatoes are tender, about 15 to 20 minutes. Drain and reserve.

Prepare the Creole mustard cream sauce. In a small saucepan over medium heat, cook the cream about 10 minutes, or until slightly reduced and thickened. Whisk in the Creole mustard until well blended. Season to taste; set aside to keep warm.

To prepare the venison hash, heat 2 tablespoons of the canola oil in a large skillet over medium-high heat. Add the sausage, onions, and bell peppers. Sauté for 3 to 4 minutes, or until cooked through. Add the reserved potatoes, hot sauce, and Worcester-shire and season to taste with the Creole seasoning. Pour in a small amount of water if needed to break up the potatoes. Stir until the mixture is sticky. Remove from heat and refrigerate until totally cooled, about 30 minutes. Preheat oven to 450 degrees.

Form the chilled venison mixture into 4 (1-inch-thick) patties. Heat the remaining 2 tablespoons of oil in a medium-sized nonstick sauté pan over medium-high heat. Sear the venison patties on both sides, turning once. Place the patties on a greased baking sheet and bake in preheated oven for 5 to 7 minutes, or until heated through. Wipe any residue left from the patties out of the nonstick pan. Spray with nonstick spray, or add unsalted butter, and fry the eggs two at a time.

To serve, place one of the patties in the center of each serving plate. Top with a fried egg and spoon a portion of the Creole mustard cream sauce over the top. Scatter some of the green onions on top as garnish.

The Driskill Hotel's 1886 Café & Bakery's Croque Madames

SERVES 2 TO 4

MAKES 2 SANDWICHES

A croque madame is a classic French sandwich that has become a popular brunch item. The sandwich is often topped with a rich and cheesy Mornay sauce, as is this heavenly version served at the Driskill Hotel's 1886 Café & Bakery brunch. Chef Troy Knapp imparts a Texas dimension to the sauce, with the addition of Pepper Jack cheese. The choice of ham is up to you, but the Driskill's version features Black Forest ham, a richly smoked ham that gives the dish a very flavorful note when combined with the assertive taste of the Gruyère cheese.

The Gruyère and Pepper Jack Mornay sauce can be prepared about 1 hour ahead of time. Gently reheat it when ready to assemble the dish.

CROQUE MADAMES

4 slices of good brioche bread,
  cut ¾ inch thick
2 eggs
6 ounces shredded Gruyère
  cheese
10 ounces shaved Black Forest
  ham
4 tablespoons unsalted butter,
  melted
Kosher salt and freshly ground
  black pepper to taste
Chopped fresh chives to garnish

GRUYÈRE AND PEPPER JACK MORNAY SAUCE

1½ ounces unsalted butter
2 tablespoons medium-diced
  yellow onion
2 teaspoons minced garlic
⅓ cup all-purpose flour
2 cups whole milk
1 cup heavy cream
2 teaspoons kosher salt
½ teaspoon freshly ground black
  pepper
1 ounce Gruyère cheese, shredded
1 ounce Pepper Jack cheese,
  shredded

Begin by making the Gruyère and Pepper Jack Mornay sauce. Melt the butter in a heavy-bottomed sauté pan on medium-low heat, and sauté the onions and garlic until translucent. It is important not to allow the onions, garlic, or butter to brown.

Remove the pan from the heat and add the flour all at once, stirring to incorporate until no traces of unblended flour remain. (This forms what is known as a "white roux.") Add the milk, cream, salt, and pepper to the pan, and place back over low heat. Whisk the mixture to incorporate the liquid into the roux. Bring to a simmer, whisking occasionally and taking care not to scorch the sauce. Simmer for 10 to 12 minutes. The sauce will thicken enough to coat the back of a spoon. (As noted earlier, this part of the spoon is also called the "nape.")

Remove from heat and whisk in the cheeses until they are completely melted. Strain the sauce through a wire strainer into a bowl, stirring with the back of the spoon to get all of the good cheesy sauce! Set aside to keep warm while making the sandwiches.

To assemble the croque madames, toast the brioche slices in butter on a large, medium-hot griddle until golden brown. Flip and brown the other sides.

Crack both eggs on an empty part of the griddle and season with the kosher salt and pepper. Cook the eggs sunny-side up.

On the same griddle, heat the ham topped with the Gruyère cheese. Once the cheese has melted, take half of the ham and cheese and place it on one slice of the toasted brioche. Place another slice of the brioche on top to form a sandwich. Repeat with the last two slices of toast and the remaining ham and cheese.

Place the sandwiches next to each other on a small platter. Ladle 12 ounces of the Gruyère and Pepper Jack Mornay sauce over the sandwiches. They should be completely covered with the sauce. Place one of the sunny-side-up eggs in the center of each sandwich.

To serve, slice the sandwiches in half diagonally and transfer to serving plates, offering a whole or half sandwich as desired. Top with additional sauce as desired. Garnish each serving with a scattering of the chopped chives.

Fonda San Miguel's Cochinita Pibil with Cebollas Rojas en Escabeche and Mole Verde

PORK COOKED IN A PIT WITH PICKLED RED ONIONS

SERVES 6

Cochinita pibil is the traditional pork barbecue of the Yucatan Peninsula, where for centuries it has been cooked in pits lined with hot stones and banana leaves. The achiote-based rub, which imparts a rich, terra-cotta color and an earthy flavor, is equally good on seafood and chicken. Cochinita pibil is a regular feature in Fonda San Miguel's Hacienda Sunday Brunch Buffet.

Because of the many steps and component parts involved, this dish must be prepared well ahead of time. Make the cebollas rojas en escabeche ahead and refrigerate. Reheat the pork in the Dutch oven in which the dish is cooked when ready to serve. Make a batch of white rice and serve.

4 pounds pork shoulder or butt, trimmed of tendons and cut into 1-inch cubes
2 tablespoons safflower oil
4 large tomatoes, sliced
2 medium white onions, sliced
2 tablespoons reserved achiote rub (see recipe below)
1 large banana leaf
Cebollas rojas en escabeche (see recipe at right)
Cooked white rice
Mole verde (see recipe at right)

ACHIOTE RUB

3 tablespoons achiote paste
¼ cup orange juice
¼ cup distilled white vinegar
½ teaspoon cumin seeds
½ teaspoon dried Mexican oregano
12 whole black peppercorns
4 whole allspice berries
8 garlic cloves, peeled
¼ teaspoon paprika
1 tablespoon sea salt

CEBOLLAS ROJAS EN ESCABECHE

1 large red onion, sliced thin
12 whole black peppercorns
3 garlic cloves, sliced
1 fresh red beet, peeled and sliced
1 cup red wine vinegar

MOLE VERDE

1 cup hulled pumpkin seeds, toasted
¼ teaspoon cumin seeds, toasted
10 whole black peppercorns
5 cups chicken broth
2 leaves romaine lettuce
1 bunch radish leaves
6 sprigs cilantro
4 sprigs epazote
Half of a medium white onion, chopped
3 garlic cloves, chopped
4 serrano chiles, chopped
4 to 5 tomatillos, husked, boiled, and drained
2 tablespoons vegetable oil or lard

Begin by making the cebollas rojas en escabeche. Combine the ingredients in a nonreactive (stainless steel or glass) mixing bowl and set aside at room temperature for 1 to 2 hours. Remove the beet slices and discard. (They are added to increase the brilliance of the onion's color.) Drain the onions and discard the pickling liquid. Transfer the onions to a serving dish and serve at room temperature, or refrigerate in a covered container until ready to use. They will keep for several days.

Make the mole verde. Combine the seeds and peppercorns in a spice grinder and process to a powder. Transfer to a small bowl, combine with 1 cup of the chicken broth, and set aside. Combine the romaine leaves, radish leaves, cilantro, epazote, onion, garlic, chiles, and tomatillos in a blender. Add the remaining broth and seed/broth mixture; puree. This may have to be done in two batches. Heat the oil in a heavy Dutch oven or soup pot over medium heat. Add the puree and cook for about 10 minutes, stirring often to prevent sticking. Keep warm while preparing the pork.

Make the achiote rub. Mash the achiote paste with the orange juice and vinegar. Transfer to blender with remaining ingredients and blend to a paste. Reserve 2 tablespoons of the paste for cooking with the tomatoes. Rub the pork cubes with the Achiote Rub and set aside.

Heat the oil in a heavy-bottomed skillet over medium heat. Add the tomatoes, the onions, and the reserved 2 tablespoons of achiote rub. Fry for about 3 minutes and set aside.

Preheat oven to 350 degrees. Have a large, heavy Dutch oven ready. Using tongs, carefully sear the banana leaf over an open flame until it is flexible. Line the Dutch oven with the banana leaf and arrange the pork cubes on the leaf. Cover the pork with the tomato mixture, folding the banana leaf over the top. Cover the pot and cook in preheated oven for 2 to 2½ hours, basting occasionally with juices from the bottom of the pot. Remove from the oven and transfer to a serving platter. Garnish with a portion of the cebollas rojas en escabeche and serve with white rice. Serve the mole verde separately.

FIVE

*Breakfast and Brunch
from the Bounty of
the Waters*

*

The fact that I love fish and shellfish probably has a lot to do with my love of fishing, or vice versa. There aren't many critters that come from Texas waters that I haven't eaten. I am a great advocate of using "by-catch" fish, often called "trash" fish, especially by anglers who prefer to keep only the more popular fish like redfish, speckled trout, flounder, red snapper, and so on, that they catch. But we are being constantly warned that these popular fish are in danger of being over-fished to the point that we won't be able to enjoy them in the future. So, when my husband and I catch an unfamiliar denizen of the deep, we like to cook it and evaluate the taste. We've discovered a lot of fish that we like equally as well as the more popular ones.

Many restaurant chefs are now sourcing "by-catch" fish for their menus, creating innovative and tasty noteworthy dishes. Some of the large coastal seafood wholesalers are buying these otherwise wasted fish from their commercial fishermen: Groomer's Seafood (located in Corpus Christi, with a distribution center in San Antonio also) and Louisiana Foods (in Houston) are leading the way in the endeavor to utilize the odd fishes from Texas coastal waters.

I have fond memories of great lakeside, early-morning breakfasts of freshly caught and cleaned whole crappie rolled in cornmeal (or not) and fried in a cast-iron skillet over an open fire until nice and crispy. What a treat for the palate to dine on a pristinely fresh fish barely 15 minutes out of the water! The taste and texture are incredible.

With our bounty of fish and shellfish, it's natural that Texans like to enjoy them for breakfast, too. I generally reserve the dishes in this chapter for brunch, as many feature elaborate—and visually beautiful—preparations. Chef friends who serve seafood dishes on their brunch menus report that they are popular with customers as an alternative to dishes with red meats.

If you're not an angler and have to purchase your fresh fish and shellfish, shop at a reputable, recommended fish market. A good market will have a smell that is not fishy but, rather, "faintly marine." Buy whole fish whenever possible so that you can look them in the eyes, which should be clear and bulging, never sunken or clouded. The gills should be bright red, never brownish, which indicates decomposition. And the flesh of the fish should be moist, never "slimy" in appearance or feel; nor should it appear dried. And again, let your nose be your guide. Fresh fish does not smell fishy. If the market selection is limited to filleted fish, examine the flesh. It should not be dry or slimy and the flakes of the meat should be tight, with no obvious signs of coming apart. It is almost impossible to cook over-the-hill fish fillets without having them come apart into flakes. Cook fresh fish as soon as possible after purchasing it. Even if you purchase pristinely fresh fish, it won't keep in the refrigerator for more than 2 days max before it becomes all of the things you avoided by buying it fresh.

When purchasing oysters in their shells, buy only from a dealer you trust. Discard any oysters that have opened shells that don't close at once when tapped. If you're buying shucked oysters in their liquor, the liquor should be clear and viscous, never cloudy or watery, and the oysters should be light tan in color and plump, never shrunken-looking. If you can, buy shrimp with the heads on. First, you can tell their freshness by how well attached the heads are. If the heads are falling off, then the shrimp are older. Second, you can collect small batches of shrimp heads (and shells) in the freezer to make a decent batch of stock once you have a sufficient number. As with other marine creatures, shrimp should not have an unpleasant odor. When you buy fresh blue crabs, they should be alive, although they may be stunned on ice. If you purchase picked crabmeat, it should never have an ammonia-like odor but, rather, should smell faintly sweet—just as fresh crabmeat should taste. Be sure to pick through fresh crabmeat to remove any bits of shell and/or cartilage before using. But do so carefully, so you don't break up those gorgeous lumps of meat that you've paid dearly for! Genuine fresh scallops, too, should not smell fishy or be slimy, and they should have firmly attached adductor muscles, which should be removed before you cook the scallops. If they don't have these muscles, then you might be buying imitation scallops that were stamped out of the flesh of less popular white fish. Fresh scallops have an unmistakable sweet aroma, so, if in doubt, give them a sniff!

Ocean Grille & Beach Bar's Crab Cake Benedict

SERVES 4

The Ocean Grille & Beach Bar opened in April 2015 to great fanfare. Restaurateur Randall Pettit and operating partner Bryan Davis brought on two Houston-area chefs to launch the casual surfside spot. Brian Peper, formerly of Urban Eats and Bellaire-area Costa Brava, is the executive chef, and Randy Evans, Pettit's longtime friend and former executive chef of Brennan's of Houston and owner of the now-shuttered Houston favorite, Haven, serves as a consulting chef. Evans is known for popularizing the farm-to-table dining concept in Houston. So it comes as no surprise that Ocean Grille & Beach Bar is focused on using locally and regionally sourced, homegrown ingredients. The restaurant sources its pristinely fresh seafood from Galveston's Katie's Seafood and its spices from Maceo's, Galveston's longtime purveyor of fine seasonings. Its ice cream comes from local ice cream producer Hey Mikey's, and Brian sources much of the restaurant's produce from the Galveston Farmer's Market.

Sunday brunch at Ocean Grille & Beach Bar has become a favorite with both island residents and tourists alike. One taste of the Crab Cake Benedict and you'll know why!

Although not many of us have the setting that comes with brunch at Ocean Grille & Beach Bar in Galveston, this popular dish from its menu is totally doable at home. You can make the crab cakes up to 1 day ahead of time and refrigerate them before cooking. The remoulade sauce can be made the day before serving, and the eggs can be pre-poached (see directions on page 32) and finished just before serving.

---

8 crab cakes (see recipe below)
Remoulade sauce (see recipe at right)
Hollandaise sauce (see recipe at right)
4 English muffins, cut in half
Clarified butter for toasting muffins
8 poached eggs (see directions on page 32), kept warm and well drained

CRAB CAKES

¼ pound jumbo lump crabmeat
¾ pound claw crabmeat
¼ cup small diced red onion
¼ cup small diced red bell pepper

2 eggs
½ cup real mayonnaise
½ cup panko bread crumbs
1 teaspoon Worcestershire sauce
1 teaspoon Tabasco
1 tablespoon freshly squeezed lemon juice
Clarified butter for sautéing

REMOULADE SAUCE

¾ cup real mayonnaise
1 tablespoon capers, well drained
1 tablespoon minced shallots
¼ cup minced roasted red bell pepper

1 tablespoon freshly squeezed lemon juice
1 tablespoon Creole mustard
Kosher salt and freshly ground black pepper to taste

HOLLANDAISE SAUCE

4 egg yolks
1 tablespoon freshly squeezed lemon juice
½ teaspoon Tabasco
¾ cup hot clarified butter
½ cup warm water, as needed
Kosher salt to taste

Begin by making the crab cakes. Combine all ingredients in a medium-sized bowl and gently fold together, blending well, but taking care not to break up the jumbo crab lumps. Cover with plastic wrap and refrigerate for about 30 minutes. Remove and portion into 8 (2-ounce) cakes. Refrigerate until ready to cook.

Make the remoulade sauce. Combine all ingredients in blender and puree until smooth. Season with salt and pepper to taste. Set aside.

Make the hollandaise sauce. In work bowl of food processor fitted with steel blade, combine the egg yolks, lemon juice, and Tabasco. Process until the yolks are thickened and light lemon-yellow in color, about 2 min-utes. Scrape down side of bowl. With machine running, add the hot clarified butter in a slow, steady stream through the feed tube until all has been added. If the sauce is too thick, add some of the water to thin to desired consistency. Process for an additional 20 seconds to form a strong emulsion. Season to taste with salt. Turn out into a bowl, cover with plastic wrap, and place over a pan of hot (not simmering) water to keep warm. Whisk well before serving.

Heat a portion of clarified butter in a heavy-bottomed 12-inch sauté pan over medium-high heat. Add the crab cakes and cook until golden brown on both sides, turning once. Set aside to keep warm.

Wipe out the sauté pan and return to heat, adding a little additional butter. Toast the English muffin halves, cut sides down in the butter, until golden brown.

To serve, place two English muffin halves on each plate, toasted sides up. Spread a portion of the remoulade sauce over each and place a crab cake on each. Using the back of a large spoon, make an indentation in each crab cake to hold the eggs in place. Gently place a poached egg on each crab cake and sauce with some of the hollandaise sauce. Serve at once.

Otto's German Bistro Gravlax with Pickled Red Onions and Horseradish Crème Fraiche

Chef Adam Yoho of Fredericksburg's Otto's German Bistro frequently serves this full-bodied version of classic gravlax at the eatery's popular Sunday brunch.

Note that the gravlax and side dishes require being made completely ahead and refrigerated, covered, for up to 3 days.

MAKES A SIDE OF CURED SALMON, ABOUT 12 TO 14 POUNDS

2 cups fine sea salt
2 cups sugar
4 tablespoons ground juniper berries
1 side of wild-caught king salmon, about 12 to 14 pounds, skinned
Capers, well drained
Horseradish crème fraiche (see recipe at right)
Pickled red onions (see recipe at right)

PICKLED RED ONIONS

1 to 12 red onions, sliced thin
6 cups red wine vinegar
1 cup sugar
1 cup kosher salt
2 tablespoons whole coriander
1 tablespoon whole cloves
2 (4-inch) cinnamon sticks
2 tablespoons whole black peppercorns
10 fresh bay leaves

HORSERADISH CRÈME FRAICHE

14 ounces crème fraiche
2 heaping tablespoons prepared horseradish
½ teaspoon kosher salt

Begin by making the gravlax. Combine the salt, sugar, and ground juniper berries in a bowl, tossing to blend well. Place a small amount of this cure in the bottom of a non-aluminum dish large enough to hold the side of salmon. Place the fish in the dish, skinned side down, and completely cover it with the remaining cure. Wrap tightly and refrigerate for 48 hours. Remove the salmon from the cure and rinse well to remove all of the cure. Pat the salmon dry and allow to sit at room temperature for 2 hours before slicing very thin on the bias, using a thin-bladed slicing knife. Place on a large platter and scatter some of the capers around and over the fish. Serve with dishes of the horseradish crème fraiche and some of the drained pickled red onions.

To make the pickled red onions, place the sliced red onions in a 5-quart crock jar. Combine the remaining ingredients in a heavy-bottomed 4-quart saucepan over medium-high heat. Bring to a full boil and continue to cook until the sugar and salt are dissolved and the brine is very aromatic. Pour over the onions in the crock, loosely cover with a clean kitchen towel, and set aside for 36 hours before using.

To make the horseradish crème fraiche, combine all ingredients in a mixing bowl and whisk to blend until smooth and well blended. Cover and refrigerate for up to 3 days.

Brennan's of Houston's Smoked Catfish Mousse

Brennan's of Houston Executive Chef Danny Trace creates mouth-watering seasonal dishes for the restaurant's iconic Sunday Creole Jazz Brunch menus. This dish is one of his personal favorites, which he likes to include as a finger food on the brunch table. In the South, catfish is praised for its delicate, sweet flesh. Here Chef Trace smokes the catfish fillets and blends the flesh with a classic Creole-style ravigote sauce. At the restaurant, they're served with sweet potato chips in paper-cone-lined silver mint julep cups for a presentation that really pops.

This dish is one of the component parts of one of the full-blown brunch menus served at Brennan's of Houston, although it makes a very tasty side dish on its own that could be served with other brunch dishes in this book. The mousse itself can be made up to 1 day ahead of time and kept refrigerated. The sweet potato chips, however, need to be sliced and fried just before serving.

SERVES 8 TO 10
AS FINGER FOOD

MAKES 2½ CUPS
RAVIGOTE SAUCE

MAKES 3½ CUPS
CREOLE SEAFOOD
SEASONING

. . . .

MOUSSE

2 pounds catfish fillets
Kosher salt and freshly ground black pepper to taste
¼ cup minced red onion
1½ cup ravigote sauce (see recipe at right)
2 tablespoons softened cream cheese
Sweet potato chips (see recipe at right)
Creole seafood seasoning (see recipe at right)
1 teaspoon minced fresh chives

RAVIGOTE SAUCE

1½ cups real mayonnaise
⅔ cup Creole mustard
1 lard-cooked egg, chopped
2 tablespoons chopped capers
1 tablespoon chopped fresh herbs (basil, thyme, oregano)
1 tablespoon Louisiana Hot Pepper Sauce
1 tablespoon Worcestershire sauce
Kosher salt and freshly ground black pepper to taste

CREOLE SEAFOOD SEASONING

¾ cup kosher salt
6½ tablespoons finely ground black pepper
4 tablespoons cayenne pepper
7½ tablespoons garlic powder
6 tablespoons onion powder
1 cup paprika
½ cup tightly packed dried thyme leaves
7 tablespoons tightly packed dried oregano leaves

SWEET POTATO CHIPS

2 medium sweet potatoes, peeled
Vegetable oil for deep frying, heated to 365 degrees.
Creole Seafood Seasoning (see recipe above) ››

Begin by making the ravigote sauce. Combine the mayonnaise, mustard, egg, capers, herbs, hot sauce, and Worcestershire sauce in a medium-sized bowl; whisk to blend well. Season to taste with kosher salt and pepper. Store in covered container in refrigerator for up to 5 days. Leftover ravigote sauce is great blended with fresh blue crabmeat for a nice first course.

Make the Creole seafood seasoning. Combine salt, black and cayenne pepper, garlic, onion, paprika, thyme, and oregano in a medium-sized bowl; mix thoroughly. If you prefer a finer mixture, combine the ingredients in work bowl of food processor fitted with steel blade and pulse a few times. Store the seasoning in a covered container and keep in a cool, dry place for up to 6 months. It's great on shrimp, fish, crawfish, and crab, and can also be used to make seasoned flour.

To make the mousse, season the catfish fillets on both sides and smoke in a smoker at 350 degrees until cooked through, about 15 minutes. Cool in refrigerator. Chop the fish coarsely and place in work bowl of food processor fitted with steel blade along with the onion, 1½ cups of the ravigote sauce, and the cream cheese. Process until smooth. Season to taste with Creole seafood seasoning. Store in refrigerator, tightly covered, until ready to serve.

Make the sweet potato chips. Using a mandolin (or a Benriner slicing box), slice the sweet potatoes into ⅛-inch-thick slices. Soak the potato slices in a bowl of ice water for 2 hours, changing the water twice to ensure that all of the starch is rinsed off. Drain well to remove excess water and blot the potatoes dry.

Fry the chips in preheated oil in batches. Frying time will vary depending on the amount of water and sugar in the potatoes. Agitate the chips in the oil to prevent them from sticking together. When golden brown and crisp, remove the chips and drain on a wire rack set over a baking sheet. Immediately scatter Creole seafood seasoning on the chips, tossing to season all of them.

To serve the dish, fill a pastry bag with the mousse and pipe into a decorative ramekin or bowl. Garnish by scattering the minced chives over the top. Serve with a basket of the sweet potato chips, or, as Brennan's does, place the chips in a paper-cone-lined silver mint julep cup!

Jeff Balfour's Southerleigh Fine Food & Brewery Brunch Cornmeal-Crusted Gafftop with Smoked Tomato, Country Ham, Fried Eggs, Spring Peas, and Béarnaise Sauce

SERVES 4

Jeff Balfour was born and raised a Texas boy in Galveston. His lifelong association with the freshest seafood money could buy, or be caught, and with sumptuous home-cooked Southern food shaped his palate and his take on Texas's cross-cultural cuisine style as a chef. Balfour began his cooking career in San Antonio in 2002 when he opened Citrus in the Hotel Valencia, which became known for its innovative menu and world-class paella. He jumped at the chance to create his own restaurant in the historic brew house at the Pearl Brewery, complete with its own brewery. When Southerleigh opened in April 2014, it had been twelve years since beer had been made in the massive space that housed the Pearl Brewery. Balfour says he is eternally grateful for the opportunity to create Southerleigh in a building that is such an important part of San Antonio's history.

The name *Southerleigh* is derived from the term used by meteorologists for the prevailing Gulf Coast breeze, giving the restaurant a proud sense of Texas place. Among the hallmarks of Balfour's approach to Texas/Southern cooking is his dedication to using not only local ingredients and grass-fed meats but also "by-catch" fish—those underutilized species, which, although delicious and plentiful, are not well-known to the average consumer. As noted, they are often referred to as "trash" fish. Growing up as an avid angler, Balfour learned about the great qualities of these fish, which are generally thrown back by commercial fishermen, never reaching the retail market, while better-known fish are being seriously over-fished. The

gafftop, or saltwater catfish, used in this recipe is a great example. It is a homely fish, with a large, sharp gaff on the back of its head—and one that is often thrown back even by seasoned Gulf Coast anglers because of the seriously slimy film that covers the flesh. However, it is an excellent fish when prepared—in just about any style—after the lateral bloodline is removed, but especially succulent when fried, or cooked into a Cajun-style court bouillon. The meat is pristinely white, tender, and flaky, with a medium oil content. This unique brunch dish is an example of Balfour's culinary genius. Pair the dish with Southerleigh Fine Food & Brewery's Watermelon–Wheat Beer Cocktail, crafted by brewmaster Les Locke (see recipe on page 10).

As is the case in many incredibly delicious chef-created recipes, this one has a lot of moving parts. It's best to plan to serve for a late brunch on a lazy Sunday. The fried cornmeal cakes can be made up to 1 day ahead of time. Reheat them in a low oven before assembling the dish. Have your *mise-en-place* entirely in place; in other words, prep all of your ingredients as instructed in the recipe, and line them up, pots and skillets ready, so that finishing and assembling the dish runs like a well-oiled assembly line.

4 fried cornmeal cakes (see recipe below)

Smoked tomato sauce (see recipe at right)

Béarnaise sauce (see recipe at right)

4 (7-ounce) gafftop filets, bloodline cleaned

Canola oil for frying, heated to 350 degrees

4 farm-fresh eggs, plus 2 more for breading, plus 2 more for béarnaise sauce

4 ounces country ham, cut into small dice, about the size of the peas

1¼ cups fresh shelled spring peas, blanched in salted water and drained

Watercress sprigs to garnish

FRIED CORNMEAL CAKES

2 cups self-rising cornmeal

1½ teaspoons kosher salt

1 tablespoon sugar

1 large jalapeño, seeds and veins removed, minced

2 cups boiling unsalted chicken stock

¼ cup bacon drippings

SMOKED TOMATO SAUCE

1 pound locally homegrown tomatoes

¼ medium onion cut into rough slices

2 garlic cloves, peeled, trimmed, and quartered

Leaves from 3 thyme sprigs

10 parsley sprigs with stems

Salt and freshly ground black pepper to taste

Wood chips for smoking

BÉARNAISE SAUCE

2 egg yolks

Leaves from 2 tarragon sprigs, chopped

1 tablespoon Crystal Hot Sauce

1 teaspoon distilled white vinegar

¼ teaspoon Dijon mustard

4 to 6 ounces hot, melted clarified butter

Kosher salt to taste

BREADING FOR FISH

½ cup finely ground corn flour

½ cup cornmeal

1 cup all-purpose flour

Louisiana-brand Shrimp Boil seasoning to taste

2 eggs beaten with ¼ cup milk (egg wash) ››

Begin by making the fried cornmeal cakes. Place the cornmeal in a medium-sized bowl and toss in the salt, sugar, and minced jalapeño. Whisk the boiling stock into the cornmeal to form a thick batter. Heat the bacon drippings in a 12-inch, heavy-bottomed (preferably cast-iron) skillet over medium-high heat. When the drippings are good and hot, use a ½-cup metal measuring cup to scoop a heaping cupful of the batter into the hot drippings. Immediately use the bottom of the cup to flatten the batter into a cake about 4½ inches in diameter. Cook as many cakes at a time as will fit in the skillet without touching. Cook for about 6 minutes, turning once, or until crisp and golden brown on both sides. Drain on a paper-towel-lined wire rack set over a sheet of parchment paper. Keep warm in a low oven while preparing the other components of the dish. Note that the cornmeal cakes can be made ahead of time and even frozen. Reheat them in the oven before serving. Do not place them in the microwave!

Next, make the smoked tomato sauce. Combine all ingredients except for the parsley and seasoning in a perforated container or oven-top smoker. Hot-smoke over medium heat for about 20 minutes until the tomatoes are beginning to cook. Pour into blender and add parsley; puree until smooth and season to taste with salt and pepper. Set aside.

Make the béarnaise sauce. Combine the egg yolks, tarragon sprigs, Crystal Hot Sauce, vinegar, and mustard. Process for about 2 minutes, or until mixture is smooth and egg yolks are thickened, creamy, and light lemon-yellow in color. With machine running, add the hot butter in a slow and steady stream through the feed tube until all has been added, then season to taste with salt and process for an additional 30 seconds to form a strong emulsion. Turn out into a metal bowl and keep warm over hot, not simmering, water.

To bread and fry the gafftop, combine the corn flour, the cornmeal, half of the flour, and the Louisiana-brand Shrimp Boil seasoning to taste; toss with a fork to blend well. Set up a breading station by lining up the other half of the flour, the egg wash, and the cornmeal/corn-flour mixture in a row next to the heated oil on the stovetop. Pat the gafftop filets dry using absorbent paper towels, then bread them—coating first in the flour, then in the egg wash, then in the cornmeal/corn-flour mixture. Coat well and shake off excess after each step. Fry the filets in preheated oil for about 4 minutes, or until cooked through; turn them once. Drain on a paper-towel-lined wire rack set over a baking sheet. Keep warm.

To assemble the dish, fry the eggs sunny-side up in a skillet at medium-high heat to achieve a browned, crispy edge. Quickly sauté the diced ham in the oil left in the skillet. Sauce each plate with a pool of the smoked tomato sauce. Set one of the fried cornmeal cakes slightly off-center in the sauce on each plate; then arrange a fish filet on the cake, extending down off the bottom edge of the cake; then place an egg on top of the fish. Blanket with a portion of the béarnaise sauce. Garnish with a scattering of a few of the blanched peas, some diced ham, and watercress sprigs. Serve at once.

HOT SAUCE: THE SECRET INGREDIENT

....

Bottled liquid hot sauce is the secret ingredient of many chefs, especially those of us from the South, where most of it is produced. Hot sauce is now a global business, and among the ten fastest-growing enterprises in the United States, with annual sales exceeding $1 billion. Splashing some hot sauce into a sauce or on a finished dish at the last minute, or stirring it into an aioli, can push flavor to the next level, adding a subtle note of heat. Hot sauce was never meant to be used in instances where it will be cooked for an extended period of time, as the flavor and heat dissipate. It's a last-minute dose ingredient. That being said, one of the best uses for hot sauce is at breakfast. When I cook a simple breakfast consisting of an egg or two—fried, scrambled, poached, or in an omelet—right before I dive in with my fork, I will splash a bit of hot sauce (generally Tabasco for breakfast) on the eggs. Starts the day with a nice little bang.

I love to visit supermarkets or specialty food stores in cities that I visit. One of my favorite sections is the hot-sauce aisle. There are so many brands of hot sauce on the market! When I find one I haven't tried, I always buy a bottle to taste. Most of the sauces are unique, made from different chiles and seasonings through various techniques. Some are cooked; others are just aged in their brine for various periods of time, as is the case with Tabasco Pepper Sauce—one of the most readily recognized brands of hot sauce. They present totally different flavor profiles and heat levels (although all are categorized within the genre of "hot"). It's great fun to experiment with using different hot sauces in your tried-and-true dishes. Louisiana-based Tabasco, produced by the McIlhenny family on Avery Island for well over a hundred years, is often a choice for Cajun or Creole dishes as its flavor profile was developed to pair with those foods. Also from Louisiana, Crystal Hot Sauce—produced in New Orleans by the Baumer Foods Company—is a favorite with many chefs for use in Creole seafood dishes. (San Antonio Chef Jeff Balfour loves Crystal Hot Sauce.) There's even a great hot sauce for using with Southwestern or Mexican foods. Cholula Hot Sauce, with its distinctive round wooden cap, originally developed by the folks at Cuervo Tequila, presents a distinctly Mexican flavor profile. The company now offers a second Cholula Hot Sauce to which lime is added. Try a splash in your guacamole.

Frank's RedHot Sauce, milder than many others, is a requirement for preparing authentic buffalo wings, which originated in Buffalo, New York; and Texas Pete's Hot Sauce, which, ahem, is not made in Texas, is the choice of many burger lovers, as its flavor profile is nice with beef. Tiger Sauce, also produced in New Orleans, is a moderately hot sauce that has an exotic note in its flavor, thanks to a unique blend of ingredients in a cayenne pepper base; it presents a sweet-and-sour profile, making it a good choice for meats, seafood, and poultry. I especially like to douse my French fries with Tiger Sauce! There are many more hot sauces, and all have their devotees. An especially popular one is the incendiary sriracha sauce, a version of traditional Thai hot sauce made from fresh hybrid jalapeño chiles, vinegar, sugar, salt, and garlic, that has been produced by Huy Fond Foods in Los Angeles for more than thirty-three years.

Vaudeville's Supper Club Sunday Brunch Crawfish Relleno

SERVES 8

Vaudeville, located in a lovely historic building replete with gingerbread trim and a second-story veranda on Fredericksburg's Main Street, is a very distinctive place. Part retail high-end home accessories store and part art gallery, bistro, and courtyard supper club, the operation has garnered both critical and public acclaim since its opening in 2012. Partner Richard Boprae handles the retail end of the operation, and Jordan Muraglia, the chef/co-owner, heads up the culinary end. The pair added a Sunday brunch to their dining options that was met with rave reviews. The brunch, with a seasonally changing menu, offers a sizable array of dishes ranging from some of the best fried chicken in Texas to the dish featured here—a fabulous fusion of Louisiana and Southwest flavors. This dish is a combination of many ingredients that Chef Muraglia loves, from places that hold meaningful memories of his upbringing. He described the brunch at Vaudeville succinctly when he told me: "Most of our brunch dishes at V Supper Club are a play on classic brunch flavors that take on new forms. This dish, and the way it's composed, has been a crowd pleaser for us; however, any of the individual elements can be prepared and enjoyed by themselves, or as components in other dishes." ››

One of the most popular items on Vaudeville's Supper Club Sunday brunch menu, this dish requires a lot of prep time. It is best to make the component parts, with the exception of the scrambled eggs, ahead of time. The chiles can be stuffed and refrigerated for up to 3 days ahead of time. Bring the stuffed chiles to room temperature. Reheat the component parts and broil the chiles, then scramble the eggs and assemble and serve the dish.

4 cups soft polenta or cheese grits (see recipe below)
8 medium-sized Anaheim or Hatch chiles
1 cup peanut or vegetable oil for blanching chiles
1 cup grated Manchego cheese
4 cups crawfish roux (see recipe below)
Tomatillo salsa (see recipe at right)
Collard greens (see recipe at right)
12 large eggs
Kosher salt and freshly ground black pepper to taste
Fresh, seasonal herbs as garnish

CHEESE GRITS

2 cups chicken stock, preferably homemade
½ cup dry white wine
Pinch of salt
1 cup stone-ground grits or polenta
½ cup whipping cream
½ cup finely grated Parmigiano-Reggiano cheese
Kosher salt and freshly ground black pepper to taste

CRAWFISH ROUX

8 cups water
1 cup dry white wine
2 cups mirepoix (mixed diced carrots, onions, and celery), divided

2 bay leaves, preferably fresh
4 sprigs fresh thyme, divided
2 to 4 pounds live crawfish, washed, or you can substitute frozen Louisiana crawfish tails and a good seafood stock
½ cup butter
½ cup all-purpose flour
½ of a green bell pepper, diced
Kosher salt, freshly ground black pepper, and hot sauce to taste

TOMATILLO SALSA

10 medium-sized tomatillos, washed (after paper-like husks are removed)
1 large onion, peeled and quartered
1 jalapeño, halved
½ cup olive oil, divided
Large pinch of salt
4 garlic cloves, peeled
1 tablespoon toasted cumin seeds
1 bunch cilantro, chopped

COLLARD GREENS

¼ cup olive oil
4 slices thick-cut bacon, diced
1 bunch fresh collard greens, washed and patted dry, thick mid-ribs removed, leaves cut into julienne strips
½ cup diced onion
Salt and pepper

Begin by preparing the cheese grits. Bring the chicken stock, white wine, and a pinch of salt to a boil in a medium-sized saucepan. Quickly whisk the grits or polenta into the stock and cook, whisking constantly until thickened, about 8 minutes depending on the type of grain used. Remove from heat and whisk in whipping cream and Parmigiano-Reggiano cheese until cheese has melted and grits are smooth. Season to taste with salt and black pepper. Set aside to cool.

Prepare the chiles. Heat peanut or vegetable oil in a heavy-bottomed deep skillet or Dutch oven over medium heat. When the oil reaches 350 degrees, add the chiles in batches and pan-fry each side for one minute. Remove the chiles from the oil and let stand until cool enough to handle. Using a paring knife, gently remove the skins without tearing the chiles. The skins should come off fairly easily; but if they don't, simply return them to the hot oil and cook a bit longer. When the chiles have completely cooled, make a 1-inch incision at the top of each chile. Carefully remove the seeds and discard. Put the cooled cheese grits in a pastry bag with a medium-sized plain pastry tip. Fill each chile, making sure not to over-fill, as the grits will expand once broiled. Set the peppers aside until ready to complete the dish. *Note:* The chiles can be prepared ahead of time and refrigerated for up to 3 days.

Make the crawfish roux. Bring the water and white wine to a full boil; add one cup of the mirepoix, bay leaves, and half of the thyme sprigs. Simmer for 20 to 30 minutes or until very

aromatic. Dump in the crawfish all at once. Cook for 2 to 3 minutes, then remove the crawfish with a slotted spoon or flat metal strainer. Remove the tails from the crawfish, reserving the rest of the bodies; set tails aside. Return the crawfish bodies to the stock and simmer an additional 15 minutes. Strain the stock, discarding solids. Peel the crawfish tails and set aside.

In a medium-sized saucepan, melt the butter and add the flour all at once. Cook, whisking constantly, for 4 to 5 minutes. The roux should be a light golden color. (If you want a darker roux, Jordan suggests substituting vegetable oil for the butter, as the butter will burn if cooked beyond light golden color.) Add the remaining cup of mirepoix and the green bell pepper to the roux. Cook, stirring, for 2 to 3 minutes. Add 5 cups of the reserved crawfish stock, while whisking. Simmer the sauce, continuously whisking and making sure the mixture doesn't scorch. Add the remaining thyme sprigs, the salt and pepper, and your favorite hot sauce to taste. Stir in the reserved crawfish tails and cook to heat through. Keep the roux warm while preparing the remaining components of the dish.

Make the tomatillo salsa. Combine the tomatillos, onion, jalapeño, and ¼ cup of the olive oil in a bowl. Toss with a large pinch of salt, then grill or broil until slightly charred. Place the vegetables in work bowl of food processor fitted with steel blade and add the garlic cloves, toasted cumin seeds, cilantro, and remaining olive oil. Pulse until fairly smooth. Season to taste with salt. Set aside until ready to plate.

Cook the collard greens. Heat the olive oil in a heavy-bottomed 12-inch sauté pan over high heat. Add the diced bacon, and cook until the bacon is almost crisp and has rendered its fat. Quickly add the julienned collard greens and onions. Sear on high heat for 3 to 5 minutes, or until the greens are wilted and slightly crispy. Season to taste with salt and pepper. Remove from heat and set aside to keep warm.

To bring the dish together, turn broiler to highest setting and place the stuffed chiles on an oiled baking sheet. Top each chile with a portion of the shredded Manchego cheese. Broil just until the edges are slightly charred and the cheese has melted, usually 2 to 4 minutes. Take care not to burn the cheese. Keep the chiles warm in a low oven while scrambling the eggs.

Whisk the eggs until frothy with a few tablespoons of water and the desired amount of salt. Scramble in a nonstick pan on medium heat. Season to taste with pepper. Set aside to keep warm.

Spoon a portion of the tomatillo salsa in the center of each plate. Add a small pile of the collard greens on top, followed by a portion of the scrambled eggs. Place a seared, stuffed chile on the eggs and ladle on a portion of the crawfish roux, making sure to include plenty of the crawfish! Garnish with fresh, seasonal herbs and serve at once.

Crave Kitchen and Bar's Crab Oscar Omelet

SERVES 4

Crave Kitchen and Bar in El Paso is one of the city's most popular dining spots, and is always jam-packed at breakfast and weekend brunch. Chef Rodolfo (Rudy) Valdes was born in El Paso to a family of restaurateurs, so it was natural that he learned at an early age to appreciate the joy that could be brought to people by a good meal. After high school, Rudy attended culinary school in Scottsdale, Arizona. He then traveled to Europe and studied at the Cordon Bleu in both Paris and London, honing his skills in fine cuisine while retaining the flavors of his Mexican heritage. Today Rudy is the executive chef/partner for the Pan Y Agua restaurant group, which includes the four locations of Crave Kitchen and Bar. The menu at Crave changes often, as Rudy creates innovative new twists on classic dishes like this egg-based version of steak Oscar topped with a classic hollandaise turned on by a shot of chipotle chiles.

12 to 15 asparagus spears, trimmed and peeled
10 tablespoons unsalted butter, divided
12 ounces lump blue crabmeat
12 eggs
Salt to taste
Chipotle hollandaise sauce (see recipe on page 129)
12 thin avocado slices

Begin by making the chipotle hollandaise sauce according to the recipe; set aside over hot, not simmering, water to keep warm.

To prepare the omelets, bring a 4-quart saucepan of salted water to a rolling boil. Add the asparagus spears and cook for 1 to 2 minutes, or just until tender. Drain at once and transfer to a bowl filled with ice water until cooled, then drain and pat dry.

In a heavy-bottomed 12-inch skillet over medium heat, melt 2 tablespoons of the butter. Add the blanched asparagus and crabmeat. Sweat until thoroughly warmed. Do not stir too vigorously, as you don't want to break up the luscious lumps of crabmeat. Set aside to keep warm.

Make the omelets. For each omelet, thoroughly beat 3 eggs at a time in a bowl with the desired amount of salt. Melt 2 more tablespoons of the butter in a nonstick skillet over medium-high heat. Add the beaten eggs and cook until the eggs are completely set. Flip the omelet and turn off the heat. Place 3 to 5 of the asparagus spears in the center of each omelet and top with about ⅓ cup of the crabmeat. Fold one edge of the omelet to the center over the filling and repeat on opposite side. Repeat with remaining eggs and crab-asparagus mix.

To serve, place an omelet on each serving plate, folded side down. Pour chipotle hollandaise sauce over each omelet and garnish by overlapping 3 avocado slices on top of each serving.

Doug Clark's Seafood Boudin Benedict

SERVES 4

YIELDS 4 CUPS
WHITE RICE

Doug Clark was my back-fence neighbor when I lived in Fredericksburg. He also happens to be a great cook. Doug is an avid hunter and fisherman, always creating innovative dishes with the bounty of his hunts and catches. He's also a sommelier and one of my best sources for help on tricky wine pairings. Doug especially loves to cook leisurely brunches for his family on weekends. The dish featured here is simply stellar. It would be a hit on the menu at even the most upscale restaurant brunch. And the great part is that the most difficult step, preparing the seafood boudin, is done ahead. The boudin is a bulk-style concoction that Doug says is a Port Arthur tradition. He calls it a *boudin blanc*, reflecting the patois of the Port Arthur Cajuns.

Prepare the seafood boudin ahead of time and refrigerate overnight before finishing and assembling the dish. The eggs can be pre-poached, according to the directions on page 32, and finished just before serving. The easy hollandaise sauce is a last-minute preparation.

Seafood boudin (see recipe below)
8 poached eggs (see directions on page 32)
Easy hollandaise sauce (see recipe at right)
Green onions, green portion only, sliced thin on the bias

SEAFOOD BOUDIN

4 cups warm cooked white rice (see recipe at right)
¼ cup bacon drippings, no cheating here with vegetable oil
1 medium white onion, finely chopped
1 celery stalk, finely chopped
1 green bell pepper, seeds and membranes removed, finely chopped
½ teaspoon ground white pepper

½ teaspoon cayenne pepper
¼ cup chopped fresh Italian flat-leaf parsley
1 teaspoon minced fresh thyme
1 teaspoon dried Mexican oregano
1 teaspoon paprika
4 garlic cloves, minced
1 pound (16 to 20) peeled and deveined Gulf shrimp, each shrimp sliced into 3 or 4 pieces
4 green onion tops, finely chopped
1 tablespoon Crystal Hot Sauce (No substitutes, please; the taste is unique.)
1 pound jumbo lump Gulf crabmeat, carefully picked through to remove any bits of shell or cartilage
Kosher salt and freshly ground black pepper

WHITE RICE

2⅔ cups water
1 bay leaf, preferably fresh
1 tablespoon butter
1½ teaspoons kosher salt
1⅓ cups long-grain white rice

EASY HOLLANDAISE SAUCE

3 egg yolks
¼ teaspoon Dijon-style mustard
½ teaspoon kosher salt
1½ teaspoons freshly squeezed lemon juice
1 dash Crystal Hot Sauce (no substitutes, please)
1 stick hot melted butter
Pinch of white pepper

Begin by preparing the seafood boudin the day before you wish to serve the dish. Cook the rice and set aside to keep warm. Combine the water, bay leaf, butter, and salt in a saucepan over medium-high heat. Bring to a full boil, then gently stir in the rice. Turn heat to lowest setting, cover the pan, and cook for exactly 15 minutes. Remove from heat and fluff the rice with a fork; set aside.

Heat the bacon drippings in a 12-inch cast-iron skillet or Dutch oven over medium heat. Add the onion, celery, and bell pepper, plus all seasonings. Sauté, stirring often, for about 5 minutes, or until onion is wilted and translucent. Add the minced garlic and shrimp pieces. Continue to sauté for another 2 to 3 minutes, or just until the shrimp turns opaque and is coral-colored around the edges. Do not overcook the shrimp.

Remove pan from heat and stir in the warm rice. Add the chopped green onion tops and Crystal Hot Sauce, stirring to blend. Add the lump crabmeat, gently incorporating, taking care not to break up those beautiful lumps of meat. Set aside to cool to room temperature, then refrigerate overnight so the flavors have time to meld together into a blissful mélange.

When ready to serve the dish, reheat the seafood boudin just to heat through. Make the easy hollandaise sauce. Combine all ingredients except the melted butter and white pepper in work bowl of food processor fitted with steel blade. Process until the egg yolks are lightened in color and thickened. With the machine running, add the melted butter in a slow, steady stream through the feed tube until all has been added. Add the pinch of white pepper and pulse several times to blend. Turn out into a bowl, cover with plastic wrap, and set aside to keep warm.

Poach the eggs according to the recipe. To serve, place a portion of the seafood boudin in the center of each serving plate and top each with 2 poached eggs. Spoon a liberal portion of the easy hollandaise sauce over the eggs and garnish with some of the sliced green onion tops. Serve at once.

Basted Fried Eggs on Wilted Greens with Curry-Fried Oysters and Coriander Sauce

SERVES 4

I love oysters. I've had them prepared in dozens of different recipes using different techniques—from poached to fried to baked, broiled, and raw on-the-half-shell, with or without sauces. Enjoyed them all. But when I eat fried oysters, I want them to be in a thin breading that gets crisp quickly when fried so that the oysters have a nice thin crust, but are still quite liquidy inside. I particularly like this recipe, which gives the oysters a quick dredge in beaten egg whites before being lightly coated with a curry-seasoned corn flour.

This is pretty much a last-minute-cooking dish. However, it's easy to put together. Just be sure that you have all of the ingredients for the separate components measured and ready to use. It's best to place them on separate baking sheets with a copy of the recipe handy.

Wilted greens (see recipe at right)
8 basted fried eggs (see directions on page 29)
Coriander sauce (see recipe at right)
16 fried oysters (see recipe below)
Chopped cilantro as garnish

FRIED OYSTERS

16 medium-sized shucked oysters
3 egg whites, beaten until frothy
2 cups fine corn flour seasoned with: 1½ teaspoons salt, 1½ teaspoons finely ground black pepper, 1 teaspoon granulated garlic, and 2 tablespoons curry powder
Canola oil for deep-frying, heated to 350 degrees

CORIANDER SAUCE

1 medium shallot, finely chopped
½ teaspoon grated orange zest
¼ cup orange juice
½ cup dry white wine
2 tablespoons sherry wine vinegar
1½ teaspoons toasted, then ground coriander
½ cup whipping cream, blended with 2 teaspoons cornstarch
5 tablespoons butter
2 tablespoons minced cilantro
Salt and black pepper

WILTED GREENS

1 small bunch mustard greens (preferably curly), thick mid-ribs removed, leaves torn into bite-size pieces
1 bunch baby kale leaves
4 slices bacon, cut into ½-inch pieces
1 fresh jalapeño, seeds and veins removed, minced
1 shallot, finely chopped
½ teaspoon crushed red pepper flakes
Kosher salt to taste
⅓ cup chicken stock
Juice of ½ lemon

To prepare the oysters, pat them very dry on absorbent paper towels. Dip each oyster in the egg wash, coating well. Then press each oyster into the curry-seasoned corn flour, coating well. Shake off all excess. Deep-fry the oysters in two batches, taking care not to crowd the pan. Fry them just until a golden crust forms. They should have a delicate, crisp crust, yet still be soft inside. Turn the oysters out on wire racks set over a baking sheet to drain. Repeat with the remaining oysters. Set aside to keep warm.

To make the coriander sauce, place the shallot, orange zest and juice, wine, vinegar, and coriander in a small saucepan and bring to a simmer over medium heat. Cook until the liquid is reduced to 2 or 3 tablespoons. While it's still hot, whisk in the whipping cream/cornstarch mixture. Cook until thickened, then quickly whisk in the butter until creamy. Stir in the chopped cilantro and season to taste with salt and pepper. Set aside to keep warm.

To cook the wilted greens, toss the torn mustard greens and kale together; set aside. Cook the bacon pieces in a heavy-bottomed skillet over medium-high heat, stirring often, until slightly crisp and fat has rendered. Stir in the jalapeño, shallot, and crushed red pepper, stirring to blend. Cook until the shallot is wilted and transparent, about 5 minutes. Add the greens in batches, tossing with tongs and adding more as they cook down. Cook, tossing all ingredients together, until the kale is slightly wilted. Add salt to taste. Add the chicken stock, cover pan, and cook just until the kale is completely wilted and the broth has evaporated, about 4 minutes. Remove from heat and stir in the lemon juice. Taste for salt, adjusting as desired.

To serve, place a bed of the wilted greens in the center of each serving plate. Top each with two basted fried eggs. Drizzle a portion of the coriander sauce over each serving. Place four fried oysters on each serving and scatter some of the chopped cilantro on top. Serve at once.

St. Charles Bay Crab Cakes and Poached Eggs on Fried Green Tomatoes with Orange-Ginger Hollandaise Sauce

SERVES 8

I created this regal brunch dish one weekend when my husband and I were spending the weekend in our RV in Rockport. We had invited some friends from Houston to drive over for brunch on Sunday. When we arrived on Friday afternoon we'd set out some crab traps, and now had a nice container of freshly picked crabmeat from our catch. I picked up a couple of green tomatoes at the outdoor market in town, and this dish emerged from those good fresh ingredients. For a really stellar presentation and a very colorful plating, place a nest of the frizzled sweet potatoes (see recipe on page 232) on the side of the plate.

The crab cakes can be made ahead and even frozen. Thaw and reheat in a low oven before serving. The tomatoes can be fried up to 1 hour ahead of time and reheated in a low oven. The eggs can be poached for 2 minutes and finished at the last minute (see directions on page 32). The orange-ginger hollandaise sauce can be made right before you finish the poaching of the eggs, and it can be kept warm over hot, not simmering, water. Whisk well before using.

8 crab cakes (see recipe below)
8 slices of fried green tomatoes (see recipe at right)
8 poached eggs (see directions on page 32)
Orange-ginger hollandaise sauce (see recipe at right)
Green portions of 2 green onions, sliced very thin on the bias, as garnish

CRAB CAKES

1 pound jumbo lump crabmeat
1 large egg
1 teaspoon Worcestershire sauce
1 tablespoon Creole mustard
1 tablespoon minced Italian flat-leaf parsley
Juice of ½ lemon
1 tablespoon Chef Paul's Seafood Magic seasoning
1 cup mayonesa (lime-flavored mayonnaise)
3 green onions, chopped, including green tops

½ cup finely chopped green bell pepper
⅔ cup finely crushed Ritz crackers
1 stick unsalted butter and ½ cup canola oil for sautéing

FRIED GREEN TOMATOES

3 large green tomatoes, sliced into ½-inch-thick slices
2 cups all-purpose flour
2 teaspoons each: kosher salt and freshly ground black pepper
¼ teaspoon cayenne pepper
2 large eggs, well beaten with 1 cup whole buttermilk (not low-fat)
1 cup panko bread crumbs tossed with 1 cup yellow cornmeal and 1½ tablespoons Chef Paul Prudhomme's Vegetable Magic Seasoning
Canola oil for pan frying

ORANGE-GINGER HOLLANDAISE SAUCE

1 tablespoon dry white wine
1 teaspoon minced orange zest
½ cup freshly squeezed orange juice
1 tablespoon minced pickled (sushi) ginger
1 medium shallot, minced
1 teaspoon whole coriander seeds, minced
1 fresh thyme sprig
4 egg yolks
Juice of ½ lemon
1 tablespoon Creole mustard, or substitute another whole-grain mustard
½ teaspoon kosher salt
Scant ¼ teaspoon cayenne pepper
1 cup (2 sticks) hot melted unsalted butter ››

Begin by making the crab cakes, very carefully picking through the crabmeat to remove any bits of shell or cartilage; take care not to break up those beautiful lumps! Set aside. In a large bowl, combine the egg, Worcestershire sauce, mustard, parsley, lemon juice, Seafood Magic, and mayonesa. Whisk to blend well. Add the green onions, bell pepper, and crushed crackers; stir to incorporate. Gently fold in the crabmeat, distributing all ingredients evenly. Form the crab mixture into 8 cakes, patting them tightly in your hands. Place on a parchment-lined baking sheet, cover loosely with parchment, and refrigerate until ready to sauté them.

To sauté the crab cakes, melt the butter in a heavy-bottomed skillet over medium heat; stir in the canola oil to blend well. Add the crab cakes, taking care not to crowd the pan. Sauté in batches if needed. Fry the cakes for about 3 to 5 minutes per side, turning once, or until golden brown and firmly cooked. Keep warm in a low oven. *Note:* The crab cakes can be made ahead of time and reheated in the oven until warmed through.

To make the fried green tomatoes, place the sliced tomatoes on a plate lined with paper towels to drain off excess moisture. Toss together the flour, salt and pepper, and cayenne in a shallow baking dish, blending well. Heat ½ inch of canola oil in a heavy-bottomed, preferably cast-iron skillet over medium heat. When ready to fry the tomatoes, dredge them first in the seasoned flour, coating well and shaking off all excess, then in the egg wash, coating well. Give the tomato slices a final dredge in the panko/cornmeal/Vegetable Magic mixture, patting the panko into both sides of the slices. Gently shake off excess. Fry the tomato slices in the hot oil for about 2 to 3 minutes per side, turning once, or until golden brown. Drain on a wire rack set over a baking sheet. Keep warm.

To make the orange-ginger hollandaise sauce, combine the white wine, orange zest and juice, ginger, shallot, toasted coriander seeds, and thyme sprig in a small, heavy-bottomed saucepan over medium heat. Cook the mixture, stirring often, until the liquid is well infused with the flavors and reduced by half. Strain the mixture through a fine-meshed wire strainer into a small bowl, pressing down to remove all liquid; set aside. Discard the solids left in the strainer. In work bowl of food processor fitted with steel blade, combine the infusion liquid, egg yolks, lemon juice, mustard, salt, and cayenne pepper. Process until the mixture is thickened and light lemon-yellow in color, about 4 minutes. Stop and scrape down the side of the bowl. With the machine running, slowly add the hot melted butter through the feed tube until all has been added. Continue to process for another minute to form a strong emulsion. Transfer to a bowl and cover with plastic wrap to keep warm. Whisk just before serving.

To assemble the dish, place a slice of the fried green tomatoes on each serving plate. Top each with a crab cake, then a poached egg. Drizzle a portion of the warm orange-ginger hollandaise sauce over each portion, allowing the sauce to ooze onto the plate a bit. Scatter a few pieces of sliced green onion over the tops and serve at once.

David Gilbert's Khai Jiao

THAI SHRIMP OMELET

SERVES 2

David Gilbert knew from the day he first peeked into his mother's first-edition copy of *Joy of Cooking*, while he was supposed to be doing his homework, that a serious interest in food had been piqued. Gilbert eventually graduated from Johnson & Wales University's culinary school and began a global odyssey as a chef, which took him to Amsterdam and St. Thomas with the Ritz-Carlton Hotel chain, then to its facility in Atlanta's Buckhead neighborhood. He worked with the Orient-Express group at the Inn at Perry Cabin, at the Park Plaza in St. Louis, and at the Eilan Hotel in San Antonio as the opening chef at Stephen Pyles's Sustenio Restaurant & Bar. But his true cooking vocation was discovered on scuba-diving vacations in Thailand, where he fell in love with the exotic foods there—foods that were not only incredibly delicious but light and healthy as well. He left Sustenio to open his own place, Tuk Tuk Tap Room, a mecca of Thai food and craft beers from around the world, in the Pearl Brewery area of San Antonio. Sadly, in 2015 the building was sold to make way for yet more condos, and Gilbert was forced to close Tuk Tuk. The spectacular dish featured here was one of the most popular on the menu at Tuk Tuk.

OMELET

¼ cup loosely packed julienned shallots

¼ cup loosely packed julienned green onions

⅓ cup loosely packed Thai basil leaves

⅓ cup firmly packed tender top cilantro sprigs

¼ teaspoon ground coriander

¾ teaspoon coarse ground white pepper

1 teaspoon tamarind-chile paste (see recipe at right)

4 ounces medium-sized shrimp, peeled, deveined, and boiled

4 extra-large eggs

½ teaspoon Thai fish sauce

3 quarts rice bran oil, or substitute canola oil

Thai sriracha sauce (see recipe at right), or use Shark-brand sriracha

TAMARIND-CHILE PASTE

1½ teaspoons crushed red pepper flakes

2 cups canola oil

½ cup minced garlic

½ cup tamarind concentrate

2 ounces fresh-squeezed lime juice

3 cups Thai fish sauce

THAI SRIRACHA SAUCE

1 pound fresh cayenne chiles or red jalapeño chiles, stems removed but green crown left

12 ounces peeled garlic cloves

1 tablespoon kosher salt, or to taste

1¼ pounds palm sugar

2 cups water

½ cup unseasoned rice vinegar ››

Begin by making the Thai sriracha sauce. Combine the chiles, garlic, salt, and sugar in work bowl of food processor fitted with steel blade. Pulse on/off to create an oatmeal-like texture. Transfer to a separate bowl and allow the mixture to sit, covered with plastic wrap, for 2 to 3 days.

Transfer the chile pulp to a heavy-bottomed 4-quart saucepan. Add water and vinegar. Reduce slowly over medium-low heat, for about 15 minutes. Strain the mixture through a fine-mesh strainer into a bowl, scraping the chiles with the back of a wooden spoon to push through as much of the pulp as possible to give the sauce viscosity. Allow the sauce to sit at room temperature for 1 day, then adjust flavor as desired with salt, sugar, and vinegar. Store in a sealed mason jar for up to 1 month.

To make the tamarind-chile paste, combine the chile flakes, canola oil, and garlic in a heavy-bottomed 2-quart saucepan. Stir to blend well. Cook over low heat to infuse the oil with the chile flakes, and slow-cook the garlic. Allow to cool, then add the tamarind, lime juice, and fish sauce, blending well. Keep refrigerated until ready to use.

To make the omelet, first assemble the garnishes. Mix the shallots, green onions, Thai basil leaves, and cilantro in a bowl. Toss the ground coriander and white pepper together. Add a hefty pinch of the mixture to the bowl, then add the tamarind-chile paste and stir to blend well. Place the boiled shrimp in warm water for 45 seconds, then mix them into the onion and herb mixture. Set aside.

Crack the eggs into a bowl and add the fish sauce; beat until frothy. Add the oil to a large wok over high heat. Once the oil is slightly smoking, add the egg mixture in a circular motion, drizzling aggressively into the oil. The eggs will puff up quickly. After about 45 seconds, flip the omelet over with a large bamboo strainer. Cook for 45 seconds on the other side, then drain off to the side, shaking off oil.

Transfer the omelet to a platter and spread the shrimp mixture over the top. Serve the Thai sriracha sauce on the side.

Note: The tamarind-chili paste and the Thai sriracha sauce can be made ahead of time and held in the refrigerator until you are ready to cook and assemble the dish.

West Table's Nola Shrimp and Grits

SERVES 4

Cameron and Rachel West, who were born and raised in the city, opened West Table on Broadway Street in Lubbock, Texas, in November 2014. The couple brought more than twenty years of restaurant experience to the table when they opened their trendy eatery, which was written up in *Texas Monthly* magazine shortly after they opened. The interior is sophisticated, but the ambiance is pure West Texas, right down to the tables, which were hand-crafted out of reclaimed wood from the West family's old cotton gin. Cameron, who is the chef, studied front-of-the-house operations at Texas Tech University's Restaurant, Hotel, and Institutional Management School, then attended the culinary program at the Culinary Institute of America's Greystone Campus in Napa Valley. After graduation he signed on with the prestigious Ritz-Carlton Hotel group, working under Chef Norman Van Aken in the Orlando Ritz-Carlton, then with Dean Fearing at the Ritz-Carlton in Dallas. The Wests are dedicated to using local ingredients in their seasonally changing menu. Their Sunday brunch has become a favorite with locals and tourists alike. It might seem odd for a Texas Panhandle restaurant to be serving shrimp and grits, but in fact it's a universally popular Texas brunch dish—and West Table's version is quite good. Keep in mind that the chef's past mentors are champions of the dish, so he learned from some of the best!

. . . .

SHRIMP AND SAUCE

- ½ cup Worcestershire sauce
- 2 bay leaves
- 1 tablespoon Cajun seasoning
- 3 tablespoons canola oil
- 20 large (16 to 20 count) shrimp, peeled and deveined, leaving tail sections intact
- 4 tablespoons water
- Juice of 2 lemons
- 1 tablespoon freshly ground black pepper
- ½ pound (2 sticks) butter, cut into ½-inch cubes
- Thinly sliced green onions as garnish

GRITS

- 4 cups chicken stock
- ¼ pound (1 stick) butter
- 1½ cups stone-ground grits (Cameron uses the stone-ground grits from Homestead Gristmill in Waco)
- 1½ cups (6 ounces) shredded Cheddar cheese
- 1 teaspoon Tabasco
- Kosher salt to taste

Begin by cooking the grits. Bring the chicken stock and butter to a boil in a heavy-bottomed 4-quart saucepan over medium-high heat. Whisk in the grits and cook for 20 to 30 minutes, whisking often, until thickened. Add the cheese and stir until smooth and well blended. Add the Tabasco, and add salt to taste. Set aside to keep warm while preparing the shrimp.

Combine the Worcestershire sauce, bay leaves, and Cajun seasoning in a small, heavy-bottomed saucepan over medium heat. Cook to reduce the liquid by ⅓. Set aside.

In a separate heavy-bottomed 12-inch skillet, heat the canola oil until it shimmers. Add the shrimp and sear them until lightly browned, about 4 minutes. Add the water and lemon juice, then add the reduction. Cook to blend well, then quickly swirl in the black pepper and butter, continuing to blend well. Whisk once or twice to be sure the butter is melted and forms a cohesive sauce. Do not allow the sauce to boil. Remove from heat.

To serve, place a portion of the grits in rimmed soup plates, making a slight indentation in the center. Pour equal portions of the sauce with 5 shrimp onto each serving. Garnish with sliced green onions and serve at once.

SIX

*Two Enticing Vegan
Breakfast/Brunch Menus
and Great Sides for
Any Breakfast*

*

I f I had been asked my opinion of vegan foods several years ago, it would not have been very high. But that was before I met Leslie Washburne, co-owner of Fredericksburg's Hoffman Haus Bed and Breakfast, who has been a vegetarian/vegan most of her life. Leslie actually studied at a culinary school specializing in all-natural vegetarian and vegan foods. Leslie can bring off a vegan brunch spread, like the one featured in this chapter, that even the most inveterate carnivore would enjoy. Sandy and I also discovered the vegan platter served at Austin's iconic Kerbey Lane Café to be quite delicious and were honored when the owners agreed to share their recipes with us.

What to serve on the side of a breakfast or brunch plate, or on a brunch buffet spread, is as important as the central dish. Side dishes can add a delightful splash of color to the whiteness of poached or fried eggs, plus the added sensory experience of complementary flavors. Consider the components of the main dish when selecting side dishes. Is the main dish spicy? Then try a side dish with a bit of sweetness like the Frizzled Sweet Potatoes, or one with a slightly sweet neutral flavor like the Honey-Baked Tomatoes. Is the main dish a poached egg dish? Perhaps a fried side like potato pancakes to add another texture and taste note. Is the main dish rich, consisting of stacked components, or one topped with a rich sauce? Then opt for a fairly bland side like just-plain grits.

I often like to serve a soup either as a brunch "first course" or in a tureen on a brunch buffet. The Driskill Hotel's adaptation of legendary Texas cook Helen Corbitt's Cheese Soup and Chef Danny Trace of Brennan's of Houston's version of the beloved New Orleans soup Gumbo Z'Herbes— both included in this chapter—are personal favorites.

Then there are days that I just want a good, hearty bowl of oatmeal. In addition to the fact that oatmeal is great for our health as an excellent source of good fiber that sops up bad cholesterol from our blood, I find it to be very palate-pleasing, as well as satisfying, especially on a frosty winter morning. Try the recipe in this chapter and create your own creamy flavor profile.

KERBEY LANE CAFÉ'S VEGAN BREAKFAST PLATTER

K ERBEY LANE CAFÉ opened in 1980, operating out of a small house on Austin's Kerbey Lane in north-central Austin. The small diner quickly became a neighborhood favorite. From the beginning, owners Patricia and David Ayer made a commitment to serving good food sourced from high-quality, local ingredients. Today, the Kerbey Lane Café empire boasts seven restaurants, scattered around Austin. The group continues to support local farms. The Kerbey Lane menu has always included a wide selection of dishes, offering something for every taste, including vegetarian, vegan, and gluten-free options.

Kerbey Lane Café has continued to offer a "safe haven" of food that is local, healthy, and affordable, while providing a memorable dining experience for its legions of fans. The café's Vegan Breakfast Platter is a favorite with customers—even those who are not dedicated vegans. Your local health-food store or Whole Foods will be good sources for ingredients.

Prepare the Soysage "Sausage" Patties ahead of time and refrigerate. Reheat in a low oven to serve. Have all ingredients for the Vegan Pancakes and Tofu Scramble prepped as listed in the recipes to make last-minute cooking easy. Serves 6 to 8.

Soysage "Sausage" Patties (see recipe on page 208)
Vegan Pancakes (see recipe on page 208)
Tofu Scramble (see recipe on page 209)
Maple syrup for pancakes
Assorted sliced fruit and/or berries

Soysage "Sausage" Patties

MAKES ABOUT
10 PATTIES

3 ounces millet

1 ounce amaranth

1½ ounces green lentils

1½ ounces brown rice

1 medium-sized beet, trimmed and peeled

1 medium-sized carrot, trimmed and peeled

1 ounce raw pumpkin seeds

2 ounces sunflower seeds

1½ ounces sesame sticks

1 ounce hemp seeds

½ ounce chia seeds

2 garlic cloves, minced

½ tablespoon each: ground cumin, paprika, onion powder

1 tablespoon kosher salt

1 tablespoon chili powder

½ cup unbleached flour

1 tablespoon olive oil

Vegan Pancakes

MAKES 6 TO 8
LARGE PANCAKES

5 ounces Earth Balance margarine

4 cups soy milk

1 tablespoon vanilla extract

6 cups unbleached flour

1 tablespoon baking powder

½ teaspoon kosher salt

1 pound turbinado (raw) sugar

Vegetable oil for frying

Maple syrup

Fruit and/or berries

Tofu Scramble

SERVES 2

1 pound firm tofu, frozen overnight to improve texture
3 tablespoons olive oil
1 tablespoon minced garlic
1 medium tomato, peeled, seeded, and diced
1 jalapeño, seeded and diced
¼ cup small diced onion

1 teaspoon chili powder
1 teaspoon kosher salt
½ teaspoon freshly ground black pepper
½ cup nutritional yeast
¼ bunch cilantro, chopped
Olive oil for pan frying

To make the Tofu Scramble, begin by thawing the tofu on a kitchen towel to soak up excess moisture. Then prepare the Soysage "Sausage" Patties. Cook the millet, amaranth, lentils, and rice until soft; drain to remove all water; set aside to cool.

Finely shred the beet and carrot. Combine the pumpkin seeds, sunflower seeds, sesame sticks, hemp seeds, and chia seeds in work bowl of food processor fitted with steel blade and pulse to chop roughly. Combine the grain/lentil mixture with the beet/carrot mixture in a large bowl. Add the chopped seeds and all remaining ingredients except the olive oil and thoroughly mix together until well incorporated.

Using your hands, form the mixture into 2-ounce patties. Heat a glaze of olive oil in a skillet over medium heat and pan-fry the patties until crisp. Keep warm in low oven while preparing the other dishes.

Prepare the Vegan Pancakes batter. Melt the margarine and add it to a mixing bowl with the soy milk and vanilla; whisk to blend well. In a separate bowl, blend the flour, baking powder, salt, and sugar. Add the soy-milk mixture to the flour mixture and stir to blend well. Set aside for 15 minutes.

Heat a thin glaze of vegetable oil in a heavy-bottomed, nonstick skillet over medium heat. Ladle in enough of the batter to cover the bottom of the skillet, about ⅛ of the total mixture. Cook until bubbles appear around the edge of the pancake. The bottom side should be golden brown. Using a flexible metal or nonstick spatula, turn the pancake and cook until browned on the other side and cooked through. Keep warm in low oven while making the remaining pancakes.

Prepare the Tofu Scramble. Once the tofu is fully thawed, squeeze it in the towel to remove the last bit of moisture. Break the tofu up into small chunks; set aside.

Heat the olive oil in a large skillet over medium heat. Add the garlic, tomato, jalapeño, and onion. Sauté until the vegetables are softened, about 5 minutes. Add the chili powder, salt, and black pepper; cook for 1 minute. Stir in the tofu, nutritional yeast, and cilantro. Cook until the tofu is heated through.

To plate and serve the Vegan Breakfast Platter, spoon the desired amount of Tofu Scramble onto each serving plate, add a Vegan Pancake, and drizzle with maple syrup. Place one or two Soysage "Sausage" Patties on each plate. Arrange the sliced fruit and/or berries as desired and serve.

LESLIE WASHBURNE'S VEGAN BREAKFAST BUFFET AT GROVE HOUSE

....

Leslie Washburne and her husband Hugh own the Hoffman Haus B&B in Fredericksburg, Texas. In 2004 the pair purchased The Grove House in Fredericksburg. As Leslie says: "It was a real fixer-upper. But the 'bones were good.'" After clearing out mountains of trash, they exposed the jewel box that is The Grove House today. Leslie teaches her hands-on vegan cooking classes there, and she and Hugh use the house for small gatherings, weddings, birthdays, wine dinners, and an occasional pop-up vegan dinner with biodynamic wine pairings—all to great reviews, even from the carnivores. Leslie has been a vegetarian/vegan for most of her life and, as noted earlier, seriously studied the craft of meatless cooking. You'll never miss the meat in this delicious buffet spread,.

Prepare the Jalapeño Cream ahead and refrigerate until ready to use. Both types of muffins can also be made ahead of time. Reheat if desired. The Minted Summer Berry Parfait can be put together early in the morning on the day of the brunch. Have all of the ingredients prepped according to the recipes for the Breakfast Chalupa Bar, the Country Hash Browns, and the Scrambled Tofu, making it easy to assemble the buffet just before serving. Serves 4 to 6.

Breakfast Chalupa Bar (see recipe on page 213)
Lemon Blueberry Muffins (see recipe on page 216)
Minted Summer Berry Parfait (see recipe on page 215)
Carrot Cake Breakfast Muffins (see recipe on page 217)
Country Hash Browns (see recipe on page 216)

....

Breakfast Chalupa Bar

Crispy chalupa shells, plus the following toppings:

Scrambled Tofu (see recipe next page)
Smoky chipotle black beans
Diced avocado
Jalapeño Cream (see recipe next page)
Thinly sliced green onions
Toasted pumpkin seeds
Pico de gallo
Fried slices of Field Roast chorizo sausage*

To arrange the chalupa buffet, pile a basket high with chalupa shells. Put each of the other ingredients in separate bowls. (Leslie likes to use white bowls to provide the perfect background for the pops of color.) To assemble the chalupas, spoon the scrambled tofu first on a chalupa shell, then follow with black beans seasoned with canned, minced chipotle chiles, diced avocado, and a generous drizzle of the Jalapeño Cream. Then scatter on the green onions and pumpkin seeds and top with a generous spoonful of pico de gallo and a few chorizo slices. ››

* Field Roast sausage comes in several flavors, with chorizo being one of Leslie's favorites. It can be found at Whole Foods Market and many health-food stores.

Scrambled Tofu

1 carton extra-firm tofu
¼ teaspoon turmeric
½ teaspoon garlic powder
¼ teaspoon onion powder
2 tablespoons Bragg's
 Nutritional Yeast*
1 tablespoon Bragg's liquid
 aminos

Drain and press as much water out of the tofu as you can. Leslie recommends using a "tofu press" (which can be found online), or just wrap the tofu up in a few layers of paper towels or cheesecloth and press gently.

Crumble the tofu into a nonstick skillet—ceramic pans are great for this. Turn heat to medium, and scatter the remaining ingredients around the pan. Stir well to coat the tofu, then sauté until the tofu is heated through, about 2 to 3 minutes.

Jalapeño Cream

MAKES 2 CUPS

Leslie notes that this is one of the most stalwart recipes in her arsenal of delicious, highly addictive sauces. It's a bit of a naughty "fooled you" for those who say the word *tofu* with extreme disdain. You would never know that tofu is the main ingredient because of the lovely marriage of the other flavors. Leslie always keeps this recipe handy, as the sauce transcends most culinary persuasions—from Mexican to French to true-blue American.

16 ounces organic silken tofu,
 drained**
2 tablespoons Bragg's Nutritional
 Yeast
½ cup pickled jalapeño slices
½ teaspoon sea salt

Combine all ingredients in a high-speed blender or food processor and blend until smooth and creamy.

* Bragg's Nutritional Yeast as a brand is a must. You can find it at Whole Foods, at most health-food stores, or online.

** You can use either refrigerated soft tofu (such as Nasoya or the Whole Foods brand), which has the consistency of silken tofu, or Mori-Nu tofu in brick packs. Both types of tofu are generally sold at regular grocery stores and health-food stores.

Minted Summer Berry Parfait

MAKES ABOUT
1 CUP ORANGE
CREAM SAUCE

Assemble these in Mason jars for a unique presentation.

2 cups sliced fresh strawberries
2 cups fresh raspberries
2 cups fresh blueberries
1 tablespoon sugar
1 tablespoon minced fresh mint
2 cups orange cream sauce (see recipe at right)
½ cup sliced skin-on roasted almonds

ORANGE CREAM SAUCE

½ cup orange juice
½ cup raw cashew halves
1 tablespoon sugar
¼ teaspoon vanilla extract

Make the orange cream sauce. Combine all ingredients in a high-speed blender, such as a Vitamix, and blend until smooth and creamy. It is important to make the sauce in a high-speed blender as a food processor just can't create the smoothness that the high-speed blender does. If you don't have one, then soak the cashews in water overnight, drain, and blend the sauce in a Cuisinart. It works, but the sauce will be somewhat grainy.

Mix the berries together and toss with the sugar and mint. Layer a tablespoon of the orange cream sauce into each jar, then scatter in some of the almonds. Repeat the layering two more times, ending with a few more almonds on top.

Country Hash Browns

1 tablespoon avocado oil
1 cup diced yellow onion
4 cups diced russet potatoes
¼ teaspoon sea salt
Pinch of freshly ground black
    pepper

Heat the avocado oil in a heavy-bottomed 12-inch skillet, preferably cast-iron. When the oil is shimmering, add the onion and a pinch of salt. Sauté for a minute or two. Add the potatoes, salt, and pepper, stirring constantly to keep the potatoes from sticking and to make sure they begin to brown evenly. Even out the potatoes with a large spoon, then reduce the heat to low, cover the skillet, and cook until the potatoes are tender and browned.

Lemon Blueberry Muffins

MAKES 12 MUFFINS

½ cup organic canola oil
¾ cup unsweetened almond milk
¼ cup freshly squeezed lemon juice
2 cups all-purpose flour
1 cup organic sugar
1 tablespoon baking powder
½ teaspoon sea salt
½ cup fresh blueberries

Preheat oven to 375 degrees. Spray a 12-cup muffin tin with nonstick cooking spray; set aside. Whisk the canola oil, almond milk, and lemon juice together in a medium-large-sized bowl, blending well. In a separate bowl, combine the remaining ingredients; toss to distribute well. Whisk the dry ingredients into the wet ingredients until a well-blended batter forms.

Spoon the batter into the prepared muffin tin, filling each cup about ⅔ full. Bake in preheated oven for 20 minutes, or until a toothpick inserted into the center of the muffins comes out clean. Remove muffin tin from oven, place on wire rack, and allow muffins to cool before removing. Serve in a cloth-lined basket.

Carrot Cake Breakfast Muffins

MAKES 12 MUFFINS

2 cups white spelt flour
1½ cups whole-wheat pastry flour
2 teaspoons baking soda
2 teaspoons baking powder
2 teaspoons ground cinnamon
2 teaspoons ginger juice
½ teaspoon sea salt
1½ cups freshly squeezed orange juice
½ cup soy milk
¼ cup organic sugar
¼ cup real maple syrup or honey
2 tablespoons organic canola oil
½ cup finely grated carrots
¼ cup pecan or walnut pieces
½ cup raisins

Preheat oven to 350 degrees. Spray a 12-cup muffin tin with nonstick spray; set aside. Mix the dry ingredients together in a medium-large bowl with a wire whisk. Mix the wet ingredients into the dry ingredients, whisking to blend well. Pour the batter into the prepared muffin-tin cups. Bake in preheated oven for about 15 to 20 minutes, or until a toothpick inserted in the center of the muffins comes out clean. Remove from oven and let cool on a wire rack before removing from muffin tin. Serve in a cloth-lined basket.

Red Cocktail Sauce with a Zing

MAKES 3¼ CUPS

This has been my all-time favorite go-to cocktail sauce most of my grown-up life for either oysters on the half shell or boiled shrimp. I may even have expounded on a version of it learned from my mother over the years. At any rate, it pairs beautifully with salted, cold raw oysters for New Year's brunch. The flavors really ping when the sauce is made at least 4 hours before serving and refrigerated.

The sauce can be made a couple of days ahead of time and kept refrigerated.

1½ cups corn-syrup-free ketchup
½ cup bottled Heinz Chile Sauce
½ teaspoon granulated garlic
½ teaspoon onion powder
⅓ cup prepared horseradish
2 tablespoons freshly squeezed lemon juice
2 tablespoons Worcestershire sauce
1½ teaspoons Tabasco
¼ teaspoon freshly ground black pepper
Kosher salt to taste

Combine all ingredients in a medium-sized bowl and whisk until well blended. Transfer to storage container with tight-fitting lid and refrigerate until well chilled before serving.

Brennan's of Houston's Gumbo Z'Herbes with Cornmeal Drop Biscuits

SERVES 6 TO 8

"Gumbo Z," as this greens-laden dish is often called in New Orleans, is generally served during the Lenten season, as it contains no meat. However, Brennan's of Houston Executive Chef Danny Trace sometimes adds pulled beef from pot roast or smoked brisket to change the entire character of the gumbo, calling it "Beef Debris Gumbo." It makes a great first course for a winter brunch. But it's also a great, hearty soup for a meal anytime.

Make the gumbo ahead of time and refrigerate. Reheat when ready to serve. Prepare the cornmeal drop biscuits just before serving.

2 tablespoons vegetable oil

1½ cups medium-diced onions

½ cup medium-diced red bell pepper

½ cup medium-diced green bell pepper

1 cup sliced fresh okra, optional

2 tablespoons minced garlic

6 cups beef stock, preferably homemade, divided

1 tablespoon Louisiana Hot Pepper Sauce

1 tablespoon Worcestershire sauce

2 teaspoons Creole meat seasoning (see recipe at right)

2 teaspoons kosher salt

3 bay leaves

6 tablespoons Creole brown roux (see recipe at right)

4 cups mixed greens (kale, turnip greens, spinach, mustard greens, collard greens, Swiss chard, and parsley), torn into 1-inch pieces

4 cups cooked, shredded pot roast or chopped smoked brisket, if desired

Cornmeal drop biscuits (see recipe at right)

2 teaspoons gumbo file powder

CREOLE MEAT SEASONING

½ cup salt

¼ cup, plus 2 tablespoons paprika

3 tablespoons granulated garlic

2 tablespoons, plus ½ teaspoon granulated onion

2 tablespoons finely ground black pepper

2½ teaspoons cayenne pepper

CREOLE BROWN ROUX

2 cups vegetable oil

3 cups all-purpose flour

⅓ cup yellow onion

⅓ cup minced green bell pepper

⅓ cup minced celery

1 teaspoon minced garlic

CORNMEAL DROP BISCUITS

1 cup all-purpose flour

¼ cup cornmeal

1½ teaspoons baking powder

¼ teaspoon baking soda

½ teaspoon kosher salt

3 tablespoons unsalted butter

½ cup whole milk

¼ cup buttermilk (not low-fat)

½ cup (2 ounces) shredded jalapeño Jack cheese

First, make the roux. In a heavy 4- to 6-quart saucepan, being careful, bring the oil to the smoking point. Add the flour, ¼ cup at a time, letting it get a dark, nutty brown, while stirring constantly, before adding the next batch. Take care not to burn the roux. When all of the flour has been added and the mixture has a nice brown color, remove from the heat. Stir in the remaining ingredients. This will start to cool off the roux, bring out more color, and add flavor. Transfer the roux to a metal bowl or container. When cool, refrigerate until ready to use. Some of the oil will come to the top; whisk it back in before using the roux.

Make the Creole meat seasoning. Combine all ingredients in work bowl of food processor fitted with steel blade and process until thoroughly combined. Transfer to an airtight container, seal, and store in a cool, dry place.

To cook the gumbo, heat the oil to the smoking point in a heavy 6-quart saucepan over medium-high heat. Add the onions and peppers, and sauté until the onions are translucent. Add the okra, if using, and sauté 1 minute more. Add the garlic and 1 cup of the beef broth, stirring rapidly to deglaze the pot. Add the hot sauce, Worcestershire sauce, seasonings, and remaining broth. Bring to a simmer; add the roux, stirring rapidly to blend well. This will give the gumbo flavor and body; it should be thickened enough to coat the back of a spoon. Return to simmer for 5 minutes. Add the greens; simmer for 1 minute to wilt.

At this point, if you wish, you can add 4 cups of cooked, shredded pot roast or chopped smoked brisket. Cook to heat the meat through.

Make the cornmeal drop biscuits. Preheat oven to 325 degrees; lightly grease a small baking sheet. Measure the dry ingredients into a mixing bowl. Cut in the butter until very fine. Make a well in the center; pour milk, buttermilk, and cheese into the well all at once. Mix together with a fork just long enough to incorporate. With a spoon, drop 6 equal portions of the dough onto the prepared baking sheet. Bake in preheated oven for 18 minutes, or until nicely browned.

To serve: Ladle the gumbo into warm bowls and top each with a biscuit. Sprinkle with gumbo file powder and serve hot.

Brennan's of Houston's Bananas Foster

SERVES 4

Bananas Foster is tied with bread pudding as one of the most popular desserts in America. Early in the city's history, bananas were shipped into the bustling port of New Orleans, making their way into many Creole desserts. The star-studded version featured here came about as a way of honoring Owen Brennan's friend Dick Foster, who, as vice-chairman of the Vice Committee, headed the campaign to clean up the French Quarter during the 1950s. The dish, which is cooked to order tableside, is pure drama. To add to the experience, Brennan's of Houston waiters sprinkle ground cinnamon from a small salt shaker into the rum as it is being ignited in the pan. The spice produces a Fourth of July sparks effect that is pure food magic! Remember the cardinal rule of cooking with liquor: *never* pour it straight from the bottle into a hot pan, to avoid the possibility of finding yourself holding a Molotov cocktail in your hand. Instead, measure the amount needed into a small pitcher and pour from the pitcher.

½ cup unsalted butter

1 cup firmly packed light brown sugar

6 tablespoons 151-proof rum, light or dark, divided

4 ripe bananas, peeled, sliced lengthwise, and halved again into quarters

½ teaspoon ground cinnamon

4 scoops good-quality vanilla ice cream

In a flat sauté pan, combine the butter, sugar, and 2 tablespoons of the rum. Cook over medium-high heat while stirring to melt the butter and sugar. Add the bananas and cinnamon. Use a fork to very lightly prick the bananas while cooking. Cook about 1 minute, or just until the bananas soften.

Carefully tilt the pan toward yourself to get the top half of the pan hot, then remove the pan from the heat and pour the remaining ¼ cup of rum over the bananas. To flambé the bananas, immediately—but carefully—ignite the rum by either tilting the pan toward the flame on the range or cautiously lighting the rum with a long taper match. But you must be quick or the alcohol will burn off and it won't ignite.

Gently shake the flaming pan with one hand and sprinkle cinnamon over the flame with your other hand. This makes the cinnamon sparkle and glow. When the flames die out, immediately spoon the bananas and sauce over the ice cream. Serve at once.

Helen Corbitt's Cheese Soup with Garlic Croutons, as Adapted by the Driskill Hotel's 1886 Café & Bakery

MAKES 1½
QUARTS

Helen Corbitt was often dubbed the "Julia Child of Texas." The original consultant/chef/menu developer for the fine restaurants in upscale Nieman Marcus stores, she penned a classic cookbook, *Helen Corbitt's Cookbook*, which remains a favorite even today. Ms. Corbitt served as the culinary director for the Driskill in the late 1950s, and the hotel has a long tradition of serving its adapted version of her famous cheese soup in its 1886 Café & Bakery. When Troy Knapp took the reins as executive chef of the hotel, he chose not to interfere with such a much-loved tradition, and the dish remained on the menu. Chef Troy reports that it's still as popular as it ever was.

Both the cheese soup and the garlic croutons can be made up to 1 day ahead of time. Refrigerate the soup and gently reheat just before serving. Store the croutons in a zip-sealing bag and serve at room temperature.

CHEESE SOUP

1 small carrot, trimmed and peeled
½ of a medium-sized yellow onion, roughly chopped
1 small celery stalk, roughly chopped
2 tablespoons butter
2 tablespoons all-purpose flour
1 cup water
3½ cups whipping cream

4 ounces mild Cheddar cheese, shredded
¾ teaspoon cayenne pepper, or to taste
Kosher salt and freshly ground black pepper to taste
Minced fresh chives as garnish
Garlic croutons (see recipe at right)

GARLIC CROUTONS

2 large slices of good-quality rustic white bread, cut into ½-inch cubes
¼ cup olive oil
1 teaspoon garlic powder
2 teaspoons kosher salt
½ teaspoon freshly ground black pepper

Begin by making the garlic croutons. Preheat oven to 350 degrees. In a large bowl, combine all ingredients together until the bread cubes are well coated with oil and seasonings. Turn the croutons out onto a baking sheet and spread in a single layer. Toast them in a preheated oven for 5 to 7 minutes, or until the croutons are golden brown and crisp. Remove from oven and cool to room temperature. Reserve to garnish the soup.

To make the cheese soup, combine all vegetables in work bowl of food processor and pulse until minced, but

not pureed. The object is to not create liquid! Melt the butter in a heavy-bottomed 4-quart saucepan over medium heat and sauté the vegetables until fragrant, about 5 minutes.

Add the flour all at once, stirring constantly to incorporate, until no traces of unblended flour remain. Add the water and then the cream. Stir to incorporate the liquids.

Reduce heat to medium-low and bring to a simmer for 10 minutes, or until thickened. Stir occasionally to prevent scorching.

Remove pan from heat and transfer half of the soup to blender. Blend with half of the cheese and half of the cayenne pepper until totally smooth. Repeat with the remaining soup, cheese, and cayenne. The soup should coat the back of a metal spoon. Combine the two blended batches of soup, and season with salt and pepper.

Ladle the soup into serving bowls and garnish with chives. Scatter a portion of the garlic croutons over each serving.

Fonda San Miguel's Escabeche de Verduras

SERVES 12

This bold and tasty blend of pickled vegetables has been a mainstay at Austin's iconic Fonda San Miguel for the forty years it has been serving authentic interior Mexican cuisine. Chances are if you dine there with a group, somewhere on the table a little pile of escabeche will be lurking near the edge of a plate. It's not only a great side for any type of food but also a regular dish at the restaurant's Hacienda Sunday Brunch.

4 tablespoons olive oil

15 garlic cloves

6 fresh jalapeños, pierced with a fork

2 dozen small boiler onions, peeled

4 carrots, peeled and cut into ¼-inch slices

1 quart water

2 medium red potatoes, cut into quarters

1 teaspoon sea salt

BRINE

2 cups rice vinegar

1½ cups water

10 bay leaves

1 teaspoon ground cumin

1 teaspoon whole black peppercorns

1 teaspoon sea salt

3 sprigs marjoram

3 sprigs Mexican oregano

3 sprigs rosemary

1½ cups fresh green beans, with ends snapped

1½ cups small broccoli or cauliflower florets

Heat the olive oil in a heavy, 4-quart nonreactive saucepan over medium heat. Add the garlic, jalapeños, onions, and carrots. Cook for about 10 minutes or until the vegetables soften.

Add the brine ingredients and bring to a full boil. Reduce heat to medium and cook for 15 minutes. In a separate 3-quart saucepan, bring the water to a full boil. Add the potatoes and cook at a brisk simmer for about 8 minutes.

Drain the potatoes and add to the vegetable/brine mixture. Add the salt, adjusting the seasonings as needed. Remove from heat and allow to cool to room temperature. Transfer to a nonreactive container and refrigerate 24 hours.

Melon and Berry Compote with Raspberry–Poppy Seed Sauce

In the spring and summer, when melons are in season, I often serve this simple fruit side dish for brunch. I like to use small, footed bowls for individual servings and a stunning clear-glass bowl when the brunch is buffet style.

The raspberry–poppy seed sauce can be made up to 3 days in advance of serving and refrigerated. The melons can be cut the night before serving. Cover tightly and refrigerate. Assemble when ready to serve.

SERVES 6 TO 8

MAKES ABOUT
1¼ CUPS RASPBERRY-
POPPY SEED SAUCE

MELONS AND BERRIES

6 cups seeded watermelon cubes, about 1 inch square, preferably Black Diamond watermelon
6 cups cantaloupe cubes, about 1 inch square
1 pint fresh strawberries, hulled and sliced
Mint sprigs as garnish

RASPBERRY-POPPY SEED SAUCE

½ cup sugar
½ teaspoon dry mustard
½ teaspoon salt
¼ cup raspberry-flavored vinegar
1 (½-inch-thick) slice of a medium-sized onion, roughly chopped
½ cup canola oil
1½ teaspoons poppy seeds

Prepare the raspberry-poppy seed sauce. Combine the sugar, mustard, salt, vinegar, and onion in work bowl of food processor fitted with steel blade. Process until smooth. With machine running, pour the canola oil in a thin, steady stream through the feed tube until all has been added. Add the poppy seeds and process just to blend. Transfer the sauce to a container with a tight-fitting lid and refrigerate until ready to serve.

When you're ready to assemble and serve the compote, combine the fruit and drizzle the desired amount of sauce on top. Toss gently to blend, taking care not to break up the melon cubes or the sliced berries. Spoon into individual small bowls or one large glass bowl. Garnish with mint sprigs and serve.

Pan-Fried Apples

When apples are in season I love to make this simple side dish to serve with breakfasts that also have eggs, bacon, and/or sausage on the plate. I think apples and pork were meant to be together.

This dish can be made ahead and gently reheated just before serving. Take care not to overcook the apples, however.

. . . .

8 medium-sized firm Granny
   Smith apples
½ teaspoon ground cinnamon
3 tablespoons bacon drippings
Light brown sugar to taste

Peel and core the apples. Cut them into slices about ¼ inch thick. Place the sliced apples in a bowl and toss with the cinnamon to coat well; set aside. Heat the bacon drippings in a heavy-bottomed 12-inch nonstick skillet over medium heat. Add the apples and stir to coat them with the bacon drippings. Cook, turning often with a nonstick spatula, and add some of the brown sugar to taste as they cook. Take care not to break up the apple slices. Cook for about 8 to 10 minutes, or until the apple slices are light golden brown but still hold their shape. Serve hot.

Fancy Lucky Peas

SERVES 8 TO 10

Black-eyed peas are traditionally served on New Year's Eve to ensure good luck in the coming year, but don't save them for just one day. Perhaps they'll bring good luck the year-round! It's important that you use fresh peas, or fresh-frozen ones, in this recipe. They are available in the produce section of most supermarkets during the holiday season. The fresh fennel is not traditional, but I love the flavor it adds here.

½ stick (4 tablespoons) unsalted butter
4 ounces sliced salt pork, cut into ½-inch dice
3 medium-sized garlic cloves, minced
2 celery stalks, chopped
1 small head of fennel, trimmed and chopped, including a few of the ferny top fronds
8 ounces cherry tomatoes, sliced in half
1¼ teaspoons freshly ground black pepper
2 pounds fresh black-eyed peas
Homemade chicken stock
Kosher salt to taste

Combine the butter and salt pork in a heavy-bottomed 6-quart pot over medium heat. Cook until the butter has melted and the salt pork is beginning to render its fat, about 5 minutes. Add the garlic, celery, and chopped fennel. Cook, stirring occasionally, until the vegetables are wilted, about 12 minutes. Stir in the cherry tomatoes and black pepper, blending well. Cook for 15 minutes, or until the tomatoes are very limp. Add the peas and stir to blend well. Add enough chicken stock to cover the peas by about ½ inch. Add salt to taste. Simmer the peas for 40 to 45 minutes, or until they are tender and a nice gravy has formed. Serve hot, and good luck!

Honey-Baked Tomatoes

SERVES 6

Not only are these honey-kissed tomatoes delicious, but they make a very nice edible garnish on a breakfast or brunch plate that begs for a splash of color. Be sure to use homegrown tomatoes in season whenever possible, and to seek out local honey. And do try to source fresh tomatoes—everyone should have at least one tomato plant growing, even if in a pot on the terrace. To bite into a tomato freshly plucked from its vine while its juices run down your arm is to truly taste sunshine!

The tomatoes can be prepared ahead of time and baked, then broiled right before serving.

6 ripe homegrown tomatoes
⅔ cup fresh coarse bread crumbs
1½ teaspoons kosher salt
1½ teaspoons freshly ground black pepper
1 tablespoon minced Mexican mint marigold, also known as "Texas tarragon"
6 tablespoons local honey
6 tablespoons unsalted butter

Preheat oven to 350 degrees. Butter an 8-inch-square baking dish. Slice off the stem ends of the tomatoes, and cut a very small slice off the bottom of the tomatoes so that they will sit flat without toppling over. Carefully scoop out the seeds and discard. Place the tomatoes, open side up, in the prepared baking dish.

Mix together the bread crumbs, salt, pepper, and Mexican mint marigold, tossing to blend well. Drizzle a tablespoon of the honey all around the cavity of each tomato. Spoon a portion of the crumb mixture over each tomato and place a tablespoon of the butter on top. Bake, uncovered, for about 20 minutes, or until the tomatoes begin to wilt a bit.

Preheat broiler and place oven rack 6 inches below heat source. Place the tomatoes under the broiler for about 2-3 minutes, or until the crumbs are golden brown. Watch them carefully so that they don't overcook. Serve hot or at room temperature.

Mexican Hash Browns

SERVES 6

This spicy, cheese-topped variation of plain old hash-browned potatoes is a delightfully different addition to the breakfast plate. Since the dish has a lot of flavors going on, I like to serve the potatoes with plain eggs—scrambled, fried, or poached, or a simple omelet—and either bacon or a simple link or pan sausage. Add a basket of hot homemade biscuits and you've got yourself a mighty fine breakfast.

¼ cup canola oil

1¾ pounds red new potatoes, cut into ¼-inch matchstick strips

½ cup ¼-inch-diced onion

1 teaspoon toasted cumin seeds, ground to a fine powder

Kosher salt and freshly ground black pepper to taste

¾ cup peeled, seeded, and tiny-diced tomatoes

2 serrano chiles, seeds and veins removed, minced

1½ cups (6 ounces) shredded quesadilla or Monterey Jack cheese

Heat the canola oil in a 14-inch, oven-proof skillet over medium heat. When the oil is hot, add the potatoes and cook, stirring occasionally, until tender and just beginning to brown, about 8 minutes. Using a slotted spoon, transfer the potatoes to a paper-towel-lined wire rack to drain for 5 minutes. Pre-heat oven to 350 degrees.

Pour off all but 1 tablespoon of the oil from the skillet and return to medium heat. Add the drained potatoes, onion, seasonings, tomatoes, and chiles. Cook until onion is wilted and transparent, and potatoes are golden brown, about 6-8 minutes. Remove skillet from heat and quickly scatter the cheese over the potatoes. Place in preheated oven and cook just until the cheese melts and begins to brown, about 7 minutes. Serve hot.

Frizzled Sweet Potatoes

SERVES 6 TO 8

These little "nests" of fried sweet potatoes are very tasty and make an interesting addition to a breakfast or brunch plate with their bright dash of color and frizzy texture. I particularly like to serve them with egg dishes. You will need either a mandolin or a Benriner slicing box that comes with a blade for making tiny, thin julienne strips of vegetables. When using either a mandolin or Benriner box, be sure to use the guard so that your hands or fingers never come close to the blades, which are very, very sharp.

3 large sweet potatoes, peeled and cut lengthwise into tiny, thin julienne strips
Canola oil for deep-frying, heated to 350 degrees
Kosher salt to taste
Chef Paul Prudhomme's Vegetable Magic Seasoning

Place the sweet potatoes in a bowl of ice-cold water and refrigerate for 1 hour before frying. Drain the potatoes, shaking vigorously in a large wire strainer, to remove all traces of water. Scatter them out on a clean kitchen towel and gently pat dry.

It's best to use a countertop deep fryer equipped with a thermostat to maintain an even temperature. Fry the potatoes in batches. Grab a handful of the frizzy potatoes and place them in the fryer's basket. Lower the basket gently into the hot oil. It will spit and sputter, so be careful of splatters. Be sure not to crowd the pan, or the potatoes won't puff up into tangled nests. Cook for about 2 minutes, or until puffed and browned. Drain on a paper-towel-covered wire rack set over a baking sheet. As soon as you turn out the batches, season them with salt and the Vegetable Magic. Repeat with the remaining potatoes, while keeping the ones that have been fried warm in a low oven. Serve hot.

Pondicheri Café's Uppma with Cilantro Chutney

SERVES 4 TO 6

Uppma, a savory pudding with vegetables, is a traditional South Indian breakfast food. It can be made with semolina, cream of wheat, grits, or polenta. Anita Jaisinghani, owner of Houston's popular Pondicheri Café, likes to top uppma with whole-milk yogurt, peanuts, and cilantro chutney.

The cilantro chutney can be prepared up to 1 day ahead of time, and at this point you can also make sure you have on hand all of the toppings you will use. The uppma itself, however, should be made just before serving and served immediately.

UPPMA

2 tablespoons canola oil
1 teaspoon black mustard seeds
8 to 10 kari curry leaves, chopped
1 medium-sized red onion, cut into ¼-inch dice
1 teaspoon ground Kashmiri chile, or substitute ground árbol chile powder
1 tablespoon pureed fresh ginger
2 teaspoons kosher salt
2½ cups water
Juice from 2 lemons, divided in half
2 celery stalks, cut into ¼-inch dice
1 cup fresh or frozen corn kernels
¾ cup semolina flour, preferably, or substitute cream of wheat, grits, or polenta
¼ cup chopped roasted and salted peanuts
2 tablespoons chopped cilantro
1 tablespoon ghee (see footnote on page 50)
Cilantro chutney (see recipe at right), peanuts, and yogurt for topping

CILANTRO CHUTNEY

2 large bunches fresh cilantro
½ of a Granny Smith apple, unpeeled, cored, and sliced
1 serrano chile, or more to taste, stem removed
½ cup unsalted dry-roasted peanuts
1 cup plain whole-milk yogurt
Juice of 1 lemon
1 teaspoon kosher salt, or to taste

Make the cilantro chutney first. Rinse the cilantro well under cold running water. Discard the bottom 4 inches of the stems, then shake the cilantro to remove excess water; set aside to drain in a colander.

Place the sliced apple, serrano chile, peanuts, yogurt, lemon juice, and salt in a blender.

Blend, beginning at low speed and slowly increasing speed to high, until completely smooth. Taste for spiciness and add 1 or 2 additional stemmed cilantro chiles as desired. Add the cilantro, ½ bunch at a time, and blend until the mixture is grainy but smooth. Taste for salt, adding more if needed. Transfer to storage container with tight-fitting lid and refrigerate until ready to use. Note that the chutney is at its brightest flavor about 2 hours after it has been made; it will keep in the refrigerator for 2 to 3 days.

To prepare the uppma, heat the vegetable oil over high heat in a deep, heavy-bottomed stockpot until shimmering. Add the black mustard seeds and let them sizzle and pop for a few seconds. Lower heat to medium and add the chopped curry leaves and red onion; sauté for 5 to 7 minutes until the onion is wilted and translucent. Add the ground chile, ginger puree, salt, water, and half of the lemon juice. Bring to a boil over high heat. Add the celery and corn and cook for another minute.

Lower the heat to maintain a simmer and add the semolina in a slow, steady stream, whisking while adding. The mixture will begin to thicken almost immediately. Lower heat further and continue cooking for another minute or two until the mixture is thick and has the consistency of mashed potatoes. Cook for about 4 to 5 minutes, then turn the heat off. Just before serving, squeeze the remaining half of the lemon juice over the Uppma and top with chopped peanuts, cilantro, and ghee. Serve immediately with the recommended toppings, or choose your own combination, but be sure to include the cilantro chutney. It's too good to miss!

Potato Pancakes

SERVES 4

Also known as *latkes*, potato pancakes are a crisp and tasty breakfast side dish that hearkens back to Texas's German heritage. I often serve them at breakfast with applesauce, as my grandmother did, which is also a German tradition. They make a good alternative to our beloved grits.

4 applewood-smoked bacon slices
2½ pounds russet potatoes, peeled
1 small onion, peeled and grated on a box grater
3 tablespoons all-purpose flour
½ teaspoon each: kosher salt and freshly ground black pepper
1 tablespoon minced Italian flat-leaf parsley
½ teaspoon minced fresh thyme
½ cup (2 ounces) shredded Brazos Valley Cheese Company's Swiss cheese, or substitute another Swiss cheese
3 tablespoons canola oil

Begin by frying the bacon slices in a heavy-bottomed skillet over medium-high heat until crisp. Remove the bacon and drain on paper towels. Reserve the drippings in the skillet. When the bacon is cool, chop or crumble it into tiny bits; set aside.

Grate the potatoes using a box grater then place them in a colander and press out all possible moisture with the palm of your hand. Transfer the potatoes to a medium-sized bowl and stir in the grated onion and flour. Stir, incorporating the flour thoroughly. Stir in the salt, pepper, and herbs, blending well. Stir the reserved bacon pieces into the potatoes along with the cheese.

Add a tablespoon of the canola oil to the bacon drippings over medium-high heat. When the fat is hot, begin to add the potato mixture in ¼-cup batches, smashing them down with a flat metal spatula. Don't crowd the pan. Cook until golden brown, flip, and brown the other side. Place the cooked pancakes on a wire rack set over a baking sheet and keep warm in a low oven while frying the remaining pancakes, adding additional canola oil as needed. Serve hot.

Tucker's Kozy Korner's "Chicken"-Fried Grits

MAKES ABOUT
20 PIECES

Tucked away on a small corner in the shadows of downtown San Antonio, Tucker's Kozy Korner has been a hidden gem in the city since 1948. It stakes its claim as the oldest African American bar in Texas. Professional athletes, entertainers, and military veterans from as far back as World War II still frequent Tucker's to have dinner and a cocktail, and to reminisce. The Sunday Gospel Brunch is legendary at Tucker's, with a Bloody Mary bar where you can build your own Bloody Mary, choosing from a plethora of add-ins, including Vienna sausages. Christopher Cullum took over Tucker's Kozy Korner on January 1, 2014, but he made few changes to the iconic establishment other than printing a new menu. One of the most popular items on the brunch menu is the "Chicken"-Fried Grits, a concoction that Cullum created in conjunction with his friend, Chef Ryan Torres. I'm giving you fair warning: these things are addictive! When I first tasted Tucker's grits I was with a group of friends, one of whom is a cardiologist (and shall remain nameless). As we all grabbed the delectable little orbs from their paper basket drenched in pimento cheese, the doc tried to hide his face—lest a colleague or patient were to see him indulging in these sinfully delicious artery-cloggers. But, you just can't stop yourself!

The grits should be made the night before, so that they form a dense texture from being chilled. You can make the pimento cheese blend ahead of time also; bring it to room temperature to use. The glaze for topping can be made up to 1 hour before using.

GRITS

4 cups vegetable stock, preferably homemade (as is Tucker's)

1 cup yellow corn grits (not instant)

3 cups finely grated Parmesan cheese

1 cup shredded Italian Fontina cheese

1 cup shredded Asiago cheese

1 tablespoon kosher salt

1 tablespoon freshly ground black pepper

2 teaspoons cracked red pepper flakes

Canola oil for deep-frying, heated to 365 degrees

PIMENTO CHEESE BLEND

6 cups finely shredded Cheddar cheese

¾ cup good-quality real mayonnaise

1 7-ounce can of whole pimentos, drained well and chopped

2 teaspoons each: kosher salt, freshly ground black pepper, paprika, granulated garlic, and granulated onion powder

1 teaspoon cayenne pepper

BREADING AND DREDGE FOR FRYING

4 cups all-purpose flour

2 tablespoons granulated garlic

2 tablespoons granulated onion

2 tablespoons paprika

1 tablespoon cayenne pepper

3 cups whole buttermilk (not low-fat), blended in blender with 2 serrano chiles and 3 jalapeño chiles until smooth

GLAZE FOR TOPPING

2 cups Texas honey

5 green onions, sliced thin, including green tops

2 teaspoons crushed red chile flakes »

Begin by making the grits. Bring the vegetable stock to a boil. Stir in the grits and cook until they are thickened and fairly stiff. Remove from heat and rapidly stir in the cheeses and seasonings. Turn the grits out into a 9 × 13-inch baking dish, spreading them in an even layer. Let cool, then refrigerate overnight to solidify.

Make the pimento cheese blend. Combine all ingredients in a bowl and stir to blend well, until the mixture is fairly mushy. Refrigerate until ready to assemble the dish.

Prepare dredge by combining flour and seasonings in a baking dish. Whisk to distribute seasoning well.

To fry the grits, scoop out golf-ball-size balls of grits, rolling them in your palms. First dredge the balls in the seasoned flour, coating well and shaking off all excess flour. Then dip them in the buttermilk blend, coating well. Dredge again in the flour mixture, coating well and shaking off all excess. Place the breaded balls on a baking sheet lined with parchment paper and refrigerate for 1 hour.

Make the glaze for topping. Combine all ingredients in a saucepan and cook until the honey is infused with the flavors of the onions and red chile flakes. Set aside to keep slightly warm.

When ready to cook the grits, spread the pimento cheese blend in a shallow serving plate or baking dish.

Fry the grits in batches in the preheated oil, taking care not to crowd the fryer. Cook for approximately 3 to 4 minutes, or until golden brown and crisp. Drain on a wire rack placed over a baking sheet. Repeat until all of the grits are fried.

Arrange the fried grits on the pimento cheese blend. Drizzle the infused honey over the top and serve.

Cajun Coush-Coush

Coush-coush is the Cajun equivalent of grits—only, I think, even tastier. It is served either as a side dish with eggs and breakfast meats or as a thick cereal. The name, which was derived from the Moroccan grain dish known as *couscous*, was given by African slaves in Louisiana. If you try it, go all out and add the butter, cane syrup, or half-and-half.

SERVES 4

2 cups yellow cornmeal
1½ teaspoons kosher salt
1 teaspoon freshly ground black pepper
2 teaspoons baking powder
1 tablespoon sugar
½ cup bacon drippings
1½ cups boiling whole milk
Butter, cane syrup (such as Steen's), or half-and-half for topping

In a medium-sized bowl, combine the cornmeal, salt, pepper, baking powder, and sugar; toss with a fork to blend. In a 10-inch cast-iron skillet over medium-high heat, heat the bacon drippings until almost smoking. Pour the boiling milk into the cornmeal mixture and stir to form a smooth paste. Spoon the mixture into the hot fat and fry until a light crust forms on the bottom, about 10 minutes. Stir the mixture, breaking up the crust and distributing the browned bits throughout. Reduce the heat to medium and continue to cook an additional 10 minutes, without stirring. To serve, scoop a portion of the coush-coush into individual bowls. Top with your choice of butter, cane syrup, or half-and-half. Serve hot.

Oatmeal

SERVES 4 TO 6

Oatmeal is really good for you. Of course, we all heard that phrase as children. But it's true. Oats are an ancient grain that provide an excellent source of fiber, both dietary and soluble, which helps lower bad (LDL) cholesterol levels. I actually love oatmeal, especially for breakfast in the winter. To those who find it boring and bland, I suggest that you try tossing in some of the flavor additives listed below. You might just change your mind. There are several types of oatmeal, but I'm including recipes for rolled oats and steel-cut oats. You can even get *savory* with your oatmeal, adding meats and veggies that are not normally associated with a grain breakfast!

ROLLED OATS

Also known as "old-fashioned oats," rolled oats have been steamed and flattened with large rollers into flakes. They take about 5 minutes to cook on the stovetop after an overnight soaking.

3½ cups water
¼ teaspoon kosher salt
2 cups rolled oats

Combine all ingredients in a non-aluminum bowl and stir to blend. Cover with plastic wrap and allow to sit overnight. In the morning, transfer the mixture to a heavy-bottomed 2-quart saucepan and bring to a brisk boil. Lower the heat and simmer, uncovered, for 5 minutes, stirring often. Remove pan from heat. If all of the liquid has not been absorbed, cover and set aside for a few minutes.

STEEL-CUT OATS

Also called "Irish oats," steel-cut oats have been cut into many pieces and steamed, but not rolled. When cooked they have a chewier consistency than rolled oats. Steel-cut oats require 25 minutes to cook.

4 cups water
½ teaspoon kosher salt
1⅓ cups steel-cut oats

Combine the ingredients in a non-aluminum bowl and stir to blend. Cover with plastic wrap and allow to soak overnight. In the morning, transfer the mixture to a heavy-bottomed 2-quart saucepan and bring to a full boil. Cover the pan and simmer the oats for about 25 to 30 minutes, or until the oats are tender and the liquid is almost entirely absorbed.

Add-ins to Make Your Oatmeal Pop

· Add a liquid other than water when you do the overnight soak, along with some chopped nuts. Perhaps apple cider with toasted pepitas (pumpkin seeds). The cider adds a richness your taste buds won't believe. To take plain oatmeal to another plane, try soaking in no-sodium, preferably scratch-made beef broth. Cook and add chopped, crisp-cooked bacon to the top. A carnivore's delight!

· After cooking, add sweeteners such as brown sugar, honey, maple syrup, or agave nectar.

· If you feel like really indulging yourself, stir some butter into the hot oatmeal and pour in some real cream!

· After cooking, scatter ground cinnamon, ground nutmeg, or apple pie seasoning on top.

· After cooking, stir in dried fruit of your choice.

· Top with your favorite nuts—toasted and chopped.

· Add flaked or shredded coconut or coconut chips.

· Add milk, half-and-half, Greek yogurt, vanilla yogurt, almond milk, rice milk, or soy milk

· Stir in some applesauce with cinnamon.

· Add crumbled sausage—and it can be any kind of sausage, from break-fast sausage to smoked to Italian to chorizo (Mexican or Spanish).

· While the oatmeal is cooking, heat a glaze of good olive oil in a sauté pan along with a little garlic and a tablespoon or so of minced shallots, perhaps a pinch of crushed red pepper, then throw in a big handful of fresh spinach, or other greens such as kale, mustard, or collards. Sauté just until the spinach is wilted and the shallots are cooked, then stir in a drop or two of good aged balsamic vinegar. Spoon your oatmeal into a bowl and stir in the spinach—or just put it on top. Scatter on some toasted pepitas (pumpkin seeds) and you might even have it for dinner!

SEVEN

Tasty Pastries for Breakfast and Brunch

*

It's hard to recall anything that makes my mouth water more than the aroma of breakfast biscuits, breads, or pastries baking in the oven or cooling on the counter first thing in the morning. Texas has a rich heritage of breakfast breads and pastries, due, in part, to the large population of Czech families who settled in the central region of the state. They brought with them the recipes for their beloved yeast-dough kolaches and klobasnikis (sausage-stuffed pastries often referred to as "pigs in a blanket"). These recipes were handed down through generations and are the

prized secrets of Czech cooks. Today, kolaches and klobasnikis are available pretty much all over the state. Texans have taken a lot of liberties with the pastries, even to the point of stuffing the klobasnikis with Cajun boudin, as Sandy and I discovered in several bakeries in Rockport! But if you want the real deal, travel to West or Caldwell, both of which are strongholds of Czech populations and, as such, qualify equally for the title "Kolache Capital of Texas." There's also a great Czech bakery on Highway 71 at Ellinger, between Houston and Austin; known by the name Hruskas, it makes very authentic Czech pastries (and a mean hamburger). Whenever any member of our family travels between Houston and Austin, Hruskas is a mandatory stop for stocking up on pastries—and one of those burgers.

On the subject of biscuits, there are probably as many styles of this doughy delight served in Texas as there are cooks who make them. Well-made biscuits are a work of art and so wonderful to savor, piled with pats of melting butter and perhaps a nice spoonful of homemade jam or local honey, especially with some of the honeycomb still in it. I find, however, that the art of biscuit making may be in jeopardy as many young cooks, including my own daughter, are afraid to tackle making them from scratch. It's really easy once you master the technique of incorporating the fat of your choice into the flour and not overworking the dough. Biscuit dough should be loose and slightly sticky, so don't be tempted to keep adding flour. Just flour the work surface, your hands, and the biscuit cutter to keep the dough from sticking. I generally pat the dough out gently with my hands before cutting to prevent overworking the dough. But if you do use a rolling pin, be sure to flour it also, and roll gently in one direction. And be sure to follow the temperature guidelines in biscuit recipes. They should be baked in a very hot oven. One of my favorite biscuit recipes is included below: Brunch Biscuits with Paula's Texas Lemon Butter. Although these little biscuits are made from a dough that is (sort of) folded and turned like puff pastry, the method featured here is much simpler and less exacting.

Sandy and I have included a cross section of breakfast and brunch breads and pastries in this chapter. Hopefully you'll find a few that will become favorites—or serve as a canvas for your own innovations.

What's a Breakfast Without Good Biscuits? And Perhaps Some Sausage Gravy?

MAKES 12 BISCUITS

SAUSAGE GRAVY
SERVES 6 TO 8

Writing a cookbook about breakfast and brunch in Texas without including a good biscuit recipe would be a gross oversight. Biscuits are a breakfast staple around Texas tables. And what makes a cowboy happier with his biscuits than sausage gravy? Quintessential Texas grub!

Many cooks are terrified of making biscuits from scratch. Yet it's really a simple task if you remember two things. Don't overwork the dough, or the biscuits will be tough. And leave the dough a bit on the sticky side. When the dough is all mixed and seems just a little sticky, don't be tempted to keep adding more flour. Just pat the dough out on a floured work surface, scattering a small amount of flour on the surface of the dough, and cut out the biscuits with a floured biscuit cutter. Carefully place them on the baking sheet. You will be rewarded with tender, fluffy, flavorful biscuits.

Biscuits freeze beautifully when fully baked and well cooled. Thaw before reheating in a low oven. The gravy is best made right before serving; otherwise, it gets too thick and turns a morbid-looking shade of gray!

BISCUITS

3 cups all-purpose flour
¼ cup sugar
1 tablespoon baking powder
½ teaspoon baking soda
1 teaspoon kosher salt
6 tablespoons unsalted butter, chilled and cut into ½-inch pieces
6 tablespoons fresh leaf lard, chilled and cut into ½-inch pieces
1 cup whole buttermilk (not low-fat)
¼ cup whipping cream
Melted unsalted butter for glazing

SAUSAGE GRAVY

¼ cup all-purpose flour
2 teaspoons minced fresh sage
2 teaspoons freshly ground black pepper
½ teaspoon crushed red pepper flakes
1½ pounds bulk-style breakfast sausage
3 cups whole milk
1 heaping teaspoon chicken base paste
Kosher salt to taste

Begin by making the sausage gravy. In a small bowl, combine the flour, sage, black pepper, and red pepper flakes. Toss to blend well and set aside. In a cast-iron skillet over medium heat, cook the sausage until it is lightly browned, about 8 to 10 minutes. Use the back of a wooden spoon to break the sausage up into small bits, so that there are no large clumps. Add the flour mixture all at once and stir to incorporate well. Cook, stirring constantly, for 2 to 3 minutes. Add the milk slowly, while stirring until all has been added. Stir in the chicken base paste. Cook, stirring, until the gravy has thickened, about 7 minutes. Taste the gravy first; then season with salt, if desired. Keep the gravy warm while making the biscuits.

Preheat oven to 425 degrees. Line a baking sheet with parchment paper; set aside. Dump the flour into the center of a large mixing bowl. Add the sugar, baking powder, baking soda, and salt. Whisk to distribute the ingredients. Add the butter and lard cubes, scattering them all over the surface of the flour. With your thumb and forefingers, use a twisting motion to blend the fats into the flour until the dough resembles coarse oatmeal. The fat particles should be about the size of green peas.

Make a well in the center of the flour and add the buttermilk and cream. Begin to stir the liquids into the flour, starting in the middle of the bowl

and continuing outward. Be sure to stir all the way to the bottom of the bowl. Continue until the liquids are well combined and a fairly cohesive dough has formed with no traces of unblended flour.

Turn the dough out onto a work surface and gather the dough together, kneading gently 5 or 6 times to form a smooth dough. Do not overwork the dough! Gently pat the dough into a circle about 10 inches in diameter and about 1 inch thick. With a 3-inch biscuit cutter, cut the dough into rounds, as closely together as possible, using firm downward cuts without squiggling the cutter. Place on prepared baking sheet. Gather the dough scraps together without overworking the dough. Pat into a 1-inch-thick circle, and cut additional biscuits.

Bake the biscuits in preheated oven until light golden brown, about 20 to 25 minutes. As soon as you remove them from the oven, brush the tops of the biscuits with the melted butter using a pastry brush.

Serve the biscuits hot. If you wish to serve them with the sausage gravy, split the biscuits in half and lay them open on individual plates. Spoon a portion of the gravy over and around them—and dig in!

Brunch Biscuits with Paula's Texas Lemon Butter

MAKES 16
2-INCH BISCUITS

I love to serve these little biscuits that are made from a dough that's sort of a lazy cook's version of puff pastry dough. They're much quicker, and the pastries have a nice puffy and light texture. Serve them with little ramekins of the spirited butter made using Paula Angerstein's delicious lemon liqueur.

These delicate little biscuits are best baked just before serving. Allow time for the dough to refrigerate for 1 hour. The Paula's Texas Lemon Butter can be made up to 1 day ahead of time.

BISCUITS

2 cups all-purpose flour
½ teaspoon kosher salt
1 tablespoon, plus 1 teaspoon baking powder
¾ cup (1½ sticks) well-chilled unsalted butter, cut into ½-inch cubes
1 cup whole buttermilk (not low-fat)
Additional ½ cup (1 stick) unsalted butter, melted

PAULA'S TEXAS LEMON BUTTER

1 cup sugar
½ cup (1 stick) unsalted butter, cut into ½-inch cubes
1½ teaspoons grated lemon zest
2 tablespoons Paula's Texas Lemon liqueur

Begin by making the Paula's Texas Lemon Butter. With the steel blade in place in work bowl of food processor, add the sugar and process until superfine. Add the butter cubes and process until well blended, stopping to scrape down side of bowl once or twice. Add the lemon zest and liqueur. Process until smooth and well blended. Pack into small ramekins and refrigerate, tightly covered with plastic wrap, until ready to serve. Soften before serving to make it easy to slather on the biscuits!

Make the biscuits. Sift together the flour, salt, and baking powder in a large bowl. Dump in the butter cubes and work into the flour mixture using your fingertips or a pastry blender, until the mixture resembles coarse meal. Add

about ¾ cup of the buttermilk and stir to form a cohesive dough, taking care not to overwork the dough. Add the remaining buttermilk if needed to form a soft, shaggy, ever so slightly sticky dough. Turn out onto a lightly floured work surface and knead about 12 times to bring the dough together. Roll out into a rectangle about ¼ inch thick. Using a pastry brush, brush half of the surface of the dough with a portion of the melted butter. Fold the unbuttered side over onto the buttered side, lining up the edges precisely. Roll the dough out again into a ¼-inch-thick rectangle and repeat the buttering. Do this 4 more times for a total of 6 turns. Wrap the dough in plastic wrap and refrigerate for 1 hour.

Preheat oven to 425 degrees and line a baking sheet with parchment paper. Roll the refrigerated dough out to ½-inch thickness. Using a sharp 2-inch biscuit cutter and a firm downward cut (no twisting), cut the dough into rounds. Place the biscuits on prepared baking sheet and bake in preheated oven for about 10 minutes, or until golden brown and puffy. Serve hot with ramekins of softened Paula's Texas Lemon Butter.

Bird Café's Cream Biscuits with Ham, Texas Horseradish-Pecan Cheddar, and Blueberry-Jalapeño Jam

MAKES ABOUT 16
2-INCH BISCUITS

MAKES 4 TO 5
PINTS BLUEBERRY-
JALAPEÑO JAM

These biscuits, made using heavy cream, are heavenly. And they are the perfect solution for those who are intimidated by traditional biscuit-making methods. Biscuits freeze well, so it would be ideal to have a bag of these gems in the freezer for busy mornings. Be sure to use a good-quality smoked ham. The Brazos Valley Cheese Company's Horseradish-Pecan Cheddar is a very distinctive cheese. You could substitute another Cheddar, but the biscuits wouldn't be the same! The cheese can be ordered online from Brazos Valley's website. Note that the dough for the biscuits is fairly damp (on purpose), so don't be tempted to add a lot of additional flour to make it completely nonsticky—as this would make the resulting biscuits heavy in texture.

Make the blueberry-jalapeño jam ahead of time and store in the pantry until needed. The recipe makes 4 to 5 pints of jam, so there's enough for other uses as well. The biscuits can be made ahead, cooled, wrapped in foil, and frozen. To reheat, bake at 350 degrees, still wrapped in the foil, until heated through. Proceed with cooking the ham and putting the biscuits together according to the recipe.

Cream biscuits (see recipe at right)
Blueberry-jalapeño jam (see recipe at right)
Smoked ham slices
Canola oil for searing the ham
16 slices Brazos Valley Cheese Company's Horseradish-Pecan Cheddar cheese

CREAM BISCUITS

2 cups all-purpose flour, plus more for rolling dough
1 teaspoon fine-grain sea salt
1 tablespoon baking powder
2 teaspoons sugar
2 cups heavy cream

BLUEBERRY-JALAPEÑO JAM

6 cups fresh blueberries, washed and picked over for bruised or damaged berries
1 jalapeño, seeds and veins removed, minced fine
4 cups sugar
2 tablespoons fresh lemon juice
1 pouch (3 ounces) liquid fruit pectin
Sterilized pint-size canning jars, seals, and lids ››

Begin by making the blueberry-jalapeño jam. Pour about ¾ of the blueberries and the minced jalapeño into a heavy-bottomed 6-quart pot and mash thoroughly. Stir in the remaining berries, sugar, and lemon juice.

Stirring constantly, bring to a rolling boil that cannot be stirred down. Immediately add the fruit pectin. Continue stirring, bring back to a boil, and continue boiling for 1 minute. Skim off excess foam, if necessary, and ladle the hot berry mixture into the sterilized jars. With a clean dampened cloth, wipe the rims of the jars. Place the flat lids on the jars, then close the caps firmly with screw-on rings. Place

the jars upside down on a clean towel until completely cooled. Press on the circle in the center of each jar lid. It either should be sunken or should "pop" into place and remain sunken. Store in refrigerator for use as needed.

Make the cream biscuits. Preheat oven to 425 degrees. Spray a baking sheet with nonstick spray and scatter flour over the surface. Tap out excess flour; set aside. Combine all dry ingredients in a large bowl. Sift all dry ingredients into another bowl. Add the cream all at once and mix with a rubber spatula, folding from the bottom over the top until the dough is relatively consistent. *Do not overmix!*

Dump the dough out onto a floured work surface. Have additional flour off to the side to add as needed. Dust your hands with flour and pull the dough together, quickly working it until it is a manageable texture.

Flour a clean work surface and roll the dough out into a ⅔-inch-thick rectangle. Fold the dough into thirds and roll out again into a ⅔-inch-thick rectangle. Add additional flour in small increments as needed to keep the dough from sticking, but leave it as sticky as possible so the biscuits will be light as a cloud. Do this for a total of 3 folds, then roll out once more to ⅔-inch thickness. Cut the biscuits with a 2-inch floured biscuit cutter using firm downward pressure. Do not squiggle the biscuit cutter. You want the cut edge to be free of dough particles. Use as much of the dough as possible, and don't re-roll the scraps. Place the cut biscuits on prepared baking sheet and bake in preheated oven for 8 to 12 minutes, or until light golden brown and cooked through. Set aside to keep warm. (At Bird Café the scrap dough is re-rolled and topped with butter, sugar, and cinnamon, then rolled up pinwheel-style, cut into 1-inch sections, and baked for staff snacks!)

Cook the sliced ham in a glaze of canola oil until lightly browned. Place a slice of the cheese on each ham slice, allowing it to melt. To serve the biscuits, slice them in half and spread the bottom sides with a liberal portion of the blueberry-jalapeño jam. Top with the cheese-topped ham and the biscuit top. Serve at once.

The Driskill Hotel's 1886 Café & Bakery's Orange-Currant Scones with Lemon Curd

MAKES
APPROXIMATELY
6 SCONES

MAKES ABOUT
1 PINT OF
LEMON CURD

Scones, which have traditionally been served with afternoon tea, have become a popular breakfast or brunch pastry—and they are easy to make. These delectable little rounds, served at the Driskill Hotel's 1886 Café & Bakery, add just the right touch to the experience of brunch at Austin's famed Driskill Hotel, especially when drizzled with its house-made lemon curd sauce

 The lemon curd must be refrigerated overnight, so it should be made the evening before you wish to serve it. Bring to room temperature to serve. The scone dough can be made and cut according to recipe directions up to 1 hour before baking. Coat with toppings and bake just before serving. ››

SCONES

⅔ cup whole milk
Full handful of dried currants
2¾ cups all-purpose flour
1½ tablespoons baking powder
⅓ cup sugar
Pinch of kosher salt
½ cup butter, softened
1 large egg
¾ teaspoon minced orange zest
½ teaspoon vanilla extract
Whipping cream for brushing
Turbinado (raw) sugar for dusting

LEMON CURD

¾ cup sugar
½ teaspoon minced lemon zest
¾ cup freshly squeezed lemon juice
½ cup butter
8 egg yolks, beaten

Make the lemon curd. Combine the sugar, lemon zest and juice, and butter in a heavy-bottomed 3-quart saucepan over medium-high heat. Place the beaten egg yolks in a mixing bowl alongside the stove. Bring the sugar mixture to a boil to dissolve the sugar. While whisking the yolks, add approximately ½ cup of the hot sugar mixture to temper them. Pour the tempered yolks back into the pan and reduce heat slightly, continuing to stir with a heat-resistant spatula until thickened.

Remove from heat and strain the curd through a fine-meshed wire strainer. Set aside to cool to room temperature, then cover and refrigerate overnight before using.

To make the scones, preheat oven to 325 degrees and line a baking sheet with parchment paper; set aside.

Warm the milk to a scald (that is, when tiny bubbles are just beginning to appear around the side of the pan). Remove from heat and add the currants, allowing them to soak for 1 hour.

In a stand mixer with paddle beater, combine the flour, baking powder, sugar, and salt; beat on lowest setting just until incorporated. Add butter, mixing only until blended. Do not overmix.

Add the egg, orange zest, and vanilla. Mix slightly, then add the milk and currants. Mix until the dough comes together. Turn the dough out onto a lightly floured work surface and work slightly by hand until fully incorporated. Gently roll the dough out into a 1-inch-thick circle.

Using a 2-inch round cutter, dredged in flour periodically to prevent sticking, cut out the scones. Place the scones on prepared baking sheet and brush the tops with some of the heavy cream, taking care not to allow the cream to puddle under the scones. Sprinkle with turbinado sugar and bake in preheated oven until lightly golden brown, about 25 to 30 minutes. Serve warm with a side dish of the lemon curd.

MargieBeth's Bake Shop's Apricot-Ginger Scones

MAKES 8 SCONES

MargieBeth's Bake Shop, a quirky little bakery with an old-world feel, was equipped with all the bells and whistles of a savvy, modern commercial bakery. The aroma of fresh-baked goods and freshly brewed, locally roasted coffee was enticing. Established in 2009 by Mark and Jacquie Frnka, longtime residents of Houston's Bellaire neighborhood, the shop offered a diverse selection of baked goods. Every food item sold in the shop was made from scratch on the premises in small batches, using the freshest, highest-quality ingredients available. Jacquie learned the craft of baking from her mother, for whom the bakery was named, developing a particular love for baking pies at an early age. The recipes that Jacquie uses have been passed down through her family and collected for several decades from various sources. Her Apricot-Ginger Scones are one of her personal favorites. They translate beautifully from the formal table to breakfast on the run.

Sadly, MargieBeth's Bake Shop was closed in the fall of 2015. Mark and Jacquie's daughter, who lives in Fort Worth, experienced severe complications during her pregnancy. When word was received that their first grandchild would be born imminently and very prematurely, arrangements were hastily made for the custom baking commitments to be met, and Jacquie, who is an RN, headed to Forth Worth to care for her daughter and her son. (The baby remained in the hospital for 102 days before going home with his parents.) While Jacquie says that making the decision to permanently close the door to her bakery was bittersweet, she has no regrets and is thoroughly enjoying her tiny new obsession.

The scones can be prepared ahead of time. Follow the recipe up to point of cutting them into wedges, and place them on a baking sheet in the freezer. Once they are frozen, place them in zip-sealing freezer bags until ready to use. Remove the scones from the freezer and allow them to come to room temperature. Place them on a parchment-lined baking sheet, and finish and bake as directed in the recipe. ››

Preheat oven to 350 degrees. Line a large baking sheet with parchment paper or a silicone mat. Whisk together the first 6 ingredients in a large bowl. Cut in the cold butter using a pastry blender or 2 forks, until the dough has the consistency of small peas. The butter particles will not be uniform and some small chunks will still be visible.

Fold in the apricots, crystallized ginger, and white chocolate chips. Add the cream and mix until the dough can be formed. Turn the dough out onto parchment-lined work surface and gather it into a circle approximately 1 inch thick. *Note*: If any dry ingredients remain in the bottom of the bowl and cannot be incorporated into the dough, add more cream, a tablespoon at a time, until the dough can be pressed into a circle.

Cut the dough circle into 8 wedges. Place the wedges on the prepared baking sheet, spacing them 2 inches apart. Using a pastry brush, brush the tops of the scones with some of the whipping cream and sprinkle with some of the cane sugar.

3 cups all-purpose flour
Scant ⅓ cup sugar
2½ teaspoons baking powder
1 teaspoon salt
½ teaspoon baking soda
1 teaspoon ground ginger
1½ sticks well-chilled unsalted butter, cut into 1½-inch dice
½ cup coarsely chopped dried apricots

⅓ cup coarsely chopped crystallized ginger
⅓ cup white chocolate chips
1 cup whipping cream, plus extra for brushing tops
Organic cane sugar for sprinkling scones

Bake in preheated oven for 18 to 20 minutes, or until tops are golden brown. Remove from oven and cool slightly before serving. Store any leftover scones in zip-sealing plastic bags at room temperature for up to 3 days, or freeze.

Sean Fulford's Buttermilk Drop Biscuits

MAKES ABOUT 10 BISCUITS

Chef Sean Fulford heads the kitchen at the Fall Creek Estate's Bistro restaurant. On weekend mornings The Bistro serves up a fine brunch menu. Chef Fulford's heavenly biscuits, made with delicious duck fat, are a signature feature of the menu. You can order duck fat from specialty meat shops. You'll probably have to buy it in a larger quantity than you think you will ever use, but it freezes well for several months. Try cooking your next batch of French fries in some of the melted fat. You'll never want them prepared any other way again!

The biscuits can be made ahead, baked, and frozen. Wrap them in foil and reheat them in a 350-degree oven until hot.

2 cups all-purpose flour
2½ teaspoons baking powder
1 teaspoon baking soda
1 teaspoon kosher salt
1 tablespoon turbinado (raw) sugar, or granulated sugar
¼ pound (1 stick) cold butter, cut into ½-inch cubes

2 tablespoons cold duck fat, cut into small pieces
1 egg
1 cup buttermilk
Additional 3 tablespoons duck fat, melted

Preheat oven to 425 degrees. Line a baking sheet with parchment paper and set aside. Combine all dry ingredients in a large mixing bowl and toss with a whisk to blend well. Place 1 cup of the dry mix in work bowl of food processor fitted with steel blade. Add the butter and duck fat. Pour in the remaining dry mix. Use the pulse feature to blend the mixture until the fat is broken into pea-sized pieces. Do not over process. Turn mixture back out into mixing bowl.

Beat the egg and buttermilk together. Make a well in the center of the dry ingredients and pour in the egg/buttermilk mixture. Fold into the dry mix gradually, using a large wooden spoon or spatula. Do not overwork the dough. The mixture will be wet and sticky. Using an ice cream scoop, scoop the mixture onto the prepared baking sheet, allowing 2 inches of space between the biscuits. Bake for 8 minutes and then brush the tops of the biscuits with the melted duck fat. Rotate the baking sheet and bake an additional 8 to 10 minutes, or until golden brown. Serve hot.

Crave Kitchen and Bar's Biscuit Donuts

MAKES ABOUT 14 DONUTS

Rodolfo (Rudy) Valdes, a native of El Paso, Texas, is the culinary genius and executive chef/partner for the Pan Y Agua restaurant group, which includes four locations of the Crave Kitchen and Bar. The restaurant's highly innovative menus change frequently, as Rudy adds new dishes that are often reconstructed versions of classic dishes. These delicious donuts are a prime example. Based on a recipe for biscuits, the biscuit dough (which is also excellent baked as biscuits, by the way) is cut with a donut cutter, then deep-fried to create a really sinfully addictive, mouthwatering breakfast treat.

Biscuit dough (see recipe at right)
Caramel (see recipe at right)
Canola oil for deep-frying heated to 350 degrees
Chopped candied walnuts (see recipe on page 84)

BISCUIT DOUGH

3 cups all-purpose flour
4 teaspoons baking powder
1 teaspoon baking soda
¾ teaspoon salt
4 tablespoons frozen butter
1 cup chilled buttermilk (not low-fat)

CARAMEL

1 cup firmly packed light brown sugar
½ cup heavy whipping cream
4 tablespoons unsalted butter, cut into 1-inch chunks

Begin by making the biscuit dough. Mix the dry ingredients together in a large bowl, tossing to blend well. Using a cheese grate, grate the butter into the dry ingredients. Stir to blend well. Add the buttermilk and stir just until the dough comes together. Do not overbeat.

Turn the dough out onto a floured work surface and pat into a circle. Wrap in plastic wrap and refrigerate to chill for 30 minutes.

While the dough is chilling, make the caramel. Combine the brown sugar and cream in a heavy-bottomed 3-quart saucepan over medium-low heat. Cook, stirring often, until the sugar dissolves, then add the butter, one piece at a time and whisking

to blend. Cook for 5 to 7 minutes, or until the desired consistency is reached. Set aside to keep warm and pourable.

Once the dough has chilled, roll or pat it out to ½-inch thickness. Using a donut cutter, cut the dough into "donut" shapes, setting the "donut holes" aside. Place the biscuit donuts on a parchment-lined baking sheet. Deep-fry in preheated oil for 30 seconds, then turn and fry for an additional 30 seconds. Take care not to crowd the oil. Cook in batches, draining each batch on a wire rack set over a baking sheet. As each batch is done, drizzle with caramel and top with a scattering of the candied walnuts. Cool slightly before serving.

UrbanHerbal's Planet to Plate Cooking School's Brioche Breakfast Buns with Scented Geranium Pesto

MAKES ABOUT 10 TO 11 BIG, PUFFY BUNS

Bill Varney is the owner of the UrbanHerbal "complex" in Fredericksburg. After selling a large herb farm and restaurant, Bill created a unique "environment," which he named UrbanHerbal. It's a peaceful place where you can stroll among raised herb, edible-flower, and vegetable beds, each with a different theme, or wander the huge greenhouse, or visit the shop where Bill sells his handmade home and personal care products (personally indulgent actually), spices, rubs, herbal teas, and other culinary condiments and herbal vinegars. Then there's the intimate and cozy little Planet to Plate Cooking School, where Bill teaches intimate, small cooking classes to locals and visitors to Fredericksburg. The luscious buns featured here, with an amazing flavor from rose geranium leaves, have always been a favorite at his bread and brunch classes. They can be made ahead and frozen before being iced. Simply reheat them in the oven and top with the glaze when you're ready to serve them. Do note that the dough must be refrigerated overnight, so add that time to your do-list when planning to prepare the buns.

. . . .

BRIOCHE DOUGH

½ cup warm (105 to 115 degrees) water
1 tablespoon instant-rise, active dry yeast
2½ cups cake flour
2 cups all-purpose flour
⅓ cup sugar
2½ teaspoons kosher salt
6 large eggs at room temperature
10 ounces (1¼ sticks) unsalted butter, cut into 1-inch cubes at room temperature
Canola oil for glazing bowl

SCENTED GERANIUM PESTO

1½ cups sugar
12 ounces (1½ sticks) unsalted butter
18 rose geranium leaves, roughly chopped
Zest from 3 oranges
¼ cup chopped pecans

GLAZE

⅓ cup unsalted butter, melted
2 cups powdered sugar
2 teaspoons rose flower water
4 tablespoons whipping cream ››

Begin by making the brioche dough. Combine the warm water and yeast in a Pyrex measuring cup. (I use a Pyrex cup so that I can look at the bottom to see if the yeast has dissolved! Then I know it's ready to use.) Set aside to proof for 10 minutes, or until the liquid is bubbly and the yeast has totally dissolved. Set aside.

Sift the flours together with the sugar. Place in bowl of stand mixer fitted with dough hook, and add the salt. Add the eggs and beat for 1 minute at low speed, scraping down side of bowl as needed. Slowly add the yeast and continue to beat at low speed for 5 minutes. Stop the machine, scrape dough from dough hook, and beat another 5 minutes.

Add about ¼ of the butter cubes at a time, beating just to incorporate after each addition. Once all the butter has been added, beat for 10 minutes at medium speed.

Oil a large bowl with canola oil and a paper towel; turn the dough out into the bowl. Turn the dough to oil all sides. Cover with plastic wrap and set aside to rise in a warm, draft-free spot until doubled in bulk, about 1½ hours.

Turn the dough out onto a floured work surface and work out the air bubbles by folding the dough over on itself several times while pressing down on it. Re-oil the bowl lightly and return the dough to the bowl. Cover with plastic wrap and place in refrigerator overnight.

Make the scented geranium pesto by combining all ingredients in work bowl of food processor fitted with steel blade. Process until a smooth paste forms. Refrigerate until ready to use, then bring to room temperature before using. Line a large baking sheet with parchment paper and set aside.

Remove the dough from the refrigerator and place it on a floured work surface. Gently smash the dough flat to remove all air bubbles. Roll the dough out into a 16 × 12-inch rectangle. Be sure to keep the corners squared off so the dough will roll evenly.

Starting 1 inch from the edge of the long side of the dough, spread the scented geranium pesto over the dough, extending it all the way to the edge on the short sides and stopping 1 inch from the top long side. Now, starting at the long side nearest you, roll the dough up like a jellyroll, making sure that you roll it evenly. When the dough is completely rolled, pinch the seam together and turn the roll so that it's seam side down. With a sharp knife, slice the dough into 1½-inch buns using forceful downward cuts. Place the buns on the prepared baking sheet, cut sides down, allowing at least 2 inches between each bun.

Cover loosely with plastic wrap and set aside to rise until doubled in bulk, about 45 minutes. Preheat oven to 350 degrees.

While the dough is rising, make the glaze. Combine all ingredients in a bowl. Whisk to make a medium-stiff paste with no lumps of powdered sugar left; set aside.

When the rolls have risen, bake them in the preheated oven until they are lightly browned and sound hollow when thumped on the bottoms, about 25 to 30 minutes. Transfer the rolls to a cooling rack set over a baking sheet. Spoon the glaze over the hot rolls, covering liberally and using all of the glaze. Allow the rolls to cool slightly before serving.

If you wish to bake the rolls ahead of time, don't glaze them. Reheat them just before serving, then spoon on the glaze and serve.

Hill Country Cinnamon Rolls

MAKES 9 TO 10
LARGE ROLLS

Big, gooey cinnamon rolls dripping with icing and stuffed with pecans and raisins are among my favorite breakfast foods. And there are bakeries around the state that have become famous for their cinnamon rolls. I particularly remember Rebecca Rather's "Jailhouse" cinnamon rolls, which she prepared at her sadly shuttered Rather Sweet Bakery in Fredericksburg. They were huge and wonderful—the stuff of legends!

I've worked with this recipe of my own over the years and am proud to say that it produces sinfully rich and delicious cinnamon rolls. I try to always have them on hand when I've got overnight guests. What better aroma to wake up to than homemade cinnamon rolls baking in the oven? You can bake the rolls ahead of time and freeze them unglazed. Thaw the rolls the evening before you wish to serve them and reheat in a medium oven just until they're heated through, then drizzle on the icing and serve hot.

2 tablespoons instant-rise, active dry yeast
1 cup warm water (105 to 115 degrees)
⅓ cup sugar, plus 1 tablespoon, divided
4 cups unbleached bread flour
1 tablespoon vanilla extract
1 teaspoon kosher salt
2 eggs
½ stick (4 tablespoons) unsalted butter, softened
Additional 3 tablespoons unsalted butter, melted

FILLING

6 ounces cream cheese, softened, and cut into chunks
1 cup chopped Texas pecans
½ cup golden raisins
1 tablespoon ground cinnamon
½ cup sugar
½ cup dark brown sugar

GLAZE

⅓ cup unsalted butter, melted
2 cups powdered sugar
3 ounces cream cheese, softened
2 teaspoons vanilla extract
4 tablespoons half-and-half, or more as needed ››

To make the dough, combine the yeast, warm water, and 1 tablespoon of the sugar in a 2-cup Pyrex measuring cup. Stir gently to blend. Set aside until the yeast has dissolved and the mixture is foamy, about 4 minutes.

Combine the flour, vanilla, remaining ⅓ cup of sugar, salt, eggs, and softened butter in work bowl of food processor fitted with steel blade. Process until all ingredients are well blended. Add the yeast mixture, scraping measuring cup to include all liquid. Process until the dough comes together and pulls away from the side of the bowl, about 20 seconds. Check the consistency of the dough, adding additional flour, if needed, by the tablespoon. Process after each addition until the consistency is right. The dough should be cohesive and not sticky. Turn the mixture out onto a lightly floured work surface and knead for about 3 minutes to form a smooth, elastic dough.

Coat a large mixing bowl with canola oil. Place the dough in the bowl, turning to coat all surfaces with the oil. Cover the bowl with plastic wrap and set the dough aside to rise until doubled in bulk, about 45 minutes.

While the dough is rising, combine the filling ingredients, except the cream cheese, in a small bowl. Toss with a fork to blend well; set aside. Place the chunks of cream cheese in a clean processor bowl and process until it is smooth and creamy. Remove to a separate bowl.

When the dough has doubled in bulk, punch it down and turn it out onto a lightly floured work surface. Roll the dough out into a 12-inch square. Spread the cream cheese evenly over the surface of the dough using a rubber spatula. Then fold the dough into a rectangle as though you were folding a letter. Now fold one end of the dough to the middle and fold the other end over to cover it, making a small square.

Add a little more flour to the work surface and roll the dough out into a rectangle of about 18 × 12 inches. Brush the dough with the 3 tablespoons of melted butter, and then scatter the filling over the dough, leaving a 1-inch border at the long sides. Roll the dough, pinwheel-style, beginning at the long side closest to you. Be sure that the roll is evenly thick in diameter. Pinch the long seam to seal the dough and turn the dough seam side down. Line a half-sheet baking sheet with parchment paper; set aside.

Using a thin, sharp knife, cut off the scraggly ends of the roll and discard. When cutting the dough, make definitive, bold downward slices and don't be tempted to squiggle the knife—as doing so will squish the bottom portion of the dough together, impeding the rise. You'll wind up with lopsided rolls. Slice the dough into 1½- to 2-inch-thick slices, depending on how thick you want the rolls to be. I like them big! Arrange the slices so that they're almost touching on the prepared baking sheet. Cover loosely with plastic wrap and set aside to rise for 30 minutes. Preheat oven to 350 degrees.

While the dough is rising, make the glaze. Combine all ingredients in work bowl of food processor fitted with steel blade. Process to make a medium-stiff paste with no lumps of powdered sugar left. Add additional half-and-half if the glaze is too thick; set aside.

When the rolls have risen, bake them in the preheated oven until they are lightly browned and sound hollow when thumped on the bottoms, about 25 to 30 minutes. Transfer the rolls to a cooling rack set over a baking sheet. Spoon the glaze over the hot rolls, covering liberally and using all of the glaze. Allow the rolls to cool slightly before serving.

If you wish to bake the rolls ahead of time, don't glaze them. Reheat them before serving, then spoon on the glaze and serve.

Pecan-Praline Rolls

These rich and gooey rolls are evocative of the hearty pastries made by the early German and Czech bakers who came to Texas beginning in the 1840s. Although it is highly unlikely that they had access to liqueurs for making tasty glazes, I'm certain they would have appreciated the flavor addition!

MAKES 12 ROLLS

CREAM PASTRY

2 cups all-purpose flour
4 teaspoons baking powder
1 tablespoon sugar
1 teaspoon kosher salt
¾ to 1 cup whipping cream, room temperature

FILLING

¼ cup unsalted butter, softened
⅔ cup firmly packed light brown sugar
⅓ cup finely chopped pecans
1 teaspoon ground cinnamon
12 pecan halves

PRALINE GLAZE

1 cup powdered sugar
1 tablespoon praline liqueur
1 tablespoon whipping cream

Preheat oven to 425 degrees. Butter 12 muffin cups; set aside. To make the pastry dough, combine the flour, baking powder, sugar, and salt in a large bowl. Stir in enough cream to make a soft dough. Turn the dough out onto a lightly floured work surface and knead gently about 15 times until the dough comes together into a cohesive mass. Roll the dough out into an 18 × 12-inch rectangle. Spread the dough with the filling butter. In a small bowl, combine the brown sugar, chopped pecans, and cinnamon; reserve ¼ cup for topping. Scatter the filling ingredients evenly over the buttered dough. Beginning on the long side nearest

you, roll up tightly, like a jelly roll. Pinch the seam to seal. Place the dough roll so that it's seam side down and cut it into 24 slices, each about ¾ inch wide. Stand 2 slices, side by side, and on the edge, in each muffin cup. Gently spread the slices apart so that they form a "v" space in the center. Spoon 1 teaspoon of the reserved brown-sugar mixture in the center of each roll. Top each with a pecan half, pressing it lightly into the roll.

Bake in preheated oven for 15 to 20 minutes, or until the rolls are golden brown.

Prepare the praline glaze. Combine the powdered sugar, the praline liqueur, and enough whipping cream to make a smooth, creamy glaze of drizzling consistency.

Remove the rolls from the muffin cups and place them on a wire rack over a sheet of parchment paper. Drizzle with the praline glaze and let stand 5 minutes before serving.

Fig Muffins with Orange Glaze

MAKES 24 MUFFINS

Just about everybody loves muffins—and they make a nice breakfast-on-the-go hand food. This tasty version takes advantage of our good Texas figs. When they ripen in the summer, it's time to make fig preserves to enjoy their taste year-round, and to make these nifty muffins, which also freeze well.

The muffins can be made up to 1 day ahead of time and served at room temperature. If you wish to reheat them before serving, add the Orange Glaze after reheating. They also freeze well. Bring to room temperature before serving.

MUFFINS

¼ cup (½ stick) unsalted butter, room temperature
½ cup sugar
3 eggs
2 cups fig preserves, finely minced, syrup reserved
1 cup old-fashioned rolled oats
1½ cups all-purpose flour
2 teaspoons baking powder
½ teaspoon baking soda
½ teaspoon kosher salt
Orange glaze (see recipe at right)

ORANGE GLAZE

1 (3-ounce) package cream cheese, room temperature
¼ cup sifted powdered sugar
2 tablespoons freshly squeezed orange juice
1 teaspoon grated orange zest

Make the muffin batter. Preheat oven to 375 degrees. Grease 24 muffin-tin cups and set aside. In bowl of stand mixer, cream the butter and sugar at medium speed until light and fluffy, about 4 minutes. Beat in the eggs, one at a time, scraping down side of bowl after each addition. Add the fig preserves, reserved syrup, and oats; beat just to blend. Sift the flour, baking powder, baking soda, and salt into a separate bowl. Add the sifted dry ingredients to the creamed mixture and just to moisten dry ingredients. Pour batter into greased muffin cups, filling each ½ full. Bake on middle rack of preheated oven until a wooden pick inserted into center of muffins comes out clean, about 25 to 30 minutes. Remove from oven. Using a small metal spatula, loosen sides of muffins; turn out onto a wire rack. Cool muffins slightly. Make the orange glaze and spread on the tops of the muffins. Set aside until cool.

To make the orange glaze, beat the cream cheese in bowl of stand mixer until light and fluffy. Add the remaining ingredients and beat until well blended and smooth.

Czech Cream Cheese and Blueberry Kolaches

MAKES 24
KOLACHES

Texas has a sizable Czech population, and many Czech foods have become an integral part of today's Texas cuisine—kolaches being one of the most popular examples. Czech immigrants from Moravia, Silesia, and Bohemia began to arrive in Texas in the early 1850s. The city of Caldwell remains a stronghold of Czech culture, having proclaimed itself the Kolache Capital of Texas, celebrating its status with an annual Kolache Festival in September. The city of West also boasts a large Czech population, and vies for top honors in kolache competitions. The delectable little pastries featured here, which derive their name from the Czech word *kolae*, meaning "cake," are traditionally filled with fruits, jams, cheese, or poppy seeds. Sausage- and cheese-filled buns, sometimes called savory kolaches, are also a Czech creation, but the proper Czech name for these pastries is klobasnikis.

DOUGH

1 tablespoon instant-rise, active dry yeast
⅓ cup sugar, divided
1 cup whole milk
¼ cup canola oil
1 teaspoon kosher salt
4 to 4½ cups sifted all-purpose flour, plus additional for work surface, or more if needed
4 tablespoons unsalted butter, softened
2 eggs, beaten
6 tablespoons additional unsalted butter, melted and cooled

CREAM CHEESE AND BLUEBERRY FILLING

8 ounces softened cream cheese, cut into small chunks
1 egg yolk
¼ cup sugar
Grated zest of 1 large lemon
1 teaspoon vanilla
8 ounces fresh or frozen blueberries
¾ cup sugar
½ teaspoon lemon juice
¼ cup water

STREUSEL TOPPING (*POPSYPKA*)

½ cup frozen unsalted butter, cut into ½-inch cubes
1 cup sugar
1 cup all-purpose flour ››

Begin by making the streusel topping. Combine all ingredients in work bowl of food processor fitted with steel blade. Process, using on/off pulses, until the mixture resembles coarse meal. Do not over-process. Turn mixture out into a zip-sealing bag and store in freezer while preparing the filling and dough.

Make the dough. Combine the yeast and one tablespoon of the sugar in a 2-cup Pyrex measuring cup. Heat the milk to approximately 110 degrees. Gently whisk half of the milk into the cup with the yeast and sugar. Set aside to proof, or until the yeast has dissolved and the mixture is bubbling and foamy. In bowl of stand mixer fitted with dough hook, place the remaining sugar, the oil, the salt, the remaining ½ cup of milk, and 1 cup of the flour. Starting on low speed, beat the mixture until the flour is incorporated; then increase to medium speed and beat until blended. Add the yeast mixture, the remaining flour, the softened butter, and the eggs. Begin again on low speed until the flour is incorporated, then increase speed to medium and knead the dough until it is very smooth and elastic, about 6 minutes. The dough should not stick to the side of the bowl. If it is too wet, add additional flour, one tablespoon at a time, beating to combine after each addition, until the dough is the right consistency.

Turn the dough out onto work surface and knead 4 to 5 times by hand, or until the dough springs back when pulled. Lightly oil a large bowl and place the dough in the bowl, turning to coat all surfaces with the oil. Cover bowl with plastic wrap and set aside to rise in a draft-free spot until doubled in bulk, about 1 hour.

While the dough is rising, make the filling. Combine the cream cheese, egg yolk, sugar, lemon zest, and vanilla in work bowl of food processor fitted with steel blade. Process until smooth. Turn out into a separate bowl and set aside. Combine the blueberries, sugar, lemon juice, and water in a heavy-bottomed 2-quart saucepan over medium-high heat. Cook, stirring frequently, until thickened, about 8 to 10 minutes. Remove pan from heat and mash the blueberries with a wooden spoon until chunky. Set aside to cool.

When the dough has doubled in bulk, punch it down and divide into 2-ounce balls. Line 2 baking sheets with parchment paper. Arrange 12 of the balls on each prepared baking sheet, placing them 3 across and 4 down. Flatten the balls with the palm of your hand. Using a pastry brush, brush each flattened dough ball with some of the melted butter, taking care not to drip butter on the parchment paper. Cover loosely with plastic wrap and allow to rise for 20 minutes.

Flatten the dough balls once more and make a deep indentation in the center of each. Spoon equal portions of the cheese filling into each indentation. Top the cheese on each kolache with a heaping tablespoon of the blueberry mixture. Scatter a portion of the streusel topping over each. Cover loosely with plastic wrap and set aside to rise for 30 minutes. Preheat oven to 350 degrees.

When the kolaches have risen, bake them in preheated oven for 30 to 35 minutes, or until golden brown. The cheese should be lightly browned and the peach preserves melty and lightly browned. Remove to a wire rack and cool slightly before serving. The kolaches can be cooled completely and frozen. Wrap tightly in plastic wrap and place in zip-sealing bags, squeezing out all of the air from the bags. Freeze for up to 6 weeks.

Polish Sausage Klobasnikis with Cheese and Jalapeños

MAKES ABOUT
28 PASTRIES

Most people in Texas know these traditional Czech pastries as kolaches. Often, they're called "pigs in a blanket." But the real Czech word for the wonderful pastries filled with sausage and often cheese and jalapeños, although the chiles are a strictly Texan addition, is *klobasniki*. According to Texas-Czech kolache expert Andy Zubick, owner of Zubick Kolache House in Austin, klobasnikis were created after Czech immigrants arrived in Texas and are an indigenous Texas pastry of Czech origin. There are also other variations of the pastry that are filled with Czech-style pan sausage and sauerkraut or cooked cabbage. If you don't get around to making your own, there's a Czech-owned bakery by the name of Hruska's, in Ellinger, Texas—on that well-traveled road from Houston to Austin—that makes heavenly kolaches and klobasnikis, including the sausage and sauerkraut or cabbage ones. You'll know you're there because of the snarl of cars jockeying for parking spaces in the small parking lot/gas pump area out front. (And also because the speed limit drops to 55 mph right before you get to the store.) There are many meat markets in rural Texas towns that make great Polish-style sausage. One of my favorites is Dziuk's Meat Market in Castroville, a charming town that offers a bit of Alsace in Texas. The Kiolbassa Provision Company of San Antonio also crafts a quite tasty Polish-style sausage that contains no MSG and nitrates, and is available in mainstream supermarkets in Texas.

. . . .

8 ounces solid vegetable shortening
1 cup sugar
1 teaspoon kosher salt
1 cup boiling water
1 tablespoon, plus 1½ teaspoons instant-rise, active dry yeast
2 eggs, slightly beaten

1 cup warm water (105 to 155 degrees)
6½ cups bread flour
3½ pounds Texas Cheddar, shredded
Sliced, pickled nacho-style jalapeños
14 good-quality Polish sausage links, sliced into about 3-inch lengths ››

In bowl of stand mixer, cream the shortening and sugar until light and fluffy, using the mixer's beater blade, about 5 minutes. Add the salt, then the boiling water. Mix on low speed until the shortening is completely melted and the mixture has cooled to between 105 and 115 degrees. Add the yeast, beating just to blend. Add the two eggs and warm water; beat until well mixed. Remove the paddle blade from the mixer, putting in the dough hook. Add the bread flour and mix with the dough hook, beginning on low speed and increasing to medium as the flour is incorporated, stopping to scrape down side of bowl as needed, until a smooth dough is obtained. Knead the dough with the hook for about 5 minutes. Place the dough in a large, oiled bowl, turning to coat all sides of the dough; cover tightly with plastic wrap and refrigerate overnight, or for at least 4 hours.

In the morning, line 3 baking sheets with parchment paper; set aside. Separate the dough into 2 equal pieces by weight. Roll each portion of the dough into a rectangle about 28 inches wide and ⅛-inch thick. Beginning at the long side of the dough, roll the rectangles, pinwheel-style, into tight rolls. Be sure the roll is uniform in thickness its entire length. Cut each roll of dough into 14 (2-inch) pieces. Roll each piece out into a round about ¼ inch thick. When rolling the dough out, use gentle strokes in one direction to avoid activating the gluten protein in the flour, which will make it very elastic and hard to roll. If the dough becomes springy and elastic while you're trying to roll it out, simply cover it loosely with a clean kitchen towel and let it rest for about 10 minutes.

Scatter each dough round with ½ cup of the cheese, leaving a 1-inch border at the edge, and place the desired number of jalapeño slices on the cheese. Place a piece of the sausage in the center of the cheese. Fold the sides of the dough tightly over the sausage and cheese, aligning the edges in a straight line; then roll the dough, starting at the edge closest to you, around the sausage tightly. Place the klobasnikis, seam sides down, on prepared baking sheets, allowing about 3 inches between each pastry. Set aside to rise, covered loosely with plastic wrap, for about 45 minutes. Preheat oven to 350 degrees.

Bake the klobasnikis for about 30 to 35 minutes, or until the dough is golden brown and firm to the touch. The cheese should be completely melted inside the dough. Cool on wire racks to almost room temperature before serving. The sausages inside will retain heat longer than the pastry.

Spudnuts

MAKES ABOUT
12 SPUDNUTS

I first tasted a *spudnut* at the Spudnut Shop in Plainview, Texas, back in 1972. It was over the Christmas holidays and I had traveled from my home in Austin to meet my soon-to-be relatives for the first time. My flight arrived in Lubbock fairly early in the morning and after the drive north to Plainview I was hungry—and probably not quite ready to go on display to the family. My fiancé took me to the Spudnut Shop on West 5th Street, explaining that he grew up eating these donuts, which were made using potatoes! I was intrigued, and the spudnuts did not disappoint with their unique flavor and great pillow-soft texture. I made it a must to get my fill of them each time we went to Plainview. Although neither the marriage nor the Spudnut Shop remains, the Spudnut Shop survived for fifty-three years under the same ownership.

1 large russet (baking) potato, about 10 ounces, peeled and cut into 1-inch cubes

2 cups all-purpose flour, sifted, plus more for dusting work surface

1½ teaspoons baking powder

1½ teaspoons kosher salt, divided

1 teaspoon freshly ground black pepper, divided

½ teaspoon ground mace

1 cup sugar, divided

2 eggs, beaten until frothy

¼ cup whole milk

2 tablespoons unsalted butter, melted

1 teaspoon grated lemon zest

Canola oil for deep frying

Place the potato cubes in a heavy-bottomed 2-quart saucepan and add cold water to cover. Bring to a boil and cook for about 20 minutes, or until the potato cubes are very tender. Drain well and pass the potato cubes through a ricer into a medium-sized bowl. Whisk the flour, the baking powder, ¾ teaspoon of the salt, ¼ teaspoon of the pepper, and the mace in a separate bowl, blending well. Add ⅓ cup of the sugar, beaten eggs, milk, butter, and lemon zest to the riced potato cubes. Transfer to bowl of stand mixer with beater paddle and beat just until

smooth. Add the dry mixture and beat just until mixed well. The secret to the pillow-soft texture is to not overbeat the dough. Set the dough aside to rest for 10 minutes.

Preheat the canola oil, preferably in a thermostat-controlled countertop deep fryer, or in a 6-quart pan, to 370 degrees. Toss together the remaining salt, pepper, and sugar in a bowl to blend well; set aside. Lightly flour work surface and pat the dough out with your hands into a 10-inch circle about ½-inch thick. Using a 3-inch donut

cutter, cut out the donuts using a firm downward cut—no twisting! Gently gather the scraps together and pat out to ½-inch thickness. Cut the scraps until all the dough is used, but don't overwork the dough.

Carefully immerse the spudnuts in the hot oil. Cook, turning once, until puffed and golden, about 2 minutes on each side. Using a slotted spoon, transfer the spudnuts to a wire rack set over a baking sheet. Let cool, until lukewarm, then toss in the sugar mixture and serve.

ACKNOWLEDGMENTS

Writing a cookbook is a somewhat daunting task. First, there's a subject to choose—one that hasn't been written to death. Or, if it actually has been, to find a new spin on it that will interest readers. Then there's the gathering and/or developing of recipes and testing them until they work perfectly and contain all the information a reader will need to execute those recipes so that they look and taste exactly as I, or their creators, intended. Last, but certainly not least, is the actual putting together of the words in an enticing manner that smacks of my personality or style. And it seems to be an endeavor that doesn't get easier with successive books, even on this, my ninth. In my own case, I figure that's because I push myself further with each new subject. Pushing further means more research, more reaching out to others for contacts and information or opinions on how the project is progressing. It becomes an intricate network without which a cookbook would never happen, or certainly not in a manner that would be very gratifying.

I owe much gratitude to all the members of my network on this book. My editor, Casey Kittrell at UT Press, is the best. He has such a talent for offering suggestions—or directions that a certain portion of the book might take—that my mind develops, turning the whole endeavor into a cognitive work. Then, the entire team at UT Press comes into play in the design, publicity, and marketing of the book. It has been a sincere pleasure to work with each and every member of that team. Julie Hettiger, food stylist extraordinaire, has once again lent her talents and suggestions for arranging my sister Sandy

Wilson's stunning photographs. I value both her friendship and her professional acumen. I wish to thank my dear friend Leslie Horne, who has been so instrumental in getting me access to the best chefs and restaurants in San Antonio and for taking her time to introduce me to them. My friend Marla Camp, publisher of *Edible Austin* magazine, has helped not only by providing great constructive ideas but also by keeping me focused during the project, and serving as guinea pig for countless breakfast dishes. I thank Nanci Taylor, publisher of *Edible Dallas/Fort Worth*, for leading me to a great breakfast and brunch restaurant in Dallas. John Griffin, co-editor of *Savor SA* online, made helpful venue suggestions. Edmund Tijerna, Food and Beverage editor of the *San Antonio Express-News*, provided some great San Antonio insider foodie information.

And, of course, there are the many chefs and personal friends who shared their recipes and their restaurants and homes for photographing their creations. I am sure those who read this book and try their recipes will appreciate them, too!

My talented sister, Sandy Wilson, makes my books what they are. Her keen eye for "the shot"—which involves layout, color, design, and expertise as a great photographer—gives life to the recipes, the people, and the places featured in this book, making them real and bringing them right into a reader's kitchen. My husband Roger works very hard long hours to support me and my love of doing what I do. And he eats even those dishes that didn't make the taste-quality cut to be included in my books. We have shared so many Texas good mornings.

Terry Thompson-Anderson
ROCKPORT, TEXAS
2017

T his project was a natural extension of the last book I worked on with my sister, Terry Thompson-Anderson. I have her to thank for the project and the coordination of recipes, restaurants, and people. Though its scope is smaller, still there are many chefs to thank for their time, kitchens, and food. Of course without the University of Texas Press and our loyal editor, Casey Kittrell, this book would not have been possible. Many thanks for their trust and support.

When I started working on the photography, I looked to Julie Hettiger, my food stylist, collaborator, and friend, not only for her great eye and wonderful, efficient kitchen but also for her tireless help in the many restaurant kitchens on the road. We shopped, cooked, styled, and photographed all of these beautiful recipes.

As in the past, I thank all my friends and colleagues who opened their doors for a night's respite to me and often Julie as well, as we traveled around the state. My friend Yvonne Sternes, culinary instructor, was also on hand to help out in a pinch when a recipe needed extra care. As always, I thank my husband, Steve Freeman, for enduring my absences and for eating all the leftovers from the shoots.

Last but not least, I need to acknowledge the loss of my dear friend Sue Heatly, who helped me through the previous book too many times to count, with an open door, a good meal, and fine company. My last visit with her was the day we presented this proposal. She was thrilled to know this latest project was in the queue.

Sandy Wilson
BELLAIRE, TEXAS
2017

INDEX